M

BARMAN

B_ARMAN

PING-PONG, PATHOS, AND PASSING THE BAR

ALEX WELLEN

HARMONY BOOKS

NEW YORK

Published by Harmony Books, New York, New York. Member of the Crown
Publishing Group, a division of Random House, Inc.

www.randomhouse.com

HARMONY BOOKS is a registered trademark and the Harmony Books
colophon is a trademark of Random House, Inc.

Printed in the United States of America

Design by Chris Welch

Library of Congress Cataloging-in-Publication Data

Wellen, Alex.
Barman : ping-pong, pathos, and passing the bar /
Alex Wellen.—1st ed.
1. Practice of law—United States. 2. Law—Vocational guidance—
United States. 3. Law—Study and teaching—United States. I. Title.
KF297.W45 2003
340' .023 '73—dc21
2003002445

ISBN 1-4000-4891-5

10 9 8 7 6 5 4 3 2 1

First Edition

FOR THE ORACLE

CONTENTS

FOREPLAY

We might as well start off with a legal disclaimer. The following is based on true events. I occasionally altered the chronology of events for clarity, and I routinely changed names and places in the interest of preserving people's privacy and for reasons that will become painfully obvious in the forthcoming pages. If only I could have changed my own name.

CONCEPTION

CHAPTER 1

I WAS GETTING a little panicked. Hundreds of unsolicited résumés and cover letters, two dozen on-campus interviews, seven callbacks, and I had nothing, *nada,* zilch. The callback interview with O'Connell & Price was starting to feel like my last hope. O'Connell & Price, based in Philadelphia, was your basic white-shoe large general-practice law firm. Most of the associates graduated from top law schools, the firm's clients were gigantic corporations and wealthy investors, and the firm handled sexy, complex legal work. O'Connell & Price was exactly what I wanted in a summer internship.

The callback interview was nothing special. Like most, it lasted four-plus hours and included five interviews, with everyone from the recruiter to a senior partner, plus lunch. Dennis Braise, a senior associate with the firm, was my fifth and final interview. He was in his early thirties. Like the rest of the attorneys I met that morning, he dressed and looked rich. He wore an expensive dark suit and was perfectly manicured. During our interview, Braise reminded me of the Cheshire cat from *Alice's Adventures in Wonderland.* At first I found his demeanor a nice change of pace, but by the third or fourth question, I wanted to smack that exaggerated grin right off his face. To be fair, by the time I met him, I was all talked out. After having given the same answers to the same questions four times, I couldn't possibly have come off as genuine. But for whatever reason, he liked me.

"I'm not supposed to tell you this," he confided as he walked me through the reception area, which looked more like a museum with its fine art and white marble floors, "but I gave you a five-point-oh. That's a perfect score. The firm doesn't even want us to give those."

"That's great. I appreciate that," I said.

Then he began whispering: "We're meeting later this afternoon to discuss everyone who has interviewed with us this week. If I learn anything else, I'll give you a call." I thanked him for the umpteenth time and stepped into the elevator feeling as good as you can about the process.

Three hours later, Dennis Braise called personally to inform me that an official summer-associate offer would arrive in a few days. I'd landed myself a superb summer job following my second year of law school. Praise the Lord.

"Meanwhile, here's to an expensive dinner on O'Connell and Price, Alex. We'd like to take you out and talk to you about the firm. How about steaks and cigars this Thursday evening at Morton's? Wear a jacket. I'll meet you at the bar."

I hung up with Dennis and scribbled down, "Thurs., eight P.M., Morton's, jacket," and, staring down at the suit that I was still wearing from the interview, I wrote and underlined, "No blue suit, no red tie." Finally, I had an offer.

I'd underestimated just how competitive these internships were. Part of the allure was that they paid remarkably well—summer associates were paid at a first-year associate's rate. The money I stood to make in one summer could subsidize an entire semester of tuition. I was relieved. I was thrilled. I was important. I mattered.

That evening I arrived fifteen minutes early. Dennis was already at the bar crouched over a drink.

"Mr. Wellen. Good to see you. He'll have a Finlandia vodka gimlet with a twist," he said to the bartender, then to me, "Let's have these, and then we can sit down at the table and feast. Have you ever had a gimlet?"

I hadn't. I thanked him for the invitation. "So, are we waiting for anyone else for dinner?"

"Maybe one other guy in Litigation. I invited him earlier this afternoon. I tried to grab a couple of other associates on my way out of the office, but no one was around. I guess that's a good thing. You see . . . eight o'clock on a Thursday night, and everyone's already left the office. The big-firm lawyer life doesn't have to be all that bad . . . just mine." He took a sip of his drink and complained about his workload and the incompetents who worked for him. We finished our gimlets, grabbed a table, and ordered another round.

The conversation started off sedate, but by the time we received our appetizers and a third round, the dialogue had become much more frank. Now Dennis was sounding off about the internal politics of making partnership, and confessing the firm's dirty little secrets.

"Yeah, it's a good thing the hiring committee smartened up and gave you an offer. For whatever reason, they haven't made any other Temple Law offers yet this year. I hope you decide this is the right place. If you don't, I'm not sure whether they'll make any more offers to Temple."

Excuse me. Why exactly did the hiring committee have to "smarten up"? Why wasn't Temple getting the offers? And why should that affect my decision?

It was all U.S. News & World Report's fault. The magazine published an annual law school survey that categorized every accredited U.S. law school in one of four quartiles. When U.S. News first published the report in 1987, it gained instant notoriety. For years the legal community had been clamoring for some guidelines. Now it had an industry standard. Dennis Braise, for example, was Tier 1. He had graduated from the University of Pennsylvania Law, one of U.S. News's top fifty schools.

On the other hand, Temple Law was not among the top fifty accredited law schools. It was one of the top schools in the next best fifty, Tier 2 (read: second rate). It didn't matter that Temple's trial advocacy program was ranked above that of Yale, Harvard, Cornell, and every other Tier 1 law school in the country. Who cared if Temple offered its students riveting lectures from accomplished professors, a diverse curriculum, and hundreds of international programs, legal clinicals, and internships? None of this improved the *U.S. News* ranking. Year after year Temple bore the same brand: Tier 2.

It seemed a Tier 2 ranking was a tough badge to shake. The most significant factor *U.S. News* used to settle on its ranking was reputation. They surveyed hundreds of influential deans, faculties, lawyers, hiring partners, and judges and asked them to rank every law school. Those personal opinions counted toward 40 percent of the total ranking. Nothing seemed to change those opinions. Temple Law, like every other non–Tier 1 law school, had a stigma attached to it. It was a self-fulfilling prophecy—once a Tier 2, always a Tier 2.

The remaining 60 percent of each ranking was divided among three factors: faculty resources, career-placement success, and selectivity. Faculty resources included everything from how much money a law school spent on each student, to the student-teacher ratio, to how many books were in the law library. From what I could tell, Temple's faculty resources were fine.

As for Temple Law's career-placement success, well, that was a problem. Over the years I'd taken some informal surveys throughout the Temple faculty, administration, and student body. My sense was that our employment rates were only slightly above average. The market was tough enough these days, but Temple Law students made it even harder. Many of my fellow students were locals. After graduation, they wanted to stay and practice in the Philadelphia area. That meant they limited their options. Perhaps if our career placement were more national in scope, our ranking would improve.

Temple's low ranking in the selectivity category was self-inflicted. The school was very selective, but not always in the classic sense of the word. The law school application read: "The Temple admissions committee is willing to recognize criteria not always reflected by grade point averages and LSATs [legal standardized admissions test scores]." This organic approach to admissions guaranteed Temple diversity, but it also guaranteed students with lower grades and lower LSATs, and accordingly, a lower overall ranking. Temple Law even admitted certain students using a discretionary process it called the Special Admissions and Curricular Experiment, or "SpACE" program. It was hardly an experiment anymore: Temple had been admitting applicants under the program since 1972. Someone who had overcome great financial obstacles or served in the Peace Corps, for example, was considered desirable despite low LSATs. There were more than a dozen other exceptions.

The fact was, I'd probably been admitted to Temple thanks to the SpACE program, likely under the category of "applicants with an undergraduate degree of unusual merit." I'd applied to Temple with an engineering degree from a state university and good grades but mediocre LSATs. I should have been the last person to complain about Temple's selectivity adversely affecting its overall ranking. But I did. To borrow from Groucho Marx, I guess I didn't want to be a part of any club that would have me as a member.

Then there was Temple's school slogan. It wasn't good: "I chose Temple." Actually, the entire slogan was: "I could have gone anywhere, but I chose Temple." The real question? Who *chose* that godforsaken slogan? It struck me as some sort of self-help expression meant to reassure everyone that Temple was a legitimate choice, that it wasn't my last choice, that it wasn't my safety school. I chose Temple, and it was a shame *U.S. News* didn't care.

I threw back the rest of my gimlet. Did I really need confirmation of my darkest insecurity? Yes. "Why do you think Temple law students are getting snubbed in the interviewing process?" I asked Dennis.

"I dunno. The senior partners are all from the Ivy Leagues, and for some reason they're on this Ivy League kick. They want more Harvards, Yales, and U-Penns. Something about increasing overall percentages as compared to the other firms in the city. Last year we hired two Temples. The year before that, three. It's now some informal, unspoken rule. Hire only from the big schools.

"Look, I'm not trying to stress you out or say that it's right," he continued, "but I think they figure if they go out on a limb to make you an offer and you decline, they'll look stupid. To whom, I don't know. But they'll take it personally. You just do what you gotta do."

The mixture of Dennis's blatantly elitist comments and the vodka gimlets was starting to make me feel nauseated. I excused myself to go to the men's room. At the sink I began throwing cold water on my face. I was alone.

"You are so drunk," I said in the mirror as I rubbed my entire face with both hands. "Soooo drunk. What am I doing? I've gotta get a grip. Got-to-get-a-grip. I gotta stay focused, not look drunk, ask smart questions."

The toilet flushed, and a waiter stepped out of a stall. He smiled. I smiled. I fixed my hair, straightened my tie and jacket, and went back to the table as composed as possible. Dennis and I finished our dinner. At the very end of the meal, he offered cigars and after-dinner liqueurs. At this point the decadence was getting obscene. I declined, and we stepped outside. It was freezing.

"So, what are you going to do now?" Dennis asked me after I thanked him for dinner.

"Tonight? I'm crashing. I have class in the morning."

"Well, I wouldn't worry about that too much anymore." He laughed. "Do you want to come back to my place?"

I paused. I couldn't be sure how long I was staring. I blinked. "Nahh," I said. "I appreciate it, definitely, but I'm just going to grab a cab and go to bed. Thanks. I appreciate it." Did I mention that I appreciated it?

"Another time, then. I just got this great *Star Trek* collector's telephone. It's shaped like the U.S.S. *Enterprise,* and it plays the *Star Trek* theme song when it rings."

"Good stuff," I said, trying to recall whether I'd feigned interest in *Star Trek* at any point in the evening. He smiled, I smiled, we shook hands, and I got into a cab.

"Ninth and Clinton," I told the cabdriver, and sank into my seat.

Oh my God. What just happened? What exactly just happened? I began piecing it together. A senior associate invited me back to his place to check out his *Star Trek* phone. Was that a euphemism? Had this man hit on me? Geez, it hadn't even occurred to me that we were going down that path.

"Oh no," I mumbled.

"Something wrong?" the cabdriver said over his shoulder.

"Nothing. Thanks," I said. Only then did it occur to me that perhaps I never had an O'Connell & Price offer to begin with. And if I had one before dinner, did it still stand? Did I still even want it?

CHAPTER 2

FIRST-YEAR LAW school they scared you, and second-year law school they worked you.

The most terrifying thing about law school was knowing the first year was the only one that mattered. Sure, law school was a three-year full-time commitment, but the path to a permanent job with a prestigious law firm was based largely on first-year grades. I called it the "rocket docket," borrowing from a federal court in Virginia that was famous for expediting legal cases.

The process was very straightforward. Law firms ignored you during your first year of law school. Then you got your first-year grades. Day one of your second year of law school, the big firms started recruiting for their summer internships. If you had the requisite first-year grades, you'd get a summer internship with one of those big firms. After your second year, you'd do the summer internship. If the people at the firm liked you, and they usually did, they hired you. In the end, the law firm would never likely see your second- or third-year grades. Strong first-year grades put you on the rocket docket.

First year they scared you, and that meant everyone. Teachers scared you by piling on the reading and never answering a single freaking question—it was known as the Socratic method, or answering a question with a question. The students scared you. On more than one occasion, for example, an important library book everyone needed to complete an assignment would go missing. Temple's Tier 2 status magnified the fierce competition. There was a need for validation among my fellow students. You felt it, dull and throbbing, like a mild migraine. It felt as if we were constantly reminding each other: "I chose Temple. I could have gone anywhere, but I chose Temple."

An incoming class was split into four sections. That meant that I took every single class with the same sixty or seventy students. It also meant that the same half-dozen students competed for every professor's attention. The rule: If you didn't know who the asshole was in the first two weeks of class, it had to be you. I kept my mouth shut.

Law school introduced me to a level of cutthroat competition that I'd never seen before. Rutgers College of Engineering was nothing like that. In engineering school the subject matter was so difficult that we all suffered together. In law school we made one another suffer. In engineering school you could easily spend a week poring over one mathematical problem. Four semesters of calculus, four of physics, two of chemistry, then statics, dynamics, and thermodynamics, and that was just freshman and sophomore years. Most engineering exams were the same: "Please take the next two hours to complete the following four problems." And the engineering exam scores? Abysmal.

"You'll notice that I did not grade problem number three," my Mechanics of Solids professor said to us after a test in my sophomore year. "As a couple of you pointed out after the exam, the hypothetical in that problem contained a physical impossibility. So your score is now out of a possible seventy-five points."

"Yeah, thanks a million, I spent an hour on that problem," my college roommate and best friend, Arjun, whispered to me as the professor handed back our exams.

"Me, too," I said. "How'd you do?"

"I got a thirty-eight! I got a thirty-eight! What's that?" he said, scanning the grade curve on the whiteboard.

"A minus," I said. "Nice. I got a twenty-seven. That's a B." There were a hundred students in the class. Next to each grade on the board was the number of students who had scored it.

"Despite the curve, as you can see, one-third of you failed," our professor told us. This was a familiar sentiment. "You'll have one more chance to raise your grade on the final." By then ten more people would have dropped the course. Engineering school was war, with casualties everywhere. During my four years at Rutgers, engineers dropped like flies. I was often reminded of that classic freshman-orientation speech: "Look to your left, look to your right. One of these people will not be here come graduation."

"Look to your left, look to your right," I whispered to Arjun during one of our last lectures in engineering school. "Now look behind you and look in front of you. None of them are here. They've all transferred to liberal arts and are now political science majors."

Because engineering was so hard, we rooted for one another. And while there was camaraderie in the trenches, there was also a hierarchy. Different engineering disciplines commanded more respect than others. Some curriculums were considered more difficult; others were more in demand. The most prestigious and desirable future employees were the biotechnology engineers. After that came the electrical, chemical, and mechanical engineers, followed by the civil, industrial, and ceramic engineers. The mechanical engineers called themselves MEs, the electrical engineers EEs, and so on.

I was a lowly IE, and so was Arjun. It's funny how career paths happen. Arjun and I were both caught off guard when the day came to narrow down our major to a curriculum. On a whim, we both picked industrial engineering. That capricious decision resulted in three years of redrafting facility layouts, evaluating ergonomic designs, and conducting time-efficiency studies. In simplest terms, industrial engineers learned how to make systems work better. By taking a few classes from each of the disciplines, along with some business courses, I learned to examine, say, a mechanical assembly line and offer solutions that increased the system's efficiency and productivity and decreased its costs. I crunched numbers. I got answers. I placed a box around them. It came naturally to me. I had inherited my father's analytical skills—he, too, was an engineer.

Law school, by contrast, had nothing to do with answers.

Occasionally during first-year law school, we'd learn a legal principle grounded in economic theory and formulas. Then, thankfully, there would be math. It happened, for example, when we examined product liability suits. In evaluating whether a particular company was negligent for a manufacturing defect in a car, I might estimate the cost to fix the fatal defect, assume certain values for human life, and approximate the likelihood of accidents. Those were the few moments in first-year law school that law most closely resembled engineering, and when I was capable and in control. When it was all about formulas, variables, and values. "Plug and chug," as we said in engineering. And, of course, the best part—box your answer.

But more often I learned that law was the opposite of mathematics. There were no answers. Legal decisions were as close as it got to answers, and law school taught you that every decision was very fact-specific. It was an attorney's job to appreciate, understand, argue, and distinguish those facts in a particular decision. If deciding a case was a matter of plugging in a few numbers, why would anyone bother with lawyers? Resolving legal matters would be a function of computers. There was very little finite about the law. Except, of course, for the U.S. Supreme Court.

First-year law school was scary. But if I had to pick one person who scared me the most that year, it would have to be me. I hadn't read a single work of fiction or written one thesis in college. Besides my engineering classes, all I'd taken in college were one writing course and three electives. I entered law school freaked out. I figured there was a good chance that I could neither read nor write. And both skills struck me as important to practice law. There were no more face-offs with illiterate mechanical engineers. First-year law school, my competition turned out to be those goddamn political science majors who transferred out of engineering. I figured I was in deep trouble.

But a year can do a lot for a law student. Second-year law school was a whole new world. I went from scared, clueless, and jobless to having six jobs. Thus the expression: Second-year law school, they work you.

My first job was being a full-time student: I had a full course load.

My second job was *Temple Law Review*. At the end of my first year of law school, I successfully wrote onto the law review. It was a huge honor. Only about forty students in my class were invited to join, based on a composite of our first-year grades and a writing competition.

My third job was law-school president. I'd always been fascinated with student government, and I'd never quite recovered from sixth-grade class elections. Damn that Andy Tucci, his free chocolate bars, and his slogan: "Tucci or not Tucci: That is the question." Since then I'd served every student body at every stage of my education. Even in first-year law school, I was elected the section rep. At the end of that year, a second-year student running for law-school president asked whether I'd like to run with him as vice president. I elected to run against him. I campaigned hard, I lobbied the night-school students, and I squeaked out a win. Now I helped coordinate student life at Temple Law. The student bar association, or SBA, was the primary voice for the student body. I attended faculty meetings and conducted student assemblies. The student bar turned out a weekly newsletter, orchestrated open houses and student orientations, and divided up the student budget among more than thirty student organizations.

My fourth and fifth jobs were teaching. I taught one high school course for school credit and one college course for cash. The high school class was called Street Law. I introduced high school seniors at one of Philadelphia's most run-down inner-city schools all about basic criminal law and procedure. At the end of the course, I presided over a full-blown trial in which the students assumed witness and attorney roles before local judges. As for the Temple undergraduate course Law & Society, I did much less teaching. I was an overpaid graduate student who kept office hours, graded papers, and occasionally ran the slide projector during lectures.

My sixth and final job was the most time-consuming. I job-hunted. It was strange. Not even halfway through law school, and my career clock was already ticking. I'd come out of the gates strong. Between good first-year grades and my law review and SBA credentials, I was a contender. The rocket docket appeared to be within my reach. I could almost taste it.

Second-year interviewing season was, to borrow from the law, "open and notorious." If you were interviewing, everyone knew it, all because of on-campus interviewing. Every day for the first two months of the fall semester, the top law firms came to interview Temple's best and brightest. The status class wore basically the same uniform. When they attended class, which was rare, they were easy to pick out of a lineup. Everyone else in class was still wearing casual clothes, except for the five or six people wearing blue or charcoal-gray suits and frantically checking their watches to ensure that they weren't running late for their next on-campus.

People hated the "suits." The suits were resented. I was a suit. We congregated on the fifth floor. That's where the Career Planning Office was located—originally called the Career *Placement* Center but changed to reflect the office's inability to promise placement, given the saturation of lawyers in the market.

This was how the process worked: The Career Planning Office would post a list of the big law firms coming to interview on campus. If a particular law firm interested you, you submitted a résumé and cover letter. Two weeks later, stapled to the Career Planning Office bulletin board, the firm posted a list of students granted first-round interviews. The most ambitious firms interviewed as many as twenty students in one day. That meant if you were lucky, and the firm wasn't running behind schedule, you had twenty minutes to dance your ass off before the firm ushered in your best friend in her best suit and best tap shoes. Then you waited. After a week or two, you got either a phone call inviting you to come to the law firm for a callback interview, or a letter indicating that you were no longer in the running.

To be anywhere near that bulletin board was excruciating. In my first month of my second year, I submitted résumés and cover letters to at least fifty law firms interviewing on campus. Twenty-two of them granted me first-round interviews. That was a pretty good average. But there were still about two dozen law students ahead of me.

Most suits dropped by the Career Planning Office a couple of times a day. As I approached the boards one morning, I saw David Markey. He and I were good friends. We had met during first-year. We were in the same section together. First-year friendships were the most likely to survive.

"Anything new up there?" I asked.

David was shaking his head in disappointment. "Tons. It's brutal," he said. "It's like they copied the same list of fifteen students over and over again, then changed the name of the firm at the top of the page."

David possessed the coveted Temple Triple Crown. He was a member of the law school's three most prestigious organizations—the law review, the oral advocacy honors society called Moot Court, and the Temple National Trial Team. Like mine, his grades were well above average, but he was not in the top twenty. That made him good enough to interview on campus but not necessarily first draft.

"Did you just interview or are you about to?" I said, referring to his dark blue suit.

"Both," he said flatly. "Do you know that Career Planning posted six new law firms up there, and Kristy Trenton is on every single list? She doesn't even want to work in a big law firm. She wants to go into public service. She's wasting one of the interview slots."

"That's rough. Any of the on-campus interviews call you back?" I asked.

"Four callbacks, but I'm not feeling very encouraged," he said. "I haven't received any offers yet, and it's getting late. What about you? How did it go with O'Connell and Price the other day?"

"Good." I paused. I hadn't heard from O'Connell & Price since my dinner with Dennis, two and a half days ago. "It went good. Jury's still out on that one."

"It's so hard to get a read on these interviews. The ones that go the best are the first ones to send me a rejection letter. I don't get it."

"Same here," I agreed. "I've been in a few interviews where you can see it all over their faces. 'Eager, seems too eager.'"

"Enthusiasm can definitely be a deal breaker," David said.

"There's nothing logical or predictable about it. These interviews usually end the way most of my relationships do—first they don't return your phone calls, then you get a two-line rejection in the mail."

CHAPTER 3

MET MOLLY IN a small, crowded coffee shop in midtown New York City. Big cities always emboldened me when it came to breaking the ice with women. Latte in hand, I studied her from across the room. She had this beautiful combination of black hair and blue-blue eyes. I needed an "in." All I needed was a scintilla of an in. I needed *something* to break the ice. Suddenly, I hit pay dirt.

"I have that *same* book," I said, referring to the spine of her familiar red hardcover law book.

"You have *The Inequalities of Women in the Law?*" she said, flipping to the cover.

"Yes, I do."

She smiled. "Have a seat," she said, clearing some papers. We introduced ourselves. Neither of us mentioned the name of the law school we attended. Saying where you went to school right away was like skipping foreplay, or like revealing your religion and political party in the first few minutes of a conversation. Plus, maybe I was a little ashamed of my Tier 2 status. These days I avoided exchanging law school names for as long as possible.

"I'm interviewing around the block. My law school sponsors New York Day—this pathetic invite-only job fair where you get one day to interview with a few big New York firms." Truthfully, I was thrilled to have been invited.

"That *is* depressing. Where do you go?"

"Temple Law. In Philadelphia." I always added the city, as if the person might not be familiar with the school. "And you?"

"Columbia."

I winced slightly. Columbia had rejected my law school application. But in general, I could deal with Columbia Law. Even though it was a Tier 1 school, at least Molly hadn't said Harvard. Harvard—God, when someone said Harvard, it just hung there in the air.

Molly and I made plans to meet that night. Confidence bolstered, I went back to New York Day. The recruiters said they'd be in touch.

Molly was typical of the type of woman I had been attracted to lately. These days I generally dated professionals, or soon-to-be-professionals. Most of the time they were law students, and always Temple Law students. Come to think of it, Molly was my first Tier 1 date. Given where I was in my life, on the cusp of my professional career, I had a whole new perspective on women, dating, and relationships. I frequently entertained the notion of marriage, if briefly. Each time I met a woman, I pondered whether she was it, the woman I would spend the rest of my life with. On paper, Molly was promising: scholarly, sexy, and sophisticated.

I met Molly at her apartment on West 119th, still wearing my interview suit. Molly had changed into jeans and a long-sleeved T-shirt that occasionally revealed a belly-button ring. I took off my tie. Molly suggested that we have dinner 110 blocks south of her apartment, in Greenwich Village. We took a cab.

In the first hour I made too many jokes. Molly was a tough audience. If she didn't think something was particularly funny, she shook her head and changed the topic.

After drinks and a fancy dinner that I couldn't afford on a student budget, she began to loosen up. I quickly learned she was an academic star. Based on her grades alone, she'd been invited to join the *Columbia Law Review,* the most prestigious writing journal in the school. I, like most law students, was asked to join Temple's law review upon successful completion of a writing competition. Even though Molly was two years younger than I, we were both second-year students. She had started school young and skipped fifth grade.

Come dessert, marriage proposals were off the table. I was still deliberating over whether I even liked her. And Molly struck me as bored. The conversation never developed into a comfortable rhythm. Long stretches of silence and small talk were interrupted by heated debates over world issues and the law. Molly liked to debate. This was typical of the female law students I dated. In just over an hour, we covered abortion, free speech, and privacy. Molly had her legal and societal philosophies carefully charted, and she pounced on me when I had different opinions or, God forbid, no opinion whatsoever. She scared me a little.

"Have you considered working for the New York State Defenders Association?" she asked, sipping her cosmopolitan. "I worked there after first year."

It bothered me that she was recommending her job from last summer. I was a second year, I was ready for something better than her leftovers. "No, not really. I'm more interested in working with a law firm." I'd always fantasized about being the cliché big-shot attorney.

Clearly, this annoyed Molly. "Aren't you being a bit solipsistic? If you're not going to make public service your career, the least you can do is make one contribution, for *one* summer, in the interest of the greater good of society. The people at the State Defenders Association are desperate for some help."

"Maybe I'll look into it." I wouldn't. I wasn't interested in becoming a defense attorney. I wasn't interested in criminal law period. If push came to shove and I had to pick some element of criminal law, I'd be more likely to investigate the district attorney's or U.S. Attorney's office. Even if you had no intention of ever practicing criminal law, you were either a prosecutor or a defense attorney. Good lawyers could always appreciate both points of view, but deep down, you were one or the other. If I had to choose, I was a prosecutor. I didn't dare say this to Molly.

"The prospect of spending an entire legal career representing big conglomerates sounds awful. What an empty experience."

Maybe she was right. I'd never done it before, but then again, neither had she. "Do you know what *you're* doing next summer?" I asked.

"I've accepted an internship with the Capital Division at the Legal Aid Society downtown."

"Congratulations. That's amazing," I said. It was. She'd landed one of the most competitive jobs in the country. She'd make virtually nothing. "What will you be doing?" I asked.

"Death-penalty cases," she said. "It's the *Capital* Division, Alex."

"Oh."

"I'll work on final appeals," she said excitedly.

I hadn't plotted out my arguments on the death penalty yet. I got nervous. "Let's get out of here," I said, feeling a buzz from my second martini. She agreed.

On the way out, we stopped in the vestibule located between the inside and outside doors of the bar and began kissing. Molly liked me. Aside from some minimal blue light spilling in from the bar, the tiny space was pitch black. Soon Molly began kissing her way down my body. Then she unbuckled my pants. What if someone I knew walked in? Thanks to New York Day, Temple students were everywhere. And we had to be breaking some municipal code.

I spread my arms and braced the inside and outside doors. No one was coming in or leaving until we finished. Our timing was perfect.

When the fire hazard was over, Molly and I took a walk through SoHo. Maybe this relationship would work out after all. Maybe Molly was just what I needed—a strong, take-charge type of woman. A life filled with passionate nights and passionate pillow talk. She looked so beautiful.

It was freezing. We ducked into a small, overpriced candle shop.

"How can these places afford to pay commercial rent on candle sales alone?" I asked Molly.

She hushed me, which annoyed me. But I persevered. "These smell nice," I said, handing her a vanilla candle.

She nodded in agreement. She hadn't said much since our interlude in the vestibule.

I walked over to a gigantic candle in the corner. "Molly, check out this wonga candle. It's immense."

"Shut up," she said sternly. "You're embarrassing us."

The salesclerk turned away, clearly uncomfortable with what Molly had said to me. I was shocked. Such harsh words from that perfect little mouth. This time it was too much.

" 'Shut up'?" I whispered angrily. "Don't tell me to shut up." No one told me to shut up. Especially someone that I'd just met.

"Well, you're being an idiot." What was with this girl? In the last fifteen minutes she had put me through exhilaration and humiliation. Did her rude remark have something to do with the vestibule? Was she angry about what had happened? Embarrassed? Empowered? Maybe she was more than I could handle. I didn't feel like talking about it, and apparently, neither did she.

"Well, don't tell me to shut up," I said, still shaken. "I'm not cool with that."

"Never mind. Can we go?"

We left the shop. I dropped her off at her apartment, took the train back to Philadelphia, and looked up the word "solipsism." A theory holding that the self is the only thing in existence.

CHAPTER 4

THERE ARE SOME professions that people seem destined for. Firefighting, police work, art, dance, music. Many of these people had their calling young. They were born with the talent and needed to develop it. Maybe they were attracted to the heroic or altruistic nature of the job, or they were encouraged to pursue the career by a family member or mentor. Ultimately, most careers come after some deep soul-searching, trial and error, and persistence. Then there are those career paths that no one could have possibly predicted.

Take coprolite experts. They're in the business of studying fossilized dung. Coprolite experts study shit for a living—literally. You give them a dropping or some great big log, and they'll tell you all about the animal's diet. Because there are so many different types of coprolites, people even specialize. World-renowned paleontologist Dr. Karen Chin, for example, can tell you anything you want to know about dinosaur dung. She is the foremost expert in the world. Could she ever have predicted that she'd one day gain major notoriety by identifying T-Rex poo? She tours the big academic lecture circuits doing shit presentations, and paleontologists from around the world send her shit. Did Chin know she had brains for shit? I think not.

Something unique must have happened that put Chin on that

career path. It could be viewed in "but-for" terms—an analysis that I picked up in law school. But-for was all about cause and effect. For example, but-for Joey wearing a blindfold when he drove the ice-cream truck, he would not have hit the large Mack truck carrying two tons of flammable explosives. I wondered what Chin's but-for was. Perhaps a career in coprolites . . . happens.

For me, but-for a broken Ping-Pong paddle, I would not have been born an attorney.

The moment of conception, as it is referred to in the law, happened during my freshman year of college. Two days before engineering classes began, Arjun and I went down to the dormitory's recreation room to play table tennis. This would be our first match in a series that would last for years to come. The sporting equipment was in sad shape. All we could find were two dilapidated paddles. Arjun took the one with the pebbled rubber hanging off one side. "Here," he said, throwing me the other paddle, which had no handle.

"What am I supposed to do with this?" I asked as I palmed the paddle in my right hand and curled my fingers around the edges. We began rallying back and forth. To my surprise, by eliminating the handle, I could take a larger, more natural, tennislike stroke and hit the ball with more momentum and strength. The racquet became an extension of my body. Because the center or sweet spot of the paddle was directly aligned with my palm, I could easily make contact with the ball at the right angle at the right time.

"See, you're fine," Arjun said. "Let's start." And with that, he served. His long arms enabled him to wind up and slam the ball across the table. I used the paddle to defend against his big forehand shots. They kept coming and coming, and I was doing fine until he hit a backhand shot. At that point I was screwed. There was no way to wrench my wrist around to return balls hit to my backhand side. After Arjun shut me out a few times, it occurred to me that what I needed was some practice—and another paddle fastened to the top of my hand.

I made a prototype. I took two table-tennis paddles and sawed off the handles, then set them parallel to each other using two small toy building blocks. Voilà: the first truly double-sided table-tennis paddle sandwich. The three-inch-high blocks allowed my right hand to slip snugly between the parallel paddles. Mounted directly on my hand, the contraption had a solid feel to it. Now when I hit the ball, it made a "pong" rather than a "ping" sound.

I followed up with some test studies. Friends agreed to meet me for games in back rooms to avoid divulging my secret paddle to the world. The novel paddle was instantly embraced. Arjun even helped me produce an instructional video illustrating the advantages of my paddle over the conventional one. He fed me questions from behind the video camera. "Will the paddle be legal?" He was referring to the official International Table Tennis Federation rules.

"Who cares," I said, with the paddle hanging off my right hand. "This paddle will *change* the rules." My research demonstrated that I had something very good on my hands—literally. What I needed was some real protection, recognizable under the law. What I needed was a monopoly on double-sided table-tennis paddles. What I needed was a patent.

Owen Thompkins didn't seem to think so, however. Owen Thompkins (Harvard Law, Tier 1) became my patent attorney out of sheer proximity. His sole practitioner office was a twenty-minute bus ride from Rutgers. In one sweeping motion, I walked into his office, handed him the paddle prototype, and popped my instructional videotape into his VCR.

"Okay, okay, I get it," he said as he searched for the stop button on his remote control two minutes in. He was extremely unimpressed, but for a fee, he was willing to pursue the idea. "We should conduct a patent search to ensure that the invention doesn't already exist somewhere else, either as a patent, by combining an assortment of patents, or as the subject of a publication. A 'prior art' search is the right way to proceed before you invest thousands of dollars in attorney fees filing a patent application."

Did someone say "thousands of dollars"? I agreed.

Three weeks later, I received a letter from Thompkins saying that, in his professional opinion, the idea sucked. Those weren't his exact words, but for eight hundred dollars, he provided me with some prior art and a short, discouraging letter indicating that my paddle wasn't quite unique enough.

He was wrong, of course. My invention was brilliant. It was much better than my previous contraptions. Maybe my wet-dry chalk-eraser vacuum or legal-size loose-leaf binders had no future, but my paddle had merit. It would reinvent the sport of table tennis. Perusing the prior art, I differed with Thompkins's legal opinion. And I didn't need a second opinion. I decided at eighteen years old that I would take the easy path and patent the paddle myself. It was a straightforward plan: graduate from engineering school, go to law school, patent my paddle, and retire on the royalties. Or something like that.

When I applied to law schools in my senior year of college, I made the paddle the centerpiece of my admissions essays. Anything to distract the committees from focusing on my average LSATs. Despite good grades, a challenging major, and extracurricular activities, my LSATs compelled me to be conservative in my selection process. Ultimately, I selected one Tier 1 (Columbia), five Tier 2s (Brooklyn, Seton Hall, St. John's, Temple, and Villanova), and one Tier 3 (Hofstra). It was important to me that the seven law schools be located within driving distance of my family in Toms River, New Jersey.

Columbia rejected me. Everyone else sent acceptance letters, except Temple. Temple, prompted by my table-tennis paddle essay, invited me to campus for an informal interview. Few law schools interviewed applicants. I guess they were on the fence about me. The Temple admissions committee took one look at my double-sided table-tennis paddle, which I'd pulled out of my empty leather briefcase, and my acceptance letter arrived later that week. I had a new lucky shirt, I thought, noticing my navy blue button-down. I'd wear this shirt to all of my future law school exams.

Reading and rereading that acceptance letter from Temple Law School, I couldn't help but think, Screw you, Owen Thompkins. Screw you.

CHAPTER 5

OLLY NEVER THOUGHT my Wall of Pain was a good idea. Neither did my mother. I, on the other hand, thought rejection could be fun.

Molly and I were still dating. Between the vestibule adventure and the shut-up incident, I left our first date feeling like I'd broken even. These days we were spending most of our time together in New York. Initially, we agreed to take turns commuting every other weekend. But in the last month Molly hadn't held up her end of the bargain. She'd made the trip to Philly once. After that she made me feel miserable about asking her to commute an hour and a half to a second-rate city like Philadelphia. It seemed tiers were everywhere.

Even though I resented her for making *me* travel, the truth was, I was happy to spend as much time in Manhattan as possible. Not so much because the relationship was going especially well—things were off to a rocky start—but I was intrigued by the possibility of practicing there. "New York is the world's center of law practice," a favorite professor told me in school. "Great legal careers either end or begin in Manhattan." Given my new second-year credentials, the city seemed attainable.

On the downside, the on-campus and callback interviews were starting to dry up, and I still hadn't heard from Dennis Braise or O'Connell & Price. It was coming up on a week. That godforsaken Career Planning bulletin board was quite a roller-coaster ride. In the last two months I'd embraced and rejected the idea of practicing intellectual property law at least ten times. One day my name would be on the board, and I'd be on top of the world—a law school superstar, convinced I could practice anywhere and anything. Why bury myself in patent-law and engineering minutiae, I'd think, when I could embark on a career as a high-powered corporate or trial attorney? Then I'd go for a few days without a mark on the bulletin board, and a career in patent law would start to sound like a pretty good option for an illiterate engineer like me. There would be much less competition:

Law students who didn't have a technical degree weren't in the running.

Because I knew it was a mistake to rely too heavily on the Career Planning Office and its bulletin board, I began an independent job search early on. Half the time I felt like a boy genius and the other half a moron, so I hedged my bets. I sent résumés and cover letters to about sixty major general-practice law firms and forty patent-law firms. Half of them were in New York City, the other half in Philadelphia. I knew it would be a long shot for a Tier 2er to secure a high-paying summer internship with a big New York firm through mass mailings and cold calls, but I had to try, and I was willing to have a sense of humor about the process.

All of the first responses were rejections. But that was the nature of letters—good news rarely arrived on paper. Requests to interview, or actual job offers, usually came over the phone. Firms didn't wait to recruit you via snail mail, they called you and arranged a meeting. But my phone never rang, and even though it was a long shot, I continued to hold out hope that a promising letter would arrive.

The harsh ones came quickly. Most of them were one-liners saying thanks but no thanks. It was almost as if those firms anticipated my application and prepared the rejection letter in advance, postage and all. One day, I'm convinced, someone will make an administrative error, and a law student will be rejected before ever sending a résumé.

New letters arrived every day. I formed a ritual. Each day I'd sit down in the kitchen with the newest batch of letters, scan them for the operative rejection word, then highlight the "unfortunately," "however," or "sorry." I even ranked the letters. The more words the law firm used before ultimately rejecting me, the higher the ranking. Every word was worth one point. Most law firms had a score of one or two points, as the typical letter started off with "We regret." But there were exceptions. One Philadelphia patent-law firm, Richmond, Falk & Doran, scored fifty-two points. The letter went on and on and on about how wonderful I was before kindly instructing me to take a hike. The gentler letters encouraged me to reapply during my third year of law school. But that was the same as being rejected: By third year it was too late. And no, there were no letters that said, "We regret to inform you that we would love to have you work for us this summer."

I taped every one of those rejection letters to a kitchen wall—my Wall of Pain. It took about a month and seventy-five letters to cover all the kitchen walls with letterhead from some of the most prominent firms in the world. I then began working my way into the living room.

It turned out that the centennial rejection was not as momentous an occasion as I'd hoped it would be. The recruiter rejected me in two sentences, and then promised to keep my résumé on file if the firm's needs changed. The notion of a Wall of Pain suddenly struck me as humiliating.

"Ahhhhhhh," I screamed at the top of my lungs. "God, damn, stupid, wall!" I ripped the letters off the wall, along with a lot of blue paint attached to the tape holding them there.

When I was finished, I rubbed my face with both hands and stared blankly at the carnage. I sank onto the floor and began vetting the letters, pulling off the straggly pieces of Scotch tape and looking for those with the highest rejection scores. If I got truly desperate, perhaps, I would reapply to those firms in my third year.

"How's the job search coming along?" Molly asked. She stood smugly in the kitchen doorway, her arms crossed.

"Oh, hey. I didn't realize you were here," I said. I'd forgotten it was Molly's turn to travel to Philadelphia. What a nice surprise.

"I used my key," she said. "No more pain wall?"

I instantly regretted having given her a key. She was the first woman I'd ever given a key. Then again, this was my first apartment.

"Yeah. The whole experiment didn't turn out to be the confidence builder I thought it was going to be," I said.

"This wall of yours raises flags on all kinds of deep psychological problems," she said, only half joking. "Can you organize those letters later? I want to celebrate."

I propped myself up and followed her into the living room.

"Wait," she said as she reached into her backpack and pulled out a bottle of good chardonnay and a thick stack of papers held together with a big binder clip. "It's a draft of my law-review article." She waited for me to pick it up.

"Geez," I said, shuffling through the pages. "This is impressive."

"I haven't slept in weeks. It's my 'comment.' It's two hundred and three double-spaced pages, with ninety-two footnotes," Molly said.

Regardless of tiers, my law-review experience and Molly's were turning out to be essentially the same. In your first year on law review, you spent half the time proofreading and cite-checking draft articles written by senior law-review writers and professors. Nearly every sentence in each article had to be attributed and footnoted. Subordinate second-year staffers like Molly and me spent endless hours making sure the sources said what the author purported. Then we Bluebooked the entire piece, which meant confirming that the format of each and every sentence and footnote conformed with *The Bluebook: A Uniform System of Citation*—the definitive source for legal citation. The book itself was blue.

Bluebooking could be a maddening process. *The Bluebook* contained thousands of special rules about punctuation, titles, fonts, and abbreviations. Most of them were arbitrary, inconsistent, and hard to apply. You had to remember, for example, that when citing an article as a source, you placed a comma after the title. But in citing a book, placing a comma after the title was wrong. Why? No particular reason. It was one of those rules that the people at Harvard, Yale, Columbia, and Stanford Law had decided were the right way to do things. Ah, the Tier 1s ruled the world. Besides the fact that four of the most powerful Tier 1 law schools published the rules of engagement, I didn't mind *The Bluebook*. Bluebooking reminded me of engineering.

We spent the other half of our time on law review writing an article. At most schools, you were given a choice: You could write either a note or a comment. The former was generally simpler and shorter. In a note, you analyzed a potentially influential, controversial, or landmark recent court decision and determined whether or not the ruling was consistent with existing case law. A comment, on the other hand, was much more extensive—it was a comment on some specific area of burgeoning law. It required the author to analyze and reconcile many different cases throughout many different jurisdictions and provide judicial or legislative suggestions, solutions, or alternatives.

Writing a comment was an admirable and impressive endeavor. Molly frequently reminded me that she was writing a comment. Then again, so was I. I was commenting on the dozen or so federal decisions that conflicted on whether federal prisoners were entitled to receive minimum wage for their work in prison. The short answer was yes. Because the federal law that guaranteed the minimum wage didn't specifically exclude them, prisoners were entitled. Of course, it would take me a thousand hours, three hundred pages, and one hundred footnotes to say that.

I flipped to the cover page of Molly's masterpiece, which read, "When Innocent Defendants Plead Guilty: How Prosecutors and Defense Attorneys Hurt the Plea-Bargaining Process, by Molly Langley."

"I know what you're thinking," Molly said to me as I scanned the manuscript. "But I take a *balanced* view of the process. It's not all about how prosecutors advance their careers by railroading plea bargains and convicting innocent defendants." In the month that we'd dated, Molly had been very clear about her take on law enforcement: The government will trample your due-process rights every chance it gets. It will routinely enter your home without notice, tap your phones without proper authority, and frisk you on the fly, simply because its agents feel like it.

"I see. This is very cool. Here you talk about how defense attorneys also abuse the process. How they push for plea bargains in order to advance their personal careers, manage their caseloads, and make a living. It's interesting." I knew that if I put the treatise down too quickly, I'd insult her. I continued to page through.

She said, "Did you know some scholars posit that innocent defendants are more likely to plead guilty than guilty ones? Innocent defendants are more risk-averse. They'll go to jail for something they didn't do because they don't want to take a chance that they'll lose at trial and get an even longer sentence. Real criminals, however, are willing to take their chances at trial because they've already demonstrated a willingness to break the law."

"That makes sense. An innocent defendant probably mistrusts the whole legal system and doesn't want to leave his fate in the hands of a jury. I guess plea-bargaining is the lesser of two evils."

"This is your copy," she said. "You can read it whenever."

"Thanks," I said, being very careful not to *promise* to read it. I took the bottle of wine into the kitchen and began uncorking it. "Hey," I yelled, "what's the title again?" She came in and read it back to me. "Hmmm. The piece focuses on prosecutors and defense attorneys, huh?" I poured two glasses. "What about the judges?"

"What about them?" she said as I handed her a glass.

I could tell from her tone that I was already in dangerous territory. I was careful with my words. "It's just that judges play such a significant role in the plea-bargaining process. And given that they're employed by the government, I figured you'd be suspicious of them, too."

She paused. "Theoretically, judges are supposed to be impartial and neutral, *not* active participants in the plea-bargaining process. But I guess, arguably, there are incentives for them to conserve judicial resources and shuffle cases through."

"Yeah, that's all I'm saying. Maybe you want to include that in your piece." Then my mind started racing. "Oh, and here's another reason a judge might push for a plea bargain," I said excitedly. "The fewer trials there are, the less likely the judge is to make a reversible error. Judges hate to get their decisions reversed. They're always so concerned about their record. That's another reason they might want the defendant to take the plea bargain. I dunno. It's just a thought."

Molly hadn't moved a muscle in thirty seconds. She sat on the couch frozen, with her glass held directly against her lower lip. Suddenly, she put down her glass, threw the article in her backpack, and began putting on her coat.

"What are you doing?" I asked. She silently buttoned her coat. She wouldn't even look at me. "Hello? What's wrong with you?"

"I'm out of here."

"You're kidding. Where are you going? You just commuted almost two hours to get here. Is this about my comment on your comment?"

"I can't deal with you right now." And with that, she threw her backpack over one shoulder and her overnight bag over the other, and walked out. I sat there for a few moments, debating over whether to chase after her.

I decided to go from one Wall of Pain to another. I took my glass of wine, sat down on the floor, and continued collating my rejection letters.

CHAPTER 6

THIS IS MARGARET Denton with the intellectual property law firm Nickel and Reed in New York. We'd like to arrange an interview with you next week, if you're available."

I sat down next to the answering machine, trying to jog my memory. All the letters and résumés I'd sent were starting to blur together. Nickel & Reed didn't ring a bell. I didn't recall sending that firm a résumé. I listened to the message again. Oh. I must have subconsciously suppressed the words "intellectual property." At least for the time being, patent law was off the table again. Three days ago I had finally received that precious O'Connell & Price offer. Dennis had come through.

Nickel & Reed was one of the few remaining IP firms that hadn't made my Wall of Pain. I pulled up their website on my computer and basked in the glory. Oh, how the tides had shifted. Thanks to a double-sided table-tennis paddle, I had an invitation to interview with one of the largest, most prestigious intellectual property law firms in the world. *Screw you*, Owen Thompkins.

But rejecting Nickel would not be so simple. Besides their prominent standing in the IP industry, the office was located in New York

City. The last time I had interviewed in New York was the day I met Molly. And New York Day ended up going nowhere—my three interviews with top general-practice firms hadn't resulted in a single callback. But now I had a new Manhattan prospect, even if it was an IP firm. As I paged through Nickel's website, deliberating over what to do next, the phone rang.

"This is Sandra Simmons. I'm a recruiter for Willis, Conrad, Schick and Beach, in New York. Perhaps Marcy Rosenblatt told you that I'd be calling. Are you available for an interview this Thursday at ten A.M.? Our schedules are tight. That's all I have."

I knew exactly who Willis, Conrad was. Willis, Conrad was one of *the* largest general-practice firms in the world, employing thousands of attorneys—six hundred plus in New York alone. Famous for high-profile cases, prominent clients, and extraordinary salaries, midlevel Willis, Conrad partners were rumored to earn nearly $1 million a year.

Thursday was only two days away, and ten A.M. was a terrible time for me—that day I had to attend class, teach class, and chair a budget meeting. "Sure, that works for me."

"We'll see you then," she said coolly. "Good evening."

Nickel may have wanted to interview me on my merits, but Willis, Conrad didn't. I'd sensed an attitude from Sandra Simmons. Perhaps that was just the way she handled all eager students. But somehow it felt personal. She'd given me no opportunity to ask questions. There was no mention of what department and with whom I'd interview on Thursday. Not even an offer to set up my train ticket from Philadelphia to New York. And then there was her particularly rigid offer. "Thursday at 10:00 A.M. . . . . That's all I have." I had to assume it was Tier 2–related—I'd heard that major firms like Willis, Conrad bent over backward to cater to Tier 1 schedules, flying them into New York from all over the country and putting them up in deluxe accommodations.

But then it occurred to me: Maybe her curt tone had something to do with the way I'd secured the interview. Simmons wasn't responding to a mass mailing, a cold call, an on-campus interview, or a callback. I wasn't interviewing with Willis, Conrad because she had identified me as a good candidate. They were interviewing me for one reason and one reason alone: because Marcy Rosenblatt had said to.

Marcy Rosenblatt (Temple Law, Tier 2) did not know me, and I did not know Marcy Rosenblatt, yet I knew exactly who she was. She'd graduated from Temple Law School within the last ten years and was now a partner at Willis, Conrad. I pulled her bio from my Temple alumni folder and confirmed the details. According to my records, she and I had even briefly spoken two weeks back.

Temple Law wasn't doing enough to help me break in to New York City. Besides New York Day, it seemed that most of Temple's career-planning resources were being used to help students secure jobs in Philadelphia—only calcifying our Tier 2 status. Those of us pursuing a career outside Philadelphia were largely responsible for conduct-ing the job search on their own, and a simple mass mailing didn't cut it.

That was where Marcy Rosenblatt came in. I'd contacted her and about fifty other Marcy Rosenblatts over the past two months using Martindale-Hubbell, a routinely updated electronic encyclopedia list-ing every attorney practicing everywhere.

The biographies varied, depending on how much each firm was willing to pay Martindale-Hubbell, which charged by the word. The more substantial bios included the attorney's birth date, the name and graduation year of every school he or she attended, the type of educa-tional degrees he or she obtained, publications, trade associations, practice areas, and every state and federal jurisdiction the attorney was licensed to practice. Before a callback interview, it was a good idea to get a list of the attorneys you were going to meet and look them up in Martindale.

Using birthdays, firm sizes, location, graduation dates, and schools, I used Martindale to narrow my search to all the Marcy Rosenblatts of the world. I searched under the same credentials—he or she had to be a midlevel partner working in a large general-practice firm in New York, and most important, each had graduated from Temple Law. I picked midlevel partners because I figured they'd be in the best position to help advance my career, but they weren't too old and crotchety to ignore me altogether.

Contacting the Rosenblatts started with a short, simple, subtle, professional letter. In it, I never actually asked for a job. "I know you receive so many letters from students graduating from Temple Law—most of them requesting a job or interview. That's not my intention. I'm writing you because I have some questions about pursuing a legal career in Manhattan, and I'd appreciate any time and advice you might be able to offer." My letter included another paragraph on credentials, then my intent to follow up with a telephone call.

But getting them to read it was a separate challenge. Between the mail room, secretaries, and recruiters, the chances of an unsolicited résumé making it onto a big-time partner's desk were low. The trick was in properly addressing the envelope.

"If you want me to read it, write 'Personal and Confidential' across the front of the envelope," a senior partner and friend of the family had told me during an informal interview two months earlier. "In the large firms, the mail room opens every letter so it can be time-stamped for litigation purposes. 'Personal and Confidential' will even make it past a secretary."

Done. From then on, I wrote "Personal and Confidential" across every envelope I addressed, and hoped for the best.

The follow-up call was all about timing. I called promptly three days after sending each letter. By then Marcy Rosenblatt had probably received the letter, glanced at the résumé, read the first sentence and half of the cover letter, and thrown it in either the "to do" or the "waste" basket. If I didn't have the attorney's direct line, I socially engineered my way past the series of receptionists and secretaries. "Ms. Rosenblatt is expecting my call," I said matter-of-factly. Once I reached her, my first few sentences were critical. I remained casual yet deferential.

"Hello, Ms. Rosenblatt. I sent you a letter the other day, requesting some career advice?" Then I added the clincher: "I'm graduating from *Temple . . . Law . . .* in the spring?"

The response generally went along the lines of "make it quick."

"If now's not a good time, I'd be glad to call back." If I sensed Marcy had a sense of humor and recognized how difficult it was to make this type of phone call, I used the same joke, "Or we could speak . . . never." The only people who ever responded to this shaky attempt at charm were the Marcy Rosenblatts. The Mark, Bob, and Samuel Rosenblatts were generally uninterested.

At that point the results were hit or miss. Sometimes Marcy made the conversation miserable. Other times she offered contacts or advice. She usually offered to forward my résumé to the firm's recruiter, and that was the whole point. A résumé delivered to the recruiter by a senior associate or junior partner always trumped blanket mailings. It was all about the reference.

And that was apparently what the real Marcy Rosenblatt had done. We must have spoken, she must have agreed to pass along my résumé, and somehow, in all the confusion at Willis, Conrad, that translated into an interview. At least now they could reject me in person and on my merits. Or because of the suit I was wearing.

I was the proud recipient of an offer to interview at Willis, Conrad, a top New York law firm. Who cared if Sandra Simmons hated me? And who needed a Career Planning Office? I was all over this job-search thing.

Given the job offer from O'Connell & Price and the interview offer from Willis, Conrad, my analysis concerning Nickel was simple. I didn't need it. Still planted on Nickel's Web page, I pulled up the firm's general phone number and called Margaret Denton to politely decline the opportunity to interview and possibly pursue a career in IP at Nickel.

"Hi, Margaret, this is Alex Wellen. You just left me a message."

"Alex, so glad you called. Tell me, does this Thursday work for you?" Denton said warmly. It never occurred to her that I was calling to beg off.

"Actually, I *will* be in New York on Thursday. Sure," I said without thinking.

"Fine. Why don't we plan on one P.M.? I'll forward your call to our travel department, and they'll arrange your trip."

"All right," I said, dazed.

Well, how do you like that? I was off to New York to interview with Willis, Conrad on Nickel's nickel.

CHAPTER 7

ARRIVED TWO HOURS early for the Willis, Conrad interview. This gave me an opportunity to grab a cup of coffee and a real New York bagel, stand around in my suit, and pretend to be a high-powered Manhattan attorney. Willis, Conrad was in midtown. The all-black contemporary design of the building was breathtaking. The firm occupied thirty of the forty-seven floors.

I checked my hair and the position of my tie in the reflection of a colossal metallic pillar near the revolving door, then took the elevator to reception on the forty-first floor.

The reception area was under construction. Tiptoeing over some throw sheets, I made my way to the woman at the front desk and gave her my best "Hello, I'm opposing counsel, here for a deposition" look. Without saying a word, she pointed me over to a waiting room clearly designated for interviewees.

In the waiting area were six other candidates, four men and two women. There was nothing to like about any of them. They all sat hunched over leather portfolios reviewing secret notes. Every last one of them wore some derivation of a blue pin-striped suit. The men had designer gel that revealed their perfect hairlines. The women wore their hair up. Their ties and scarves were conservative, elegant, and expensive, but not too expensive. They wanted to look polished but not too polished. Confident but not too confident.

I took two quick steps backward toward the reception desk and looked down at my suit. For the love of God, what had compelled me to wear glen plaid? Was I on crack?

I knew I shouldn't have worn the glen plaid. But I was so damn tired of wearing the same two dark suits to every one of my interviews—one blue, the other a gray pinstripe. After two months of grueling interviews, I'd treated myself to a new suit. For the first time I passed on Today's Man and went straight for Boyds, one of Philadelphia's most elegant men's clothing stores. That was where I found the gray-black-and-white-checkered glen plaid. Even though it was a good $250 outside my student budget, I had to have it. It was snappy. And I'd been waiting for just the right occasion to wear it. This interview, it pained me to admit, was not it. Had I been wearing a seersucker or a tuxedo, I might have felt more comfortable.

The other candidates were too consumed by their preparation to pay much attention to me. One or two of them glared over at me in my death shroud and immediately went back to practice interview questions. I could hear them rehearsing their perfect answers under their minty-fresh breath.

Scanning the room, I named the six of them: Okay, you're Harvard, you're Columbia, you're Yale, and you're NYU, Cornell, and Stanford. I assumed most of them were here for interview week—a designated time offered by some Tier 1 schools when normal classes were suspended to allow second- and third-year law students to schedule as many big-firm interviews as possible. Temple didn't have interview week, presumably because landing a job from a Tier 2 took over a week. And "interview month" never really caught on.

After about forty minutes, my turn came.

"Are you Sandra Simmons? I think we spoke on the phone," I said timidly.

"No," she said, annoyed. "I'm Judith Alexander. Sandra doesn't meet our interview candidates. She's in an entirely different part of the building. I'm bringing you to meet a senior partner, Henry Fundguard."

"All right. Will I be meeting with Marcy Rosenblatt? She recommended that I interview with the firm. She and I spoke on the phone—"

"No. She's on the twenty-seventh floor." Apparently location was important. "And if you know her, you wouldn't be interviewing with her. Anyway, no one told me you were supposed to meet with her."

We zigzagged our way through Willis, Conrad's narrow, poorly lit hallways, passing books piled on photocopiers, secretaries in cubicles buried under stacks of legal documents, and two or three attorneys crammed into tiny offices meant for one. Apparently the entire floor was under construction. So much for the luxurious big-firm lifestyle.

I didn't know a thing about Henry Fundguard, and Judith wasn't volunteering. Had I known his name the day before, I could have at least plugged him in to Martindale-Hubbell.

We arrived at the corner office, I waited in the doorway, and Judith delicately walked up to his desk. Fundguard was busy signing something. His law diploma hung on the wall behind him (Stanford Law, Tier 1).

"Henry," she said sweetly, "I'd like you to meet Alex Wellen. He's your ten-forty-five candidate." She turned to me. "As I mentioned, Henry's a senior litigation partner in our products liability department." This was news to me. Fundguard looked up and waited for me to do something.

"Hello," I said nervously. He put down his pen and stretched out his hand but didn't rise from his chair. I awkwardly bent over the large desk and gave him my best firm handshake.

"I'll be back in twenty minutes, Henry," Judith said as she walked out.

"Let me just . . . finish . . . this." Fundguard paged through the document in front of him. I scanned the room for an icebreaker and landed on some preschooler drawings that wallpapered the room at eye level.

"So, I see you're an artist," I said with an approving nod and smile.

"No, those are my son's paintings," Fundguard replied shortly.

"Of course. Right," I said, trying to recover from my failed attempt at humor. "He's very good."

"Fine. Have a seat, Alexander." Okay, Hank. He ran me through all the "why" questions. Why did I go to law school, why did I study engineering in college, why wasn't I pursuing intellectual property work, why did I want to practice in New York, and, of course, why was I Willis, Conrad material?

He seemed unimpressed with my answers. That was par for the course. I figured that his blatant apathy was encouraging, since the good interviews always ended with a quick rejection. Judith arrived a few minutes early to shepherd me through two other uneventful interviews. I promised myself that I would check in with Marcy Rosenblatt and thank her for making this pleasure ride possible, but an impromptu offer to have lunch with two Willis, Conrad junior associates preempted that notion.

Rupert Fuller, a third-year associate (University of Chicago, Tier 1), and Oliver Richtel (University of California, Berkeley, Tier 1), a second-year associate, were my hosts. Recruiters will tell you that the point of dining with junior associates is for you to get down and dirty— to ask them the questions that you might not feel comfortable asking firm partners or senior associates. But that was a farce. Lunch interviews weren't for you; they were for *them*. There was no "insider perspective"; it was one more setting for the firm to scrutinize you in. I always felt you should be Mirandized before a lunch interview: "I have the right to remain silent, everything I say can and will be used against me in a firm evaluation."

Besides the risk of self-incrimination, lunch interviews also meant observing strict eating etiquette. Knowing what to order, how to eat it, and how to carry on a conversation between bites definitely took some negotiating. Over the course of the last two months, I'd picked up a few rules about law firm luncheons.

The first one was simple: Don't order the stringy kind of pasta, like linguine or spaghetti. It was too noisy, too messy, and tended to splatter. Chunkier pastas like ravioli and lasagna were better, but it was best to avoid pasta with tomato sauce altogether. The second rule: Drink iced tea, and don't ask whether it's presweetened, a sign of weakness. The third rule: Don't salt your food before trying it. From a philosophical point of view, salting too early intimated impatience and hasty judgment. And from a practical point of view, perhaps the dish was plenty salty to begin with. Since I'd already diverted from the dress code that afternoon, I embraced these three rules steadfastly.

We walked to a restaurant that was too fancy—the Willis, Conrad cadets were obviously trying to make an impression. Both Fuller and Richtel were nice enough. It quickly became apparent that Richtel was along for the free lunch. The way Fuller explained it: The recruiting department picked a junior associate to dine with an interview candidate, and that junior associate got to bring a law firm friend. Given Richtel's motives, or lack thereof, he made no efforts to engage me in the standard interviewing dialogue. That was a relief.

Fuller, on the other hand, knew he'd have to fill out an evaluation once he got back to the office, so he did his best to do some reconnaissance.

"Feel free to ask me whatever you'd like; I'm not going to include any of this in your evaluation," he promised. And he didn't do a half-bad job of selling it. But I knew better. I played along with the charade and, in the most informal way possible, asked him about his hours, the type of work he performed, and how much responsibility he was given during his first few years with the firm.

The casual luncheon atmosphere emboldened Fuller to ask me informal, inappropriate questions. Who else was I interviewing with? Did I have any offers with other firms, and with whom? And what was *my* impression of his boss, Fundguard? I showed restraint.

He wasted no time, however, in telling me how much he despised working for the man, and how bored he was with product liability. He said all he'd done in his first year with the firm was review documents and summarize deposition transcripts. That was about the time Richtel chimed in. In what appeared to be a form of hazing, the two of them began competing with each other in the all-nighter category. Large law firms like Willis, Conrad were notorious for keeping extensive hours.

"Last week I slept on a conference table. It was brutal," Richtel said.

"No kidding?" Fuller countered. "Well, the day before we filed that huge Chevrolet appellant brief, I slept in the storage closet. I'm pretty sure that's the only place where you can't hear the paging system."

I played impressed, but felt worried. There was nothing glamorous about sleeping in the supply closet.

"You know," Richtel said in a bragging tone, "there are two cots and two showers on the tenth floor."

"Really?" I jumped in.

"Yeah, but they're always being used," Fuller said. "You have to sign up for those beds. Plus, it's kind of creepy down there, with all of that fluorescent lighting."

Realizing the two of them were going a bit overboard, Fuller then made a feeble attempt at rehabilitating things. "Listen, these all-nighters, they don't happen that often. Isn't that right, Olly?" Richtel nodded. "Actually, the firm treats us pretty well. We get great perks. Like, say you're working and you want lunch or dinner, all you have to do is fill out one of these hanging tags, put it on your door like a hotel, and the cafeteria will deliver a meal to you twenty minutes later."

"The firm will even do your laundry," Richtel added. "It's delivered right to your office. There's also a fitness center that provides clean gym clothes. All you need to bring is your sneaks."

"You can even get shoe shines at your desk," said Fuller. "That's Thursdays." The image made me uncomfortable.

When the dessert menus finally arrived, it dawned on me that I might be running late for my interview with Nickel—possibly very late. I casually put my right hand under the table, pulled up my sleeve, and glanced at my watch.

It was one-fifteen P.M. I was already fifteen minutes late to the Nickel interview across town.

I excused myself. Huddled in a corner by the rest rooms, I took out my cell phone and dialed Margaret Denton. As it rang, I planned out my apology and ultimate cancellation.

"I'm sorry, but I'm running late." I cupped the phone and took a few deep breaths. I was rushing.

"That's fine." As she'd done before, Margaret immediately put me at ease. "Where are you?" she asked curiously.

I paused. "Actually, I've been interviewing with another firm this morning." Oh, the horror. I decided not to name the firm. "And we're at lunch."

"No problem."

"It's Willis, Conrad," I blurted out uncontrollably. I instantly regretted saying it. God, I sounded desperate for validation.

"When should we expect you?" she said nonchalantly. I could hear her paging through her planner. "Does two o'clock work for you?"

It was déjà vu—this was the second time I had tried to cancel on Nickel, and the second time Margaret Denton had stolen my thunder. She was using a well-known Jedi mind trick. "Yes, I will interview with you," I said in a monotone. "I mean that sounds good. Sorry if I've thrown off your schedule."

"Don't give it another thought. That's the nature of the business," she said.

I went back to the table rejuvenated, even excited, about the Nickel interview. I continued to make small talk with Tweedledee and Tweedledum, spooned through some exquisite crème brûlée, thanked them both, and dashed for a cab.

CHAPTER 8

HAILED A CAB outside the restaurant. As I got in, I realized that I'd forgotten to get cash. I didn't have enough money to pay the cabdriver. I begged him to wait while I darted across the street to get money.

"Come on, come on, come on," I said as the ATM considered dispensing me money. The machine spit out five twenties, I grabbed them, reached into my pocket for my car keys, pointed them at the

ATM, and unconsciously pressed the button that would ordinarily turn on the car alarm. "What am I doing?" I whispered. Was I actually trying to *lock* the ATM? The man waiting to use it next looked embarrassed for me. Suddenly, my cabdriver decided he'd waited long enough and took off.

Between hailing another cab and traffic, I arrived at Nickel at two-twenty P.M.—twenty minutes late to the interview I'd already rescheduled. I took the elevator to the twenty-first floor and frantically rushed up to the reception desk.

"I have a two o'clock appointment with Margaret Denton," I said, out of breath. I felt like a wreck but looked like a million bucks. Even though I deeply regretted wearing the glen plaid, it had held up nicely through my first interview and the nightmare commute across town. The receptionist gave me a kind smile and asked me to take a seat. Two minutes later, Margaret rounded the corner to greet me. She seemed excited and surprised at the same time. "Sharp suit," she said with a wink. Denton had good taste.

We sat in her office for the preinterview. Margaret looked younger than I'd expected, in her mid-thirties. She had short, bushy blond hair parted on the side and big blue eyes. I liked her right away. And in the way she spoke to me, Margaret was unlike any recruiter I'd ever met before.

"The way I see it, you're here to interview us," she said. "We already know we want you. Meet our attorneys. Ask them anything. And if you can, try to envision yourself practicing here. Oh, and by the way"—she glanced at a highlighted copy of my résumé—"I see here that you interned with Judge Lexington last summer."

My clerkship with Judge Barry Lexington was the most expensive job I'd ever had. It paid nothing. And because the courthouse was located on the eastern tip of Long Island, the summer internship had required me to move temporarily to Merrick, Long Island, live on my uncle's couch, and rent a car. All told, I must have dropped a couple of grand. On the upside, it wasn't simply a job with a judge. It was a federal internship, and in prestige, federal always trumped state. I'd applied for the internship because I'd read that Judge Lexington sponsored one of the largest summer programs in the country, accepting as many as twelve interns each summer. Why he ultimately chose me over some other Tier 1 student I didn't know. But thank God for the internship. It leapt off my résumé.

"We just won a huge case before Judge Lexington. So now we like him," Margaret said. "Anyway, before we get started, let me ask you one standard interviewing question: Why do you want to practice in New York?"

I thought about it, a tactic I'd picked up in law school. You have to think about the judge's questions, even if you've prepared and rehearsed your answers a thousand times before. "Well, I'm originally from the Bronx, and I have family in the city and in Brooklyn." That was the beginning of my stock answer. And because Margaret made me feel so comfortable, I added, "The truth is, I really can't explain it. I've always been drawn to the power and intensity of this city—you can feel it as you walk through midtown, it comes up through your feet. Deep down, I've always known this was where I would practice." I hated my answer. The room was remarkably quiet.

"You're going to fit in here nicely," she said. "Let's get started. Which reminds me. I've changed your first interview. You *were* scheduled to meet John Madison, our seniormost partner and star litigator. He runs the place. Unfortunately, you just missed him, so I have you down with Donald Concannon, a partner in our trademark-prosecution department." She led me out of her office.

This was disappointing news. I had no intention of practicing trademark prosecution. In fact, I had no intention of practicing any form of prosecution—a legal term of art that meant drafting applications to secure trademarks or patents. When people say that practicing intellectual property law is boring, they're usually referring to prosecution. And patent prosecution was the worst. Patent applications themselves read like stereo instructions: fully technical descriptions drafted according to tens of thousands of special patent-prosecuting rules. Even the simplest devices sounded complex in a patent application. I remember being shocked by the lengthy table-tennis patents—the prior art—that Owen Thompkins had sent me.

To draft a patent, you not only needed a technical degree, you also had to pass a special test called the patent bar, and it was rumored to be brutal. It was a six-hour multiple-choice exam that tested on all the many rules associated with drafting patents and prosecuting them before the U.S. Patent and Trademark Office. Even though it was an open-book exam, I'd heard there was no time to research the correct answers. The infamous pass rate was typically below 50 percent, and you had to correctly answer at least seventy out of the hundred questions. Unlike engineering school, there was no scaling. I was having none of this exam.

If I still possessed any interest in practicing patent law, it was in litigation. Patent litigation was sexy. "Sexy"—a term more and more attorneys were using to describe complex, important legal matters where a great deal of money was at stake. Who gets to own the patent to the human genome? Now, that's sexy. The fantasy of trying a major patent case before a federal jury excited me. The image of sitting behind a desk drafting tedious applications didn't.

"This is Donald Concannon. He heads up our trademark department," Margaret said.

Donald Concannon (Duke Law, Tier 1) was old. Old old. I wasn't sure if he was going to make it through our interview. His face was bright red. The room smelled of alcohol, but I gave him the benefit of the doubt.

He grinned. "Pull up a chair." I reached for the big brown leather chair in the corner, and I began dragging it across the room. I was mid-drag, with my back to him, when he asked, "So tell me, what do you know about trademark law?"

I whipped my head around. Now he was really smiling. He looked like he was about to say "I'm just kidding." But he didn't. He patiently waited for my response.

Everything I knew about trademark law, I learned from clerking for Judge Lexington. And that was not a lot. My trademark experience was limited to trade-dress law. I panicked. What was the name of that Supreme Court holding on trade-dress law? Oh yeah, *Two Pesos*. I quickly tried to jog my memory on the facts and holding of the case.

But how long would that get me into the conversation? Two, three minutes, tops?

I sat down in the chair, farther away from his desk than I would have liked, and began babbling. "Well, I'm familiar with trade-*dress* law. That is, the trade dress that refers to the overall image, impression, or look and feel of a product or its packaging. Last summer I drafted an opinion for Federal Judge Barry Lexington of the Eastern District of New York on the topic of trade-*dress* law." I had said Lexington's full title in the interest of stretching. "In that opinion, I held—I mean, the judge held—that is, I determined that the allegedly infringing product was not infringing." Wait, did I just say "infringing" twice in the same sentence? I took a moment to catch my breath and come up with something more. But I couldn't. My trade-dress monologue was over.

I began to go down in flames. In a stream of consciousness, I started dropping technical trade-dress terms in no specific order or sentence structure. Donald looked on like a true theatergoer. "Secondary meaning, suggesting source, the *Two Pesos* case." I took another breath. "So, what about you? Are you familiar with trade-dress law?"

I paused. Not good. Of course he's *familiar* with trade-dress law. He's a trademark partner in one of the largest intellectual property firms in the world. Donald disappeared behind his desk. It appeared my question had actually knocked the wind out of him. I could hear him grunting, presumably struggling. Please be resting, I prayed. I'd been so obsessed with how hard this interview process had been on me. What about Donald? After hundreds of interviews, mine had finally done him in.

Then his little wrinkled hand appeared, and he pulled himself and an enormous brown volume up onto his desk. He turned the spine toward me, smiling. It read: *Trade-Dress Law* on one end and *Concannon* on the other end.

Concannon. Concannon. There was a name that rang a bell. Dear God, *he's* Concannon. The Concannon who wrote the definitive text on trade-dress law, the ultimate source for law students and attorneys alike. Come to think of it, I had cited his text in the legal opinion that I drafted for Judge Lexington.

Donald didn't take offense to my inability to place the name with the face. Apparently, he didn't get recognized on the street as much as you'd think—even when toting around a 750-page treatise with his name on the spine.

The rest of the interview went smoothly. Donald was an impressive man, and unless I was mistaken, he was coming off a liquid lunch.

Margaret Denton escorted me to my next two interviews. After each one, she asked me how it went, seemed interested in my answers, and briefed me on the next meeting. We were on the same team. I'd never felt that way about a recruiter before.

After finishing the third interview, I was spent. Between Willis, Conrad and Nickel, I'd given the same garden-variety answers at least ten times—I just couldn't be sure whether I'd said them to ten different people.

"Ready for one more?" Margaret asked.

Enough was enough. "I'm going to have to pass, Margaret. I've got to be heading back to Philadelphia. I hope that's not a problem."

"Not at all," she said, and with that she escorted me to reception. At the elevator, we exchanged a travel voucher for a writing sample and references, and I thanked her for being a true professional. I walked out of the building a bit disappointed in myself: came late and underprepared, left early and overextended. It was a shame.

In the cab to the train station, I checked my messages on the cell. There was one from Molly. We hadn't spoken since she stormed out of my apartment nearly a week ago.

The message said: "Hey, what's going on? Call me. It's been a while. And you'll be happy to learn that my law review adviser recommended that I add a *short* section to my comment concerning a judge's role in the plea-bargaining process. You'll have to forgive me. I was working on too many days with no sleep. Call me. I'll make it up to you. I have two specific ways in mind."

I called. "Hey, what are you doing?" I said.

"An appellate brief," she said sweetly. "Where are you?"

"I just finished interviewing with Willis, Conrad and Nickel and Reed."

"I didn't realize those firms interviewed on campus."

Hoping I could ride out some of the goodwill from her voice message, I confessed, "Actually, I interviewed with them in New York." I closed my eyes and braced for her response.

"You're a real piece of work, Alex. You were in New York today, and you didn't even call."

"I'm calling now. Hey, *you* were the one who stormed out on *me* the other day. I had no idea where we stood."

"What, were these phantom interviews? Did they just spring up? You knew you were coming to New York. Why didn't you give me some notice? We've hardly seen each other lately."

"I know, but heartness makes the fond go grander," I said, using the botched-up line that had become a joke between us. I was famous among my friends and family for malapropisms and mixed metaphors.

"It's incredible how quickly you can get me out of the mood." She paused. "Why are you even interviewing with Willis, Conrad? They're a total sweatshop. And Nickel is an intellectual property firm. Didn't you decide that you weren't *doing* intellectual property law?"

"Yeah, yeah. I did. But Nickel is a top firm," I started. "Face it, Molly. You're never going to be thrilled about the big firms."

"Well, you should've given me some notice."

"Look, I apologize. It was a commando mission. I was in and out. I have to get back to Philadelphia. I'm in the cab right now, almost at the train station. Can I call you when I get home?"

"You're in a cab on your way to Penn Station? Good. Take the West Side Highway to the West Ninety-fifth Street exit. Then take a left onto Riverside Drive to One-fifteenth Street."

"Yeah, I know the address." Again I had to travel to her. "I don't even have clothes," I said. "And I have a student bar meeting in the morning. I've already postponed it once."

"I'm not asking you to stay. Just visit."

The cabdriver dropped me off at her apartment. I walked in, we said hello, had some brief, satisfying sex on her draft appellate brief, and fifty minutes later, I was on the 10:11 P.M. train back to Philadelphia.

CHAPTER 9

ICKEL OFFERED ME a place in its summer internship two days later. Between leaving early and running late, I had figured I was out of the running. Perhaps my interviewers interpreted my exhausted, low-key attitude as inflated self-confidence. Lately, I'd done a decent job of toning down my eagerness.

Maybe, I thought, the offer had something to do with my dropping Willis, Conrad's name in the preliminary conversation with Margaret Denton. But that was ridiculous. Yeah, the Nickel recruiters got in a room and decided to make me an offer because I'd interviewed with Willis, Conrad: "I don't know what it is, but that Alex Wellen has *something*. I mean, *Willis, Conrad* wants him." In the end, I guess Nickel wanted me, and the interview was an academic exercise to confirm that I wasn't completely out of my gourd.

Deciding whether to accept the offer was a big decision, and I needed counsel. I turned to my legal advisers, the Oracle and the Optimist: my mother and father, respectively.

"The Oracle" was a name my high school friends came up with for my mother, and it stuck. She liked it, even though she never said so. Everyone looked to her for wisdom. Whatever the dilemma, whether it involved love, secrets, fear, family, death, dreams, she had a way of dispensing good advice, even if you'd heard it a hundred times before. Sometimes she packaged it in life instructions: "Don't let a stranger inflict you with his pain." Other times it was a prophecy: "You seem to spend a lot of time in your relationship talking about how to make it better. If you're asking me, it seems like that relationship is over." Most times it was truths: "I am going to be dead for a very long time."

The Oracle believed in God, religion, and spirituality. The Oracle did not believe in ghosts. "If ghosts existed," she told me as a child, "objects would be flying all over the place, and people would be talking to them all the time. Dead artists, poets, and musicians would make appearances in the media, and the government would have found a way to tax them."

Then there was the Optimist. My father was always ten minutes away from our final destination, it didn't matter if we were pulling out of the driveway for a cross-country trip. When will we be there? "In about ten minutes." He made simple advice work. "You'll do fine." "I like it." "It's perfect. Leave it." "It's only money." "It'll grow back." "Don't worry." And, of course, his stock expression: "Sounds good." My dad was an electrical engineer, but he should have been a doctor. He possessed the perfect bedside manner. He also didn't hesitate to dispense expired prescription medicine from the medicine cabinet to anyone in pain.

The three of us made plans to convene and reconnoiter in our usual forum, the Toms River Diner. When I arrived, they were already at our regular booth.

"Where's the Child Prodigy?" I asked them as I sat down.

"SAT camp," my mother said. Of course. My fourteen-year-old brother, Mike, otherwise known as the Child Prodigy, had enrolled himself in a weekend course that consisted of round-the-clock SAT drills, exercises, and practice exams. He was easily the youngest guy in the class.

"So now that you have the Nickel offer, you can use it as leverage to get one with Willis, Conrad," the Optimist theorized.

"I tried that already," I said. "Willis told me that they're not interested in rushing a decision. In fact, the recruiter said that I'm on the waiting list. Isn't that lame? I've never heard of such a thing in a law firm. The whole place rubs me the wrong way."

"Don't go to Willis, Conrad," the Oracle piped up. "I'm almost done reading *Willis*—that tell-all book about the firm's inner workings. The place sounds awful." It was normal for my mother to do independent research like this. "For example, do you know about their support services?"

"I guess," I said, a bit embarrassed that she knew more about the firm than I did.

"The firm has psychiatrists and social workers at your disposal to help work out personal problems," my mother continued.

"Really?" I said, impressed. That was uncharacteristically civil of

Willis, Conrad. "I guess a mentally grounded attorney is a productive one."

"You don't understand," she said. "The therapists are not there for you. They're for your wife, your father, your brother, or whoever is having any sort of mental meltdown or physical ailment. They deal with it so you don't have to."

"Geez." Any employer that was worried about me being too distracted by real life to do my job was not for me. Sure, I wanted the high-profile, hardworking, young-New-York-attorney lifestyle and image. And yes, I was prepared to make many sacrifices and work long hours, including some all-nighters. But did I really want to knowingly enter into a relationship with the sweatshop of all sweatshops that required me to check my life at the door?

"Yeah, you're right," I told them. "This support-services thing is the needle to break the camel's back."

"Straw," my mother said.

"Plus, Nickel will give you a chance to use your engineering degree," the Optimist added. "And they're big enough."

"And what about the Ping-Pong paddle? I thought you were going to patent it, and we were all going to retire on the royalties?" My mother was very familiar with my paddle. Years ago I'd asked her if she'd do some drawings illustrating different embodiments. The Oracle was an artist, master of all mediums. I had grown up with her artwork all around, which was like having another sibling in the house. Her watercolor, acrylic, and oil paintings filled every wall; her clay and stone sculptures adorned every shelf. Her realism was wonderful, but it was her contemporary figurative and abstract work that was exceptional. It was no wonder that I was an inventor who had chosen to pursue a career in patent law, seeing that I had a trained artist and an engineer for parents.

The Oracle and the Optimist were right. I was getting off track, forgetting about the paddle and the master plan. On my drive home to Philadelphia, I left two voice messages—both similar in nature, both with recruiters. The first was to O'Connell & Price, politely passing on the firm's offer to spend my career working next to Dennis Braise. The message for Willis, Conrad was curter. I instructed the firm to take my name off that freaking waiting list. My decision to go with Nickel was now irreversible. Monday morning I phoned Margaret Denton and accepted their generous offer.

Nickel *was* the Willis, Conrad of intellectual property. The firm housed smart and accomplished attorneys, represented impressive clients, and had a long and successful history in the practice. No other firm in the world had as many skilled intellectual property attorneys under one roof. And now was a good time to practice intellectual property law. The field had gotten a big shot in the arm with the proliferation of the Internet. The Web was streamlining people's ability to steal ideas (which increased demand for lawyers). But even before the Net came along, stealing intellectual property had always been in style— maybe because it was intangible, maybe because it was somehow easier on the conscience to steal intellectual property than to swipe someone's personal property or squat on their real estate. Nowadays copyrighted music, trademarked logos, and patented designs were just a point-and-click away. New intellectual property laws and legal quandaries were beginning to take shape. That interested me.

Besides, I didn't have to commit to a career in intellectual property law. I had eleven weeks to try out the job, salary and all, before deciding whether to pursue it as a full-time gig. None of my non-technical law school colleagues would ever have an opportunity to experience this career. Plus, while patent *law* might sound boring, patent *litigation* was *sexy*. The Nickel offer put me on the career rocket docket.

CHAPTER 10

TWELVE WERE TIER 1s, and four were Tier 2s. That was the breakdown of the summer associate program at Nickel. The Tier 1s came mostly from New York schools like Columbia, NYU, Fordham, and Cornell, with a few thrown in from the University of Virginia and Georgetown. Then there were the Tier 2s, from St. John's, Rutgers, and Temple. Nickel was more tolerant of Tier 2s because many were already accomplished engineers, doctors, and scientists.

At Nickel's orientation, I immediately gravitated to Hayley (NYU Law, Tier 1). She had shoulder-length chestnut-brown hair, big hazel eyes, and a perfect smile. She was medium height with a killer body. Hayley, who was summer-interning in the Nickel trademark department, seemed fashionably out of place. In a world of geeky intellectual property attorneys, most of them males, the trademark attorneys were the cool kids in school. After that came the patent litigators, and finally, the patent prosecutors. From day one Hayley attracted a lot of attention. Male partners and associates descended on her like fresh meat. She had no shortage of legal assignments.

She and I were inseparable that summer. We felt instant chemistry that neither of us acted on. With all the vultures around, I figured it was better that I be someone she considered a friend. Plus, she had a boyfriend back at NYU Law. And I was still unavailable, despite the fact that Molly and I were barely keeping it together.

The summer associate program was a breeze. We were assigned basic legal research and writing projects. It was a very low-maintenance deal, no pressure and very boring. When we finished one assignment, we had to ask for another; otherwise we could sit around and do nothing all day. Some of the Tier 1s did just that. Senior associates told us that unless you killed a partner, a permanent offer at the end of the summer was guaranteed. Some interns got the chance to sit in on depositions, client meetings, or court proceedings. I didn't. Hayley got the rare opportunity to go on a bust with a firm partner, some senior associates, and police. They recovered a warehouse full of counterfeit toys. The firm routinely went on these trademark-infringement stings.

All summer long Nickel wined and dined us. Maybe it wasn't like the booming eighties, when summer associates were rumored to be swept away to Atlantic City and given spending budgets, and perhaps

Nickel's program wasn't quite as lavish as some of the big general-practice ones, yet I was still floored. Every week they had something different planned. One week bowling, another week pool, the next week a professional baseball game. The firm frequently took us to New York's most expensive restaurants. They even bused us to the New Jersey Six Flags Great Adventure amusement park and sponsored a private picnic.

Nickel topped off the summer with a private cruise around Manhattan.

"This is making me sick," I whispered to Hayley, as we sipped champagne in the corner of the cabin.

"What? The boat?"

"I'm not sure. I can't tell whether it was dinner, it's the sloshing waves, or all this sucking up that's making me feel nauseous," I said. Inside the boat's cabin, summer interns could be seen engrossed in partner conversations, laughing at partner jokes.

"Look at them," Hayley said. "They're ridiculous. What makes them think they're not going to get an offer? Everyone gets an offer."

"I guess that's just it," I said. "None of them wants to be the exception to the rule. It would be humiliating." This was the last night of our internship. Tomorrow we'd pack up our stuff and say good-bye. Offers to work with the firm after graduation could come at any time. But they weren't happening tonight. It was getting late and Nickel would have made the offers already. The firm purposely kept us in the dark. Nickel never promised us that we'd know before leaving the program. I'd heard of firms that waited as late as October to make permanent offers.

"Let's go up on deck," I suggested. It was cool on the deck, and the fresh air did me good. Besides the one summer associate vomiting off the side of the boat, Hayley and I were the only ones up there. I gave her my coat, and we stared at the breathtaking Manhattan skyline.

"Will you accept if Nickel makes you an offer?" she asked.

"Definitely," I said.

She took a pause. "Me, too," she whispered. Our faces were dangerously close. Then we heard people approaching. In unison, we took sips of our drinks and turned back to the skyline.

Once the boat docked, Hayley and I shared a Nickel-sponsored Town Car back to Greenwich Village. We were staying in the Mercer Street Residence Hall, part of NYU Law's housing. Every summer thousands of law students flocked to the city to participate in their decadent summer associate programs, and many of them stayed in NYU housing. Occupancy was tight. Rooms not occupied by overpaid summer associates were filled with recent graduates studying for the New York bar examination, and NYU law students like Hayley, who lived there all year round.

As I held the door open for her to Mercer Hall, it was times like these that I fantasized about living in New York, attending a Tier 1 law school like NYU, and dating someone like Hayley.

Hayley and I got into the elevator. My studio apartment was on the fourth floor. Hayley was on the seventh. The seventh floor had a beautiful terrace where law students sunned themselves. Still high on drinks, I wanted to hit the stop button on the elevator, turn to Hayley, pin her up against the wall, and give her a long, hard kiss. Instead, the elevator doors opened, I gave her a kiss on the cheek, and we said good night. Perhaps I'd change my mind and be knocking on her door in fifteen minutes. Maybe she'd knock on mine.

I walked into my four-hundred-square-foot studio, and a gush of cool air from the air conditioner swept over me. I had this glorious, fully furnished room for a total of twelve weeks. The apartment was pitch-dark, except for the blinking red light on my answering machine. The message was from Molly: "It's me. Call." The length and frequency of our messages were getting progressively shorter. Now we both lived in New York and there were only 110 blocks separating Columbia from NYU. Unfortunately, our proximity hadn't improved the deteriorating relationship. It seemed we were on two very different legal paths, and the public versus private nature of our internships had driven another wedge between us. Our summer internships had ended up being all-consuming, but for different reasons. Molly worked long hours at Legal Aid, but when her workday was over, it was over. My work hours were reasonable—that was part of the big-firm dog-and-pony show—but there were always social events that extended into the night. It seemed I never had time for Molly. Before Nickel, I'd blamed it on my job search and interviewing. Now firm responsibilities occupied my free time. The truth was, I was avoiding her because I knew the relationship was over. It was time to take the final step and end it. A part of me thought she might be a bit relieved.

It was early evening on Tuesday. I figured that if I broke it off with her tonight, there was still plenty of time for each of us to rehabilitate the week. She answered the phone with a big hello, but when she realized it was me, she became sullen. I considered reminding her that she'd originally called me, but I didn't want to start a fight.

"I just got back from a Nickel event," I said. I knew she despised the whole big-firm mentality, so I was always vague about my extravagant evenings. That summer Molly received three credits for her internship. I earned in excess of twenty thousand dollars.

"What was it this time?" she asked out of courtesy.

"A cruise around Manhattan."

"Are you drunk?"

"No." I'd had two, maybe three drinks. I wasn't drunk.

"Was Hayley there?" Of course she was. "Why don't you ever introduce me to her?" Molly asked.

"You've never expressed an interest in meeting *anyone* from the firm." I paused. "Can I change topics? Can we talk about us? I have a few things on my mind."

"If this is a breakup speech, I'm really not in the mood. That's what this is, isn't it?"

"You tell me. Is this still fun for you? You don't seem to be having fun. Maybe we should take a break."

"You've got to come up with something more creative than that. Look, this *thing* we're doing has never been exclusive. You can date other people. You can sleep with other people. I really don't care. I just don't want to know about it. But there's no taking things down a notch. If you're saying that you don't want to see me anymore, period, then say so." Before I could answer, she said, "Does this have anything to do with Hayley?"

"No, I swear. All I'm saying is things are a bit strained lately. I don't think it's working anymore. I say all this with a heavy hand."

"It's 'heart.' 'Heavy heart,'" she said. There was a long pause. "Okay, then I want a refund," she said flatly.

"That's very funny."

"I'm not being funny. I want back the year I've wasted with you. I've been victimized. I want to be made whole again. I want a complete re-fund for the telephone calls, the train tickets, everything."

Another long pause. "You're kidding, right? You want restitution for our relationship?"

"Yeah, I want restitution."

I thought about it. "How about five hundred dollars?" I said. "Is that a fair settlement? Do you take checks?"

"Alex, listen carefully, because this is very important. The next sound you will hear is me hanging up on your ass."

"Wait, wait, wait! Don't go anywhere. Hold on. Please, Molly. Hold on."

"What?"

"I was totally, utterly wrong. I blew it. You're right. You are *definitely* someone I want to be in a serious relationship with."

Then the phone went dead. I was free.

THE NEXT MORNING there was an e-mail waiting for me, inviting all the Nickel summer associates to a decadent dinner at the Rainbow Room on the sixty-fifth floor of the GE Building at 30 Rockefeller Plaza. As dessert was served, Margaret Denton handed each of us an offer letter.

"Woo-hoo, I just won the lottery," I said to Hayley, who was sitting next to me. It was truly an incredible thing. I'd secured a permanent job with a major law firm before even starting my third year of law school. All thanks to strong first-year grades. The rocket docket had successfully landed me on the moon. I checked what shirt I was wear-ing. Mental note: White button-down Kenneth Cole shirt, good luck.

"Your letter mentions an offer?" Hayley asked. "Mine doesn't." Summer associates on either side of us were cheering, laughing, and crying. Nickel would never reject someone in such a public way. If a person didn't make the cut, he or she simply wouldn't have been in-vited to the luncheon. Hayley was kidding.

"That's a shame," I said, pretending that she'd been swept up into a law-firm nightmare. "Waiter, waiter, another refill on my champagne?" She showed me her offer. We hugged.

"A toast. To us working together at Nickel, and to your patent," Hayley said. That week I'd filed a patent application for my double-sided table-tennis paddle with the U.S. Patent and Trademark Office. Had I interned at any other law firm that summer, the paddle would have gone nowhere. But Vincent Bertucci (Brooklyn Law, Tier 2), a senior partner in the firm's patent-prosecution department, liked the idea and offered to educate me on writing a patent, using my paddle as an example. We collaborated on a variety of potential embodiments, and I added him as a named inventor.

"And to Owen Thompkins," I said, "screw you for being no help at all."

CHAPTER 11

FIRST YEAR THEY scared you, second year they worked you, and third year they bored you.

I'd gone academically numb. The Nickel offer set the tone for the year. Having a job locked up so early gave me very few incentives to work hard. It had taken me my entire academic career, but I'd finally done it: For my last semester of school, I'd designed the perfect schedule—one class. That one class required me to be present in the law school three hours a week.

The rest of the time I did my other "for credit" obligations. Those included an internship with the U.S. Attorney's Office Criminal Division, an independent study, and a clerkship with a federal judge.

It was so nice to intern with the U.S. Attorney's Office without having to explain myself to Molly. She would have hated the clinical aspect. One day a week we role-played with the interns in the Federal Defender's Division. The semester culminated in a full-blown trial in which I prosecuted a fictitious John Doe for fictitious armed robbery and felony-murder. I got my first chance to prepare witnesses, argue pretrial motions, make an opening statement, prepare and examine witnesses on the stand, and deliver a closing argument before a jury of my peers. I lost. My peers all happened to be future defense attorneys.

Then there was my independent study. It was like so many independent studies, all smoke and mirrors. I spent the entire semester independent of the study until I realized that I had three weeks to turn it in, so I cranked out a thirty-page piece over the course of four all-nighters. It was a shame that I rushed it. I'd had such great intentions at the outset. The project dated back to my days as SBA president, when there were a few complaints about on-campus stalking. Working with the students, faculty, and administration, the SBA attempted to draft a provision that prohibited stalking. Ultimately, we failed. We couldn't agree on language that reflected a balance between a person's constitutional right to freedom of movement, and conduct that constituted harassment. For three credits, my independent study was intended to help Temple find some closure. I surveyed a number of other law schools and proposed some new language. The grade would appear on my final report card, but the proposal itself wouldn't see committee until next fall, and by then I'd be long gone.

Finally, there was my clerkship. Temple had a fantastic internship program with Philadelphia's federal courthouse. On a lottery basis, the program hooked up Temple law students with more than two dozen federal judges. You received three credits for a one-day-a-week obligation. Depending on the judge, you attended trials, drafted legal opinions, and sat in on private conferences held in the judge's chambers. I got matched up with Archibald Hudson (Cornell Law, Tier 1), a senior judge. All that meant was that he was close to retirement, accomplished, well respected, and well, not interested in becoming my friend or, for that matter, my mentor.

My internship with Hudson was much like the one I'd had with Judge Barry Lexington following first-year law school. It seemed that Hudson, like Lexington, didn't appreciate me romping around his chambers and courtroom, even if I was free labor. For Judge Hudson, in his late seventies, every intern was a pain in the ass. Our legal instincts were wrong, our questions were moronic, our requests to attend court proceedings or negotiations in his chambers were a complete imposition, and compliments were rare and backhanded.

"Students from the non–Ivy League schools try harder," he told me on my first day. "I find that many of the judges in this courthouse don't hire law students from the secondary schools. I don't think it's fair to rule them out." Screw him. I already had a six-figure salary set up with Nickel.

After that uplifting speech, Hudson's full-time law clerk, Sharon, gave me a short tour of the law library. Apparently, when it came time for Hudson to hire *his* full-time clerk, he was all talk: Sharon graduated from Yale Law (Tier 1).

"We have two computers that you can use for legal research," Sharon told me. "The federal court system has a contract with Westlaw for unlimited access to its online legal databases."

Most days I sat in Hudson's courtroom and watched him rip in to the attorneys who appeared before him. Often it felt like he was showing off. In general, he wanted nothing to do with me. Aside from brief exchanges of pleasantries on his way from the courtroom to his private chambers, we never spoke.

Instead, I dealt with Sharon, who assigned me mundane research and writing assignments. Because she knew that I would be practicing with Nickel, Sharon would throw me an occasional obscure trademark or copyright issue. That semester Hudson didn't have any patent cases on his docket.

"Any developments in your latest mission?" law school friend David

Markey asked me over lunch one day. He was also in the federal-internship program.

"Not really," I said. For the last three weeks I'd been drafting a legal opinion concerning social-security benefits. My "brief" was already twenty-two pages. In the end I'd be lucky if Sharon found any of my legal research and writing helpful. She was the one who usually wrote the judge's legal opinions. Hudson just signed off on them, flexing his muscle in court. Like any ghostwriter, Sharon didn't get a byline. But if she adopted any of my legal reasoning, I was determined to get some credit.

I took a piece of crumpled-up paper out of my pocket and flattened it out on the table. "This is the best that I could come up with," I said to David. " 'The *Younger* court couldn't leave well enough alone.' What do you think?"

He stared at it. "You're a fool. There's no way you're ever going to get your last name in a published federal opinion."

"But I'm only a 'well enough' away from getting 'Wellen' in there."

"It ain't gonna happen," he said.

"Yeah, you're right. I hear the music."

"Face the music." David was right. Not only did Sharon cross out that sentence, she crossed off the entire page. I did manage to get the words "all extraordinary" published—if you combined the first two letters of each word, it spelled "Alex."

When I wasn't drafting anti-stalking legislation, pretending to be a federal prosecutor, or embedding my name in a federal opinion, I was in my one class, Federal Courts and Jurisdiction, with Professor William McGovern. My independent study, internships, and clinical were all graded pass/fail, only McGovern's class was letter-graded. Whatever I got in his class was my grade-point average for the semester. But it didn't much matter. Five previous semesters of grades had sealed my fate. Unless I failed his course, I was going to graduate cum laude. No higher, no lower.

By the time the final lecture rolled around, I'd gone from apathetic to antsy. Someone get me out of here. Then it finally happened. McGovern delivered the last word of our last lecture, in our last class, on the last day of our formal education, and the classroom erupted in applause.

I instantly wanted to do what I'd done the first time my parents took me to an R-rated movie. I was nine years old at the time, and I'd persuaded them to take me to Stanley Kubrick's *The Shining*. It wouldn't be *that* scary, I pleaded. But then there was that little boy whispering "redrum" (the word "murder" backward) as he bent his pointer finger in time; dead people in bathtubs; axes; tidal waves of blood; bloodcurdling screams; and Jack Nicholson's infamous "Here's Johnny," and I was toast. Before we walked out, I spent most of the movie kneeling on the floor, peering through the slit between the seats with both thumbs in my ears, chanting to myself quickly "la-la-la-la-la-la-la." I can't hear you. I'm not listening.

If only I could do that right now and drown out the applause, I thought. I was sure most of my fellow students were just being polite, as it was customary to clap for the professor at the end of his last lecture. I'd never been crazy about the idea. It always felt contrived, maybe even a bit excessive. I'd never clapped for a teacher at any other stage of my education, why should I now? Plus, most of the time, the smattering of applause usually amounted to no more than simple courtesy.

But the clapping this time seemed pretty genuine. For all intents and purposes, it was a momentous occasion. Besides, there was no better person to close than William McGovern, the quintessential law professor.

McGovern was every great law professor you had ever read about, seen on television, and met, rolled into one. His credentials were unmatched. He graduated from Harvard Law summa cum laude, clerked for two U.S. Supreme Court judges, and possessed thirty-plus years of teaching experience. He looked the part. He was six foot four and completely bald, aside from a few wispy pieces of hair. He wore thick glasses that looked like binoculars mounted backward on his face. When he made his way to the lectern each day, the room hushed. We knew the law came from God to McGovern to us.

That semester, I looked forward to his lectures every Tuesday and

Thursday. They were always captivating, passionate performances in which McGovern darted back and forth across the room, spewing nontraditional legal theories. When it came to convoluted legal principles, he'd wildly diagram them on the board into accessible bullet-points of law. He taught the school's most challenging courses and, as a result, attracted some of the sharpest, most curious, and diligent students. I'd gotten a taste of McGovern during first-year, and I was thankful that I had one last chance to study before him. Even though I'd spent my whole life with talented teachers, William McGovern was my first scholar.

His final lecture was highly anticipated—professors and students alike celebrated McGovern's parting words. As expected, more than a dozen students who weren't even taking the course filed into the back of the room to catch some brilliant insight into the overall meaning of jurisprudence and the practice of law.

If he said it, I missed it. I was too busy calculating how many classes I'd taken over the last twenty years. I probably should have been taking notes for my final final exam, but about ten minutes back, he'd started babbling uncontrollably, and I knew it wasn't exam-worthy material.

My legal pad looked a lot more like one of my engineering notebooks from undergrad than it did notes from a law school lecture. At the bottom of my pageful of calculations, I'd written "18,424" and put a box around it. This class was number 18,424. At least that was the most accurate guess I could come up with. I assumed 184 days of class per year, with 4 to 6 classes each day for a total of 20 years of schooling, going all the way back to nursery school. (My final number included nap time, as well as milk time, dodgeball, show-and-tell, field day, and the elementary school science fair.) I'd had enough of being a student, living on a student budget, and doing student things. Legal internships, externships, and clinicals were all the same: free labor. It was time for a career; time to make some real coin; time to be a grown-up.

Real life was three months away. In September Nickel would start paying me a fortune. The firm had agreed, in writing, to promote me from my current salary of zero figures to six. Between my promising career prospects, the finality of the moment, and McGovern's passionate parting shots, I had every reason to applaud. Yet there I sat, unable to muster the energy. I hadn't practiced a day in my life yet I was already disenchanted with the legal profession. I couldn't pinpoint when, but somewhere along my law school career, the charming idealistic beliefs that I had about the law practice had fallen by the wayside. These days the public perception of lawyers seemed to have hit an all-time low. It wasn't like hating lawyers was something new. (Everyone hates lawyers until the police offer you one phone call from jail, and you're scrambling to think of the name of your second cousin's lawyer friend you met two weeks ago.) But lately, hating lawyers had become more than a simple American pastime; it was now a sport.

I knew things had gotten bad when my nine-year-old cousin cheered as the tyrannosaurus ate the lawyer in *Jurassic Park*. The downhill had gotten a kick-start from the O. J. Simpson trial and picked up momentum with those looping late-night 1–800–INJURED infomercials. I was finding myself too embarrassed to disclose my career choice at parties. What are ten thousand dead lawyers at the bottom of the sea? "A good start," I would preempt the person telling the joke. In fact, there were so many lawyer jokes that I'd rejected the pejorative career term. In the United Kingdom I could have become a "barrister." That sounded much nobler. I split the difference. "Attorney," I corrected friends and family. Attorney, I thought, somehow commanded more respect than lawyer.

Universal disdain for the profession and an overwhelmingly litigious society still hadn't dissuaded tens of thousands of young, sprightly college students from going on to law school every year. If one more person told me that there were more students in law school than lawyers currently practicing, I planned to sue for intentional infliction of severe emotional distress. Was my degree worth the paper it was printed on? It depended on whom you asked.

In the end, McGovern gave me a B—a blah grade for a blah attitude. Exams were graded anonymously, but perhaps he sensed that I was the person at the other end of that blue book. I'd lost my passion for the law and school, and it showed in my essays. I wasn't clapping on the inside, either. Then again, maybe my answers were lame.

I hoped that putting on my graduation cap and gown would inspire me, that marching into the auditorium and waving to my family would help me feel more like the occasion was in fact momentous. Losing the election for graduation speaker was a blessing in disguise. I was the wrong person to do an uplifting speech: "Now, go show the world what you're made of, you bloodsucking Tier Two lawyers."

The keynote speaker was Federal Court of Appeals Judge Judith McGowen (Northwestern Law, Tier 1). From the looks of her, she didn't seem the type to appreciate a good Judge Judy joke. She was one of the first black women in U.S. history to be appointed to a federal-appeals court. She was a self-assured, distinguished woman in her sixties.

She stepped up to the podium. "Good afternoon. I'm going to talk about something that may make many of you uncomfortable," she began. "There is no worse way to start off a legal career than to fail the bar. I'm sure you plan to take it very seriously, but I'm here to underscore that point."

The audience gasped in unison. I glanced over at my parents. My mother was shaking her head in disbelief. Friends, family, faculty, and graduates began fidgeting in their seats. Can we change the topic to something less uncomfortable, like social diseases?

"Passing means focusing," she continued. "Do not fool yourself into thinking that you can work and take the bar at the same time. You can't. Studying for the bar is a full-time commitment. For those of you who have a conflict, I suggest that you contact your future employers and change your start date. Otherwise, they may quickly turn into your former employers."

I was smiling to disguise my discomfort. But the good news was that I had the entire summer to study—my start date was mid-September. Also, Judge McGowen had assisted me in a breakthrough. I finally understood why I wasn't in a clapping state of mind these days. It wasn't simply the Tier 2 ghetto, feeling like I was a second-class citizen. It wasn't because schools were flooding the market with lawyers, and I was about to share a profession with money-grubbing ambulance chasers. The reason I wasn't clapping was that my juris doctorate was worthless without a license. And getting a license meant taking and passing the bar exam. It was only then that I could add those three pretentious letters, "Esq.," after my last name.

That double-sided table-tennis paddle had taken me far. Maybe one day I'd sell the invention and live off the royalties. I'd recently received word that I was one step closer—the U.S. Patent and Trademark Office had granted me a limited monopoly on double-sided table-tennis paddles.

But the more likely scenario was that paddle had given birth to an attorney. Or at least to a wanna-be attorney who would have to wait nine months for the results.

FIRST TRIMESTER

CHAPTER 12

THERE WAS NO way that I was going to study for the bar in Philadelphia. I could think of no worse place to prepare for the hardest exam in the world than in the concrete-no-window walls of the Temple Law School library, surrounded by the very neurotic people whom I'd just warmly bid good-bye. I needed a new environment. I needed new neurotic people.

I was off to live with the Oracle, the Optimist, and the Child Prodigy in Toms River, New Jersey. The Oracle would keep the bar in perspective, the Optimist would provide that much-needed positive slant, and as for the Child Prodigy—misery loved company. I just wasn't sure who was "misery" and who was "company." In the three years of law school leading up to the bar, Mike was preparing for his own exam. In the fall he'd take the PSATs, and his virginal experience with a standardized test was destined to be different from mine.

To look at us, Mike and I were constructively the same. Pictures of me were simply age-progressed pictures of him. We were both medium height and weight. We both had fair skin, hazel eyes, and jet-black hair with highlights of premature gray. For both of us, the hereditary gray hair began in sixth grade. We also lived the same life with the same parents in the same home. We'd grown up in a loving and supportive family where each person admired the other more than the next.

Overall, my parents seemed very happy with the way I turned out, but in staggering Mike and me by eleven years, the Oracle and the Optimist got a chance to do a few things over. I got a surreal glimpse into the *childhood that could have been*. With me, the Oracle had severely underestimated the importance of standardized test scores. All my life she watched me struggle with some version of Tier 2 due to mediocre scores. First it was the PSATs, then the SATs, and finally the LSATs. She decided early on that Mike wasn't going to face the same struggles. The Oracle prophesied the birth of the Child Prodigy.

"This will be fun," she told Mike as she handed him an SAT prep book in sixth grade. For the next three years, Mike participated in weekly quizzes in which our mother asked him to put commonly tested SAT words in complex sentences. Every night she'd read to him. Sometimes a chapter from classic literature, other times from the Princeton Review's SAT strategy books.

"Leonard Huber is trying to mess you up," she'd say. The strategy books personalized the SAT experience. Leonard Huber was the Educational Testing Service employee responsible for writing the reading-comprehension questions. "Leonard's thrown in answer 'B,' but you're too smart for Leonard. You know from chapter four that by working backward, you can narrow it down to 'A' or 'C.'"

The Child Prodigy grew up petrified of one day becoming Joe Bloggs, the Princeton Review's token average test taker. Bloggs got all the easy questions right, half the average questions right, and all the hard questions wrong. Mike wasn't about to become Bloggs, and if that meant taking radical steps, so be it. It was this notion that compelled the Child Prodigy to enroll himself in the SAT sleep-away camp. "That particularly traumatic experience diminished my overall SAT score by one hundred points," he told me later.

I'm sure there were times that Mike wished he'd never heard of the SATs, that there wasn't a five-year ramp-up to the exam, and that he'd become acquainted with the SATs like I did—upon impact. I know there were plenty of times I envied Mike and what he knew when. I routinely fantasized about how things might have been different had I improved my standardized-test-taking skills. I suppose scores were the stuff of sibling rivalry, but we never experienced any. Partly because we weren't brought up that way and partly because we were so close and admired each other so much. Another part of it was the eleven-year age gap. I often celebrated Mike's successes more like a parent than a brother.

Between the Oracle, the Optimist, and the Child Prodigy, I'd have a full-time life-support system for the bar. There was virtually no better place in the world to become one with the exam. In Toms River I could get free meals, physical and mental space, laundry service, love, air-conditioning, hot water, and cool breezes from the bay fifty yards away.

I'd taken my law school graduation speaker's advice very seriously. Per Judge Judy McGowen's instructions, I'd make studying for the bar exam my only responsibility. The good news was that my working conditions would be flawless. The bad news was that my working conditions would be flawless. If I couldn't pass the bar in this utopia, with no distractions or other responsibilities interfering, how would I ever pass?

CHAPTER 13

T IS VIRTUALLY impossible to pass the bar exam without taking a prep course. The commercial courses know this and extort thousands and thousands of dollars from law students in exchange for a seven-week course, a two-foot stack of reading materials, and tens of thousands of practice questions. None of my textbooks or notebooks from law school would likely be any help on the exam. I left them in storage. Eventually, they'd make nice shelf decorations.

Nickel, like most big firms, picked up the cost of the course as part of my employment package. I'd always hoped that a big firm would absorb that cost. If you didn't have a big law firm in your future and didn't want to cough up thousands for a course, one option was working for one of the major bar-review courses. Most reps received a salary plus a free course. As a bar rep, you either sold courses two or three days a week in the law-school hallways, or you helped orchestrate things at the prep course location once classes began.

Because all the reps were also students, when it came time to select a bar-review course, they were in no position to give me answers to substantive questions about the exam. And what little knowledge they did possess revolved around the Pennsylvania bar, since most of my colleagues were intent on practicing in Philadelphia. So for the New York bar, I was stuck. Everyone who had taken the New York exam had already graduated and was off practicing somewhere. And the few lawyers I was able to track down seemed to have blocked out the experience altogether.

The good thing was that for the New York bar, selecting a course was pretty straightforward. BAR/BRI was really the only game in town. It was the predominant player in the industry, boasting more than thirty years of experience and, according to its marketing campaign, more than 750,000 passing scores. Missing from the reams of BAR/BRI materials, however, were the real statistics. Such as the number of bar applicants who tossed their cookies before, during, or after the exam. The number who cried. How many multiple-choice questions they guessed on. How many essays they faked. How many applicants waited until the last month, or the last week, to start studying.

BAR/BRI did provide one very important statistic: how Temple students did on the New York bar. According to BAR/BRI's supercomputers, every Temple Law graduate in last year's graduating class passed the New York bar exam after taking BAR/BRI.

I expected my prep class size to be small. How many people in Toms River, New Jersey, could be studying for the New York bar?

It turned out BAR/BRI wasn't taught in Toms River. It was taught in Asbury Park, about an hour away. I pulled into the hotel parking lot and noticed that the letters "R" and "A" from the old Ramada sign were peeking out from underneath the new Holiday Inn banner. This place had a history of failure. Bad sign.

Blue arrows directed me to the Lily Conference Room. Tulip, Daisy, Carnation, Lily. I turned the corner to discover a long line of candidates waiting to receive study materials. I stepped up and began scanning the line to ensure that no one looked familiar. Anonymity was one of the chief reasons I'd come to New Jersey to study for the exam.

An even longer line began to form behind me. I spun around, scanning my BAR/BRI classmates. Five people back, a striking young petite girl with olive skin and auburn hair smiled my way. No smiling, I reminded myself. Stay focused on the task at hand. I smiled back.

I began eavesdropping on the conversation behind me. The excuses were starting already:

"I'm working all summer, so I won't have a chance to study much."

"Yeah, I know, I'm studying for the New Jersey and the New York bar this summer."

"Did either of you guys take trusts, wills, or tax in law school? I didn't. I'm screwed."

A voice called my name from the front of the line. I whipped my head around to find a man jumping around and waving in my direction. He looked faintly familiar. I smiled and tipped my chin toward him. "Hey, good to see you," I said through clenched teeth.

"This is great!" he yelled over the ten people between us. "Have you spoken with anyone from the firm?"

The firm. That's where I knew him. We'd interned together at Nickel last summer. There were sixteen of us. Even though his name escaped me, I remembered three things about this guy. One, he'd graduated from Georgetown Law (Tier 1). Two, he drank too much on the summer associate cruise around Manhattan and spent half the night vomiting off the side of the boat. And three, he was a "splitter": That is, he split his summer between two law firms—the first six weeks with Nickel and the next five weeks with a firm in Washington,

D.C. Many firms frowned on students who hedged this way. Apparently, Nickel didn't seem to mind, seeing that he was standing in line to receive his New York bar-review materials.

He held his spot in line with the tip of his toe, twisted his body toward me, and closed the gap between us by three people. "I'll save you a seat inside," he said.

I checked in with the BAR/BRI rep and got my books, plus the name of the guy from Nickel, Sam Weaver. On my way into the conference room, I swung the heavy blue BAR/BRI bag over my shoulder and caught the petite girl's attention once more. We both smiled.

Inside, fourteen tables were set up, seven per row, all in front of a twenty-seven-inch television on a cart in the center of the room. That was the instructor. That was all the instructors. Each table sat seven or eight. The tables were long eighteen-inch planks covered with tablecloths. Two water pitchers sat in the center of each table.

Sam waved me over. He was hard to miss, tons of red bushy hair and he was sitting front-row center. There was an empty seat next to him. The seating was tight. Sam was a big guy. He was in my personal space.

The BAR/BRI representative welcomed everyone to class, loaded our first very expensive videotape into the VCR, and sat down with that "I got a free BAR/BRI course" shit-eating grin. The tape began and the race was on.

"Six and a half weeks of class and nearly a thousand hours of studying will come down to twelve hours and fifteen minutes spread out over two days," the virtual professor explained. "The New York bar is administered on Tuesday, July thirtieth, and Wednesday, July thirty-first." Despite my proximity to New York City, where the exam was being administered, out-of-state applicants like me were required to travel six hours north and sit for the exam in Albany.

"Let's start out with the question on all of your minds. When will this all be over?" the professor asked. "The results will arrive in late November, early December."

I let out a soft moan. "Four months," Sam whispered to me. "We have to pretend to be attorneys at Nickel for three or four months before we know if it's all an act. It says here that the retake or the swearing-in ceremony, whichever applies, happens three months later, in February." Sam was reading directly from the BAR/BRI background materials.

"Day one is the New York Law Examination, or the NYLE, which tests candidates on law specific to New York. The NYLE consists of five essays, fifty multiple-choice questions, and one Multistate Performance Test, or MPT, administered over six hours and fifteen minutes," the professor said.

"Day two is the Multistate Bar Examination, or the MBE. The MBE is a six-hour, standardized two-hundred-multiple-choice-question examination administered nationally. That means you will have about one-point-eight minutes per question. Every multiple-choice question has four answer choices. Forty-eight of the fifty states require applicants to take and pass the MBE. New York is one of them. If you're curious, Louisiana and Washington are the exceptions." Sam was taking notes. He wrote down the two exceptions.

"Now, this part is important," the virtual professor said. Sam stopped writing. "The national average raw score on the MBE is one hundred twenty-five out of two hundred." Sam and I exchanged a look of hope. We both liked the fact that you could get more than seventy questions wrong and still be considered average. "The committee that grades the MBE is made up of law school professors and practitioners nationwide. Through a psychometrically approved scaling procedure, the committee converts those national average *raw* scores into *scaled* scores." Had there been a professor standing in front of me at that point, and not a VCR, I would have asked what "psychometrically approved" meant.

"If you're wondering what 'psychometrically approved' means," the professor continued, "according to the *American Heritage Dictionary*, it's a branch of psychology that deals with the design, administration, and interpretation of quantitative tests for the measurement of psychological variables such as intelligence, aptitude, and personality traits. If that doesn't help, join the club. Simply put, the committee adds between ten to twenty points to the *raw* scores to settle on *scaled* scores that land somewhere between one hundred thirty-six and one hundred forty-five."

"I hear the people who grade the MBE dump faulty questions," Sam whispered. "Yeah, sometimes they forget to put in the right answer," he said. "Other times the questions are ambiguous. And every so often they even include multiple correct answers."

"Something else to keep in mind," the professor said. "We've observed a 'wrong makes right' phenomenon to the bar. If the majority of applicants pick the *same wrong answer*, the committee may choose to accept the wrong answer as correct."

"Does that mean if everyone agrees to answer every one of the two hundred MBE multiple-choice questions with B, we all get perfect scores?" Sam whispered. I wished Sam would shut up. Everyone was giving us dirty looks.

The virtual professor went on to explain that we'd start off with the MBE topics. According to BAR/BRI, the two hundred multiple-choice questions revolved around six legal topics that we'd covered in some form or another in law school:

1. **Torts** (*34 questions*): These involved the most interesting fact patterns. The issue was always the same: Is Bob liable? Bob punches Chuck in the nose. Bob slanders Chuck. Bob hits Chuck with his truck by mistake. Bob's dog bites Chuck. Bob's car explodes and kills Chuck's dog. Bob's got problems.

2. **Contracts** (*34 questions*): Here you had to ask yourself: 1) Did the parties create a contract? 2) If so, was the contract enforceable? But what if Harvey was drunk when he made the offer? What if the contract was oral? What if Harvey wanted to take the offer back? What if Clarence accepted the offer without saying anything?

3. **Constitutional Law** (*33 questions*): How do you impeach the president? Who can declare war? What can Congress spend money on? What type of speech is protected? Which laws discriminate on the basis of race, gender, or sex?

4. **Evidence** (*33 questions*): Admitting evidence at trial was an elaborate process accompanied by hundreds of rules. Was the evidence

relevant? What was the evidence being offered to prove? Was the evidence authentic?

5. **Criminal Law and Procedure** *(33 questions):* The crimes: battery, assault, kidnapping, embezzlement, robbery, extortion, theft, forgery, arson, murder, rape, burglary, and larceny. The criminals: aiding, abetting, counseling, soliciting, conspiring, attempting, and, of course, committing. The defenses: self-defense, insanity, intoxication, infancy, mistake, entrapment, duress, and mistaken identity. The police: searching, seizing, stopping, frisking, chasing, and arresting. The process: confessions, attorneys, judges, juries, pleas, and prison.

6. **Real Property** *(33 questions):* Can I sublet my apartment? Must my landlord fix my broken washing machine? What if my brother breaks his leg in my landlord's hallway? What if my apartment has rats? Can I take the cabinets when I move? Can I walk across my neighbor's yard to get to my house?

After an hour and a half of orientation, class got started. The VCR professor started off with criminal law and procedure. I'd taken both courses in law school, yet most of the material was new to me. The law-school version took a year. The BAR/BRI version would take two days. During my three ten-minute breaks, I watched Sam recopy his notes and the petite girl doodle and stare at the ceiling. Four hours later, my first BAR/BRI class was over. I'd severely underestimated this exam.

CHAPTER 14

O N THE SECOND day of BAR/BRI class, I struck up an inane conversation with Gwen, the attractive girl I'd noticed in line that first day of class, and on the third day I asked her to dinner. Gwen had graduated from Seton Hall Law (Tier 2). In the fall she'd start a prestigious one-year clerkship with a state judge in Newark, New Jersey.

Gwen accepted my dinner proposal "as friends." I wouldn't be so easily dissuaded—I proposed we start studying together. Up until now, history would demonstrate, I hadn't "group-studied." In law school, study groups never struck me as productive, and a few bad experiences crystallized that point of view. Like first year, when I wasted four precious hours the day before my property-law exam philosophizing with my study group about the exceptions to the Rule Against Perpetuities. Half the group turned out to be underprepared eavesdroppers looking to pick up some last-minute study tips. By the end of the session, I was more confused than ever.

But I had to have this woman. And if it meant studying together for the bar, so be it. Gwen had pheromones. The combination of her Italian olive skin, auburn hair, light peach-smelling perfume, and perfect smile left me helpless. I made studying together as easy as possible for her. We'd go back to her place in Howell, New Jersey, just ten minutes from class. Like me, Gwen was living at home with the " 'rents." We'd sit by their pool, spend part of the time studying for the bar and most of the time complaining.

Two weeks into BAR/BRI, that all changed. It was a humid New Jersey afternoon. We were out by the pool. Suddenly clouds moved in, and rain began to pour down. We ran inside. Gwen suggested that we call it quits for the day; apparently our synergistic study machine was solar-powered. As I ran for my car, I slipped on the wet lawn and fell square on my back. She ran out to me, first to confirm that I was okay, then to laugh in my face. She was wearing a loose-fitting light sundress, and as she bent over, I caught a glimpse of her entire exquisite, ballet-perfected body. She wasn't wearing anything but the dress.

"Can I help you?" she said, remaining bent over me in the rain. I grabbed her hand, pulled her down to me, and gave her a long, soft kiss. We stayed there on the lawn kissing. For the next few days, we couldn't get enough of each other. We grabbed and groped every moment we could. The only time we showed restraint was in class. Even there, we had a debate over how best to use our ten-minute breaks. In a false attempt to stay focused, I refused to sit with Gwen in class. Instead, I sat with Sam, who had a seat waiting for me every day.

Gwen preferred to sit in the back of the room. My tactic of ignoring her generally backfired. I spent half the class turning around to watch her taking notes. The virtual teacher failed to tell me to keep my face forward and pay attention.

Perhaps God was putting me to a test: Let's see what kind of restraint you have—here is the most important, challenging exam of your life on the one hand, and the most seductive woman of your life on the other. Sometimes I cursed God for this conflict. Most times, usually in a compromising position, I thanked him. Sometimes even out loud.

Since we were both living at home, it was tough to find any privacy for that sort of thing. We used the bar exam as a pretense as often as possible. "Going upstairs to study with Alex" is what got us in Gwen's bedroom one night. It was high school all over again.

"Wait, wait, wait," I whispered to her. "Someone is coming up the steps. Listen."

"Fine," she said. We quickly got dressed and fanned out some property-law flash cards on her bed. BAR/BRI's study kit didn't include flash cards. The Oracle had bought them for me from an online law bookstore. Adjusting ourselves, we picked up our conversation midstream.

"And that's the difference between an equitable servitude and a covenant running with the land," she said. I agreed. The door was closed. Her mother walked by the bedroom without incident. Gwen rolled her eyes and smiled. Clearly, she got some pleasure out of the timing.

But we needed to find a better place, either to fool around or to study, because we weren't getting anything accomplished. Our chemistry put us in a physical groove and a study funk. Over the last three days, we'd elected the former. Attraction always trumped ambition when it came time to hit the books.

"Now what?" she said, sitting on her bed.

"Strip-criminal-law flash cards?" I said. "I get one right, you lose a piece of clothing. I get one wrong, you keep your clothes on. And vice versa." Together we were wearing four articles of clothing.

"You're ridiculous." Gwen paused. "Can we do strip *constitutional* law instead?"

"No. You studied constitutional law last night. We're sticking with strip criminal law. Neither of us knows criminal law very well."

Gwen began paraphrasing from a flash card: "After patrolling the warehouse, Security Guard Roy falls asleep on the job. Meanwhile, Joey Bag of Doughnuts comes along and lights the place on fire. Roy dies. Has Joey committed arson, first-degree murder, both, or neither?"

"You're so naked," I said. "Joey is guilty of both arson and first-degree murder."

"Wrong and wrong! If you don't start concentrating, we're never going to have sex. First off, no on arson, because for it to be arson, you have to light a 'dwelling' on fire. And even though Roy fell asleep on the job, BAR/BRI says a warehouse is not a dwelling."

"Right," I cut her off. "And it's not murder under the felony-murder rule, because there's no underlying felony. Under felony-murder, you can charge someone with first-degree murder only if death results from an underlying felony like arson. And without the arson charge, you can't charge him with first-degree murder. So Joey is free to go. Do I get partial credit?"

"No, 'fraid not," Gwen said flatly. "Keep your pants on."

We came to know this legal insanity as the bar. In any jurisdiction across the United States, lighting a warehouse on fire would be considered arson, but under the law tested on the MBE, it wasn't. This was the bar administrator's attempt to level the playing field. By establishing a special set of laws, what I referred to as the "bar code," nearly every law student—regardless of curriculum—was theoretically on equal footing. No one was any more or less prepared for the exam.

The bar code was an imaginary set of tens of thousands of outdated, antiquated laws that everyone needed to be familiar with for the single purpose of passing the bar. For most of us, the laws were inconsistent with anything we'd learned in school and would have no practical application when it came to practicing law.

The MBE laws were based on two general categories of law: statutory law and case law. Statutory law, otherwise known as "black-letter law," was straightforward. These laws regulated certain types of conduct. Statutes were drafted by the legislative branch of government, generally approved by the executive branch, and interpreted by the judicial branch. The government in question might be as small as a municipality or as large as the federal government. Although legislators worked hard to spell out statutes with excruciating clarity, it was a lawyer's job to interpret them. In fact, that was how most attorneys spent their careers—dissecting statutes, making hypertechnical distinctions in language and phraseology, identifying ambiguities and vagueness, and interpreting terms, phrases, definitions, and omissions to their client's benefit. (That was where the expression "don't be such a lawyer" came from.)

Judges also did quite a bit of interpreting. But when they did it, it was with regard to case law—the other body of law that contributed to the MBE. Local, state, and federal judges interpreted statutes and developed or expounded upon new or existing legal doctrines or theories and then wrote legal opinions—together, those hundreds of thousands of decisions were considered case law, which was decided based on the legal principle called precedent, one of the fundamental concepts of American jurisprudence. Under that principle, lower courts were bound by the legal opinions of higher courts. State trial courts followed state appellate courts, federal trial courts followed federal appeals courts, and everyone followed the U.S. Supreme Court, the highest court in the land.

But the rule of precedent wasn't as straightforward as it appeared. Since no two fact patterns were ever exactly the same, the party for whom precedent was not helpful always argued the case was distinguishable, so judges rendered new legal opinions, and the case law continued to grow and grow and grow.

That was the MBE's bar code: a conglomeration of statutes and cases based on precedent taken from different jurisdictions across the country from different periods of time. BAR/BRI got the big bucks because it did the near impossible: Its people summarized, in a logical way, the tens of thousands of rules concerning the six MBE topics and then incorporated them into various educational tools, including legal outlines, questions, and essays.

Now I picked up a flash card. " 'One afternoon, while Roger is at work, Linus walks in the front door of Roger's home. The front door happens to be wide open. Inside, Linus picks up Roger's television and walks out. Which of the following crimes has Linus committed: breaking and entering, robbery, and/or burglary?' "

"The fact that he walked through an unlocked, open front door doesn't matter," Gwen said. "It's still breaking and entering. It's not robbery, because robbery involves a person. Linus isn't stealing from a person. As for burglary, read the question again."

"One afternoon—" I said.

"Stop. It's not burglary because it didn't happen at night. Under MBE common law, burglary has to happen at night. Your pants, please." I shook my head in defeat, smiled, and turned off the light on the nightstand.

CHAPTER 15

SPENT THE HOUR drive to class every day listening to bar-review tapes. It got me pumped up for class.

No.

Okay, I *occasionally* listened to bar-review tapes. The fact was that every waking moment was starting to feel like one more missed opportunity to memorize a different legal cause of action.

The format of the BAR/BRI lectures had been the same for weeks. We sat there, watched the videotape of the day, and took notes. Many of us used laptops to take notes. Even if you were only an average typist, you could keep up with the bar professors because they purposely lectured in outline form, slowly enumerating the elements of a crime or cause of action. By contrast, law school wasn't conducive to taking notes on a laptop. Most law school lectures rarely included such specific information, and thanks to that damned Socratic method, law school questions were generally answered with more questions. Bar-review teachers provided answers and more answers.

Today I was going to travel forward in time. I was on my way to New York City to see a live taping of the lecture. How exciting.

The lectures were originally performed before twenty-five hundred law school graduates in the auditorium of the Javits Center in midtown. After that, BAR/BRI distributed the live lectures—what I referred to now as "dead" lectures—to remote locations like mine. Anyone attending the live lectures had about a one-week advantage.

I'd always been curious about the live lectures. Hayley, who'd studied for the bar in Manhattan, said they were something you had to experience firsthand. I agreed to meet her at the Javits Center. As for my dead lecture in Asbury Park, I'd get the notes from Sam. The visit to New York would also give me a chance to do some apartment hunting with Arjun. Not since engineering school had we lived together. Since then, we'd both abandoned engineering: Arjun was getting his graduate business degree at New York University. We agreed that if we lived together, we could defray costs, plus get a bigger place. In Manhattan, size mattered.

"Wow, you look great," I said, kissing Hayley on the cheek. This was the first time we had seen each other since the summer internship with Nickel. Until now I'd always seen her wearing business suits. Today she was wearing summer clothes—a denim skirt and red tank top. She was tan and wore sunglasses with blue lenses.

"Thanks. See, if you studied here, you could enjoy this oppressive heat every day," she said. It was about ninety-five degrees. "Tell me that it's cooler on the Jersey shore." We went inside the conference center, which was as she had described: thousands of students listening to this little speck lecturing at the center of the room.

For the students at the Javits Center, this was lecture twenty. Yesterday, in New York City, BAR/BRI had finished teaching the last of the six MBE courses. It was now time to focus on the New York courses.

"Before we start the wills lecture, I want to answer some of your questions about the New York portion of the exam and give you some background on a new section," said the real-life professor. "Like dozens of other states, New York has added the Multistate Performance Test, or the MPT, and it counts as ten percent of your overall score. Even though you'll take the MPT the same day you take the New York portion, it doesn't test on New York law. Unlike every other part of the bar exam, the MPT doesn't test on *any* law. As the name suggests, the MPT tests you on your ability to *perform* as an attorney—to 'think' like an attorney."

By now I'd heard plenty about the MPT. This was the one part of the exam where we didn't need to regurgitate the law. For the MPT, we could focus on what it took to be an attorney; problem solving, analyzing facts, identifying legal issues, and researching the law. For this section, we'd be provided a case file containing background resource materials, the facts of the case, and a memorandum from a supervising attorney that described a hypothetical assignment. Usually, the assignment was to write a client opinion letter, a brief in support of a motion, or some other legal document. The exercise, intended to simulate a real situation encountered by a new attorney, struck me as very fair.

"Next week BAR/BRI will conduct an MPT workshop where you'll be instructed on deciphering the files and libraries presented, analyzing the various types of problems, and managing your time," the professor added. I was glad BAR/BRI would prep us for the MPT, but if law school hadn't done the job already, you were in pretty sad shape. Between my legal writing and research classes, exams, clerkships with federal judges, and law review, I felt ready to "perform" like an attorney. At least as far as the MPT was concerned.

"Now let's turn to the New York Law Exam, or the NYLE," the professor said. "The NYLE accounts for the largest portion of your composite bar exam. As you know, the MBE is worth forty percent, the MPT ten percent, and the NYLE fifty percent. The New York bar exam does not have minimum score requirements for the MBE, MPT, or NYLE. States like Pennsylvania require a minimum MBE score. New York creates a composite score based on a weighted average of the MBE, MPT, and NYLE. So theoretically, a spectacular MBE score can compensate for a pitiful NYLE, and vice versa.

"Last summer the overall New York pass rate was seventy-one percent. But the prognosis for first-time candidates is always higher. The pass rate for first-timers on that exam was actually about seventy-eight percent. By comparison, the overall pass rate in Utah was ninety-one percent. Then again, only three hundred people took the Utah bar earlier this year. Nearly ten thousand people took the New York bar last year.

"The New York pass rate has a lot to do with the NYLE. The NYLE tests on twenty-five topics that deal specifically with New York law. No other bar in the country has this many topics. Only Virginia and Mississippi come close."

"New Jersey is a cakewalk in comparison," I whispered to Hayley. "They have six topics. BAR/BRI is prepping people for the New Jersey bar exam at the same hotel that I go to for the New York videotapes. They're still watching tapes on criminal law." Hayley rolled her eyes. "And they don't even have to study New Jersey law. They can answer the essays using the law from the MBE bar code."

"It is sheer breadth that you'll have to overcome," the professor went on. "Please pull out your syllabi. Of the twenty-five topics, ten are most commonly tested. Five of the most commonly tested subjects have the same names as five of the MBE topics: torts, contracts, real property, criminal law and procedure, and evidence. But you'll have to appreciate the distinctions between the MBE and New York versions."

"That'll be the death of me," Hayley said to me.

"A very simple illustration," the professor said. "You may remember from your criminal-law lecture for the MBE that lighting a warehouse on fire is not arson. But under New York law, it is."

"There's going to be thousands of these distinctions, and somehow we're going to have to keep them separate in our mind," I said.

"Yeah, and then be sure to purge them in between Day one and Day two of the exam," Hayley said.

"There are five other New York topics also commonly tested. The first is New York practice. It's unlikely that any of you have ever taken this course, even though many of you studied here in New York. As you learned in lectures three, four, and five, New York practice is a collection of thousands of specific New York civil-procedure requirements—the who, what, when, where, why, and how of filing a civil lawsuit in New York.

"As for the other four remaining most commonly tested subjects, you'll probably have some working knowledge of them from law school. They are New York wills, trusts, domestic relations, and corporations."

I'd known this day would come. I'd taken corporations in law school, but I had no excuse for not taking wills, trusts, and domestic relations. Although Temple Law wouldn't have taught me the New York versions, at least I'd be familiar with the general legal concepts and terms of art. I'd just never gotten around to taking them, and by the time I realized how important they were, it was too late.

"Can you write a codicil to my will?" my uncle Stephen asked me late in my third year of law school.

What's a codicil? I remember asking myself. I looked it up and realized it was simply an amendment to a will. Not good. This was something that I should have known. How could I possibly graduate from law school not knowing how to write a basic will, set up a trust fund, or finalize a divorce? Not taking these courses was very poor judgment on my part.

It would have been enough trying to get my head around these ten most commonly tested topics—the primaries—but the professor began listing off the secondaries, and I panicked.

"The fifteen secondary topics cover everything else under the New York sun," the professor said. I looked over the list; few of them were familiar. I didn't dare say this to Hayley. "Once you pass the bar, you will be licensed to do it all. You can buy and sell property in New York, draft a loan, finance a lease, and record a New York mortgage. Thanks to this course, you'll know how to file a New York trademark infringement suit, New York taxes, and a New York worker's compensation claim."

The professor began her lecture on New York wills. An hour later, she was winding down. "After the break, we'll continue with wills, and tomorrow we'll begin on estate taxation."

"Watch this," Hayley whispered to me.

"All right, people, take ten minutes, and then we'll get started again. Please try to restrict the break to ten minutes. We have a lot to go over." All of a sudden it was chaos—a total media frenzy. No fewer than fifty students began racing toward the professor and her podium. Tripping over one another, they surrounded and engulfed her, then began firing questions.

"This will go on anywhere from half an hour to forty minutes," Hayley said casually. "They'll make the professor answer a dozen different hypothetical fact patterns and ask for legal explanations with excruciating detail."

"These are the same students you hated in law school," I said.

"Bingo," she said. "These are the people who will be wearing red and inhaling bananas at the exam."

I'd worn red ties to plenty of job interviews. Red, a "power" color, was supposed to symbolize assertiveness and self-confidence. "Bananas?" I asked.

"They're brain food. Rich in complex carbohydrates," she said. "They're supposed to have a calming effect and give you brainpower for problem solving and memory." I made a mental note to start eating bananas. "I deal with these fanatics accosting the professors every day," Hayley said. "How does it translate on your end?"

"Oh, it's a pleasure compared to this," I said. "BAR/BRI edits them down. All I hear is the professor say, 'Let's take a ten-minute break,' then some elevator music comes on, and a big clock appears on the television screen with a timer that counts down from ten."

"This is the price of getting the lectures one week ahead of you," Hayley said.

"Yeah, I think I'll forgo the press conference, stick with my virtual teachers, and continue to rent the videotapes for a few thousand dollars."

After class I took the subway downtown to meet Arjun. We planned to look at an apartment on Broadway and Bleecker in the Village. "It's a good space," he'd assured me. From there we'd check for more list-ings in *The Village Voice*.

Given my bar obligations and his proximity to the city, Arjun had been kind enough to take the laboring oar in our search for residence. My two requests were an elevator and air-conditioning. Over the past three weeks Arjun had scouted nearly twenty apartments. All of them were a wash—either the neighborhood was too seedy, the space was insufficient, or the public transportation was inadequate.

Where in the city do you live? How much rent do you pay? How many square feet do you have? These were the three most popular ice-breakers in Manhattan. New Yorkers took no shame in asking these questions. "Upper East, twenty-seven hundred dollars, seven hundred fifty square feet," you would overhear someone brag in a dimly lit, overpriced New York bar. Descriptors like "loft," "high ceilings," and "view" commanded respect. Your apartment relegated you to a class.

I was glad that fate had enabled Arjun and me to be roommates again, but I didn't expect things to be the same. We'd drifted apart over the years, and I worried there was too much distance between us. Three years of law school had changed me. I'd become accustomed to living alone. I considered myself more private and guarded. Plus, the school phase of my life was over, while Arjun was still in the throes of academia. In the fall he'd enter the second year of his MBA program, or "b-school," as he referred to it. We were still best friends, but only out of habit. Still, familiarity can be a great comfort when you're faced with so much uncertainty.

Arjun and I greeted each other with a hug. "That place we're supposed to see is already rented," he said. "New York apartments are like moving targets. There's another place a few blocks from here. We can walk."

"No problem," I said.

"You brought your checkbook, right?" Arjun asked. "If we see any-thing we like, we'll have to immediately put down first month, last month, one month's security deposit, and sign a one-year lease."

"Got it. I guess it makes sense that we sign a one-year lease. None of these places rents month-to-month, do they?" I asked. He gave me a look. "I didn't think so."

"Is this about the bar?" he asked.

"I'm just being ridiculous. Signing a year lease assumes I pass the bar, that's all," I said. Every contingency of the bar filled me with anxiety.

"You're going to pass." Everyone said this, and it was maddening. Everyone assumed I'd pass. You'll see, I'd think. I'll fail, and then you and everyone else will realize that I'm an idiot, a fraud. "And so what if you don't pass? Worse-case scenario, you take it again. You're allowed, right?"

"Nickel expects me to pass on the first try. I didn't ask how many times I could take it before getting the boot. That probably wouldn't have exuded the level of confidence I was going for."

"Could you venture a guess?"

"The rumor is three times," I said. "Pass on the third try, or do not pass go, do not collect two hundred dollars, and do not let the door hit you in the ass. After that, I guess I pack my bags and drag my sorry ass back to Philadelphia or Toms River. Or, better yet, sit in our expensive Manhattan apartment eating the one-year lease.

"And every place is different," I continued. "David Markey tells me that the New York DA's Office has a 'two strikes and you're out' rule. New York *State* has *no* limits on the number of times you can retake the exam. But I imagine after failing it two or three times, you might want to take some time off to regain consciousness."

"My friend Harold Franklin? You met him. He went to Rutgers with us and dropped out of engineering. He went to Villanova Law [Tier 2], took the New York bar last year, and failed. And he was a smart guy," Arjun eulogized. "He did fine in law school, but I guess he missed class the day they taught the bar."

I'd heard this joke before, but I didn't appreciate it coming from Arjun. He had no idea what I was going through. Was it really a good idea for us to live together?

Why *had* Harold Franklin failed? I wondered. Did he have bad professors, or had he taken the wrong courses? Maybe he'd gone to a bad law school. Was Tier 2 at work again? It didn't make sense.

Arjun and I turned the corner to see a small crowd gathering outside a brownstone. It was the building with the apartment for rent. We got in line.

CHAPTER 16

MY STOMACH HURT. Every time I took a bite of food, I could feel it travel from my lips to the bottom of my throat. Then the food would sit there, below my rib cage, building up pressure. My doctor said it was heartburn and put me on a prescription dose of Pepcid AC.

My teeth hurt. They all hurt. I figured that was a good sign, since I couldn't possibly have thirty-two cavities. My mouth and stomach problems were just as well. I think of all the time I saved by not eating. I was definitely losing weight.

Oh, and my eyes were going. After overwearing my disposable contact lenses for three weeks straight and infecting my right eye, I was now in glasses. The optometrist said another few days, and I would have created an ulcer on my cornea.

Until now denial had enabled me to ignore my various ailments. But four weeks into the bar-review class, anger—the second phase of classic trauma—began to sink in, and I realized I was falling apart because I was angry about the exam. There was simply too much information to memorize and not enough time. I was too busy attending lectures, recopying notes, preparing outlines, answering practice questions, having sex, and drafting practice essays.

BAR/BRI's study materials included an ideal study schedule. Had I stuck to that plan, I would have completed more than two thousand practice MBE questions, read more than a thousand pages of legal outlines, and completed nearly one hundred practice essays. But like so many of my compatriots, I'd abandoned the BAR/BRI schedule early on. Few of us could keep up.

For the practice essays, BAR/BRI told us, "Put away your books, clear the room, set the clock for forty minutes, spend ten to fifteen minutes reading and outlining the question and twenty-five to thirty minutes writing your practice essay under simulated test-taking conditions." I never did that. To me, "simulated test-taking conditions" meant being paralyzed with fear, interrupted by lapses of nausea. This was not a state I needed to practice.

I didn't have time to do practice essays. Besides, I'd written plenty of essays in law school. All I had to do was make sure I stuck to BAR/BRI's CIRAC format: conclusion, issue, rule, analysis, and conclusion. For every single issue in a fact pattern, BAR/BRI told me to write out the legal conclusion, then discuss the relevant legal issue, apply the applicable rule of law, analyze why the law applied, then repeat the conclusion. CIRAC.

Writing the conclusion first was tough—often I didn't know what it was until after I completed the analysis. Anticipating this problem, BAR/BRI told us to leave a couple of lines blank at the beginning of each paragraph, then fill in the conclusion after the fact. In law school, I'd learned the mnemonic as IRAC. My professors didn't find it necessary to state the conclusion twice. IRAC, CIRAC, BIGMAC, it was all the same.

I devoted the time that I would have used in writing out practice essays to memorizing. BAR/BRI's brilliant schedule did not allot time to memorize the tens of thousands of rules of law that it taught. I guess they assumed we would memorize content upon impact. I, like everyone I knew, threw out the ideal study schedule after the second week.

I had my own routine. My day started around eight A.M. I spent the morning studying BAR/BRI outlines and doing practice questions in my mother's art studio, which I'd commandeered. It hardly resembled a studio anymore. Bar books, outlines, flash cards, and notebooks were sprawled everywhere. In the afternoon I went to class, then usually to Gwen's, and back home for evening devotions.

The first half of my evening was spent memorizing. I'd lie on the living room couch for hours, getting up only to air off my midsection from the hot batteries of my laptop. Those were the moments I tried to desperately convince myself: It's called a *laptop.* They couldn't possibly design and name it a laptop if it made you sterile when you placed it on your lap.

For the second half of the evening, I'd move over to the big wooden dining room table to rewrite, expand, and consolidate my notes. The phone rang one night. Most of the calls these days were for the teenager in the house.

"I'll get it," I said, and as I jumped up, I stubbed my toe on the table. "Frick!" I screamed, avoiding the obvious alternative. Mike contained himself, but I could hear the Oracle laughing in her bedroom. Since my departure for law school, my parents had replaced the table in the dining room. The table I'd grown up with sat on two bases. The new table was much bigger and was stabilized with four legs. Every time I got up these days, without fail, I stubbed my toe on one of those legs. My family found this entertaining.

I answered the phone. "Hey, David," I said, rubbing my toe. "Good to hear from you." This was the first time I'd heard from David Markey since graduation. I figured he was the only person I'd keep in touch with from Temple. He had stayed in Philadelphia to study for the bar exam, but we were both headed to New York in the fall. I'd gone the private route, David the public. He had a prestigious job as an assistant district attorney.

"I figured I'd check in," he said. "How's it coming?"

"Poor," I said. "This whole thing is so grueling. I'll finish memorizing one topic, then I'll forget another. Sometimes I'll be studying a topic, and I'll draw a complete and absolute blank. I can't ever remember what topic I'm studying. You?"

"I'm all right," he said flatly. "It's a job. You wake up, you study, you sleep." He was rarely affected, consummately mature, and always grounded. That was how he approached law school, and that was how he approached the bar. "Chill." "Calm down." "Relax." He told me these things in law school, and they had the very opposite effect. His cool sensibilities could perhaps be attributed to the two years he'd taken off between college and law school. I'd gone straight through school with no sabbaticals.

If anyone was going to painstakingly stick to BAR/BRI's ludicrous schedule, it would be Markey. He seemed unmoved by the bar exam experience. I, on the other hand, did my best to hide my shock.

"Come on, you have no other pressing responsibilities this summer," he said. "It's the ultimate excuse. 'Can you clean out the gutters?' 'Sorry, got to study for the bar.' 'Can you help me move into my new apartment?' "

"Nope, got to study for the bar," I parroted.

"You've seen the Temple Law graduation statistics for the last five years," Markey said. "Ninety-something percent of our graduates pass this thing. Think of all the idiots we went to school with. We're going to pass."

"You make some compelling arguments. I guess it's just a matter of seeing the trees through the forest," I said.

"Forest through the trees."

"Exactly," I said, walking over to the dining room table. "Then rationalize this." I picked up a sheet of paper. "BAR/BRI has a sheet of mnemonic devices. You've seen them, right? Well, under 'Evidence,' there's an acronym called 'DAMP RIM.' Can you kindly explain to me what in the hell a DAMP RIM is?"

David was the right guy for this question. In his third year, he won the national trial-team competition and was chosen by the judges as the country's most promising young trial attorney. Temple Law may have been Tier 2, but we were number one in the country for trial advocacy.

"Ah, DAMP RIM. You're right. That one is absurd," he said. "Obviously there's no such thing as a DAMP RIM, and neither word has anything to do with evidence. DAMP RIM deals with hearsay, right? I made a point of ignoring that mnemonic." I was amazed. David had actually memorized what he'd ignored. Hearsay evidence was an out-of-court statement made by someone other than the person testifying and offered to prove the truth. In other words, if Joey was on the witness stand and wanted to testify about what Corey said, he couldn't. Corey's out-of-court statement was considered hearsay. The law preferred for Corey to come say it himself.

There were, of course, legal exceptions. Exceptions existed because certain statements were presumably true by their very nature. For those types of statements, the law was willing to make an exception and admit the hearsay as evidence. For example, I could testify that Cindy screamed, "That guy is running the red light," because her statement might fall under the "excited utterance" exception to hearsay. She "uttered" the statement during the "excitement" caused by the accident, and her statement was presumed true because it was unlikely that she had time to lie right before the accident. It was still hearsay, but the law made an exception for such excited utterances.

There were about two dozen other exceptions, all of which we needed to memorize. And that was where DAMP RIM came in.

"It says here DAMP RIM is a mnemonic for the 'unavailable' element of the hearsay exception," I said, reading from BAR/BRI's study materials.

"Okay, so Pat wants to testify as to what Soupy says," David explained. "Soupy should obviously show up and testify for herself, but she may be 'unavailable.' DAMP RIM tells you whether or not Soupy is *really* unavailable. We did this all the time on the trial team. But we had our own rules. I don't know what BAR/BRI's DAMP RIM stands for. Remind me."

"Sure. There are seven letters and seven ways Soupy can be unavailable. Soupy is truly unavailable if she's D, as in *dead*. She's unavailable if she's A, as in *absent*. Meaning Soupy can't be subpoenaed or brought into court in a reasonable manner."

"She's unavailable if she's 'M,' as in *memory*, right?" David said. "All that means is Soupy lacked the memory to testify on the subject matter. And she's unavailable if she's 'P,' as in *privileged*." That meant Soupy was part of a special relationship that afforded her the privilege of refusing to testify. Doctors and patients; attorneys and clients; and spouses all had this type of relationship.

"Which leaves RIM. Soupy is unavailable if she's 'R'—she *refuses* to testify," I said, still reading from the BAR/BRI materials. "Now, here's where it gets trippy. Soupy is unavailable if she's 'I,' as in she has a physical *inability* to testify. What's that all about? Physical inability is the best they could come up with? I guess 'P,' as in *physically* unable to testify, didn't work. Yeah, DAMP RPM makes no sense whatsoever."

"Or DAMP RUM, *unable* to testify," David added. "Don't worry about the I—what are the chances you'll get an exception to the hearsay rule on unavailability and it will have to do with the person's *inability* to testify due to a physical challenge?"

"Knowing my luck, pretty good odds," I said. "That is assuming that I can recognize that the fact pattern is asking me to recall the 'I' in DAMP RIM. But the fact that we're even having this conversation will help me memorize it."

"Oh yeah. What's the M stand for? *Mental* inability to testify?" David asked.

"Exactly," I said. "You're a ninja."

"Thanks. All right, I'm done. When I called you, I had no expectation of reviewing the finer—or rather asinine—points of evidence. I'm sure we'll talk again before the exam. When you and Arjun find an apartment, give me a call. I'm going to start looking next week. Ultimately you'll find me somewhere on the Upper East Side."

The conversation had been thoroughly therapeutic. I'd always admired David's willingness and ability to jump right into a legal discussion. Perhaps the angry phase of my trauma was drawing to a close. Maybe the third phase—bargaining—was at hand. I could hear myself: "Please let me pass. I'll do anything. I'll give up my job at Nickel. I'll live in Queens. Please just let me pass. By a point, even. Round my score up if you must."

If not, I was destined for depression and eventually acceptance, the final two phases.

CHAPTER 17

SOMETIMES I WOULD forget that I was studying on the Jersey shore. The bar was like a tiny tropical island. And on the Isle of Bar, there was this vacation resort where all the activities revolved around the exam. Maybe you'd like to suntan on the beach while you do a practice exam. Or perhaps take a dip in the pool while you memorize the Rule Against Perpetuities?

Gwen was with me on the island. And it felt like a relationship in vacation mode. There were no obligations to family or friends. There were no bills or shopping. Food and lodging were provided and paid for. It didn't matter what was happening in world affairs. There were no newspapers or television. We spent our days in the sun doing bar-related activities, and our nights having sex in one of our bungalows.

We weren't in love. We liked each other. We lusted after each other. When it came to talking about the relationship, I was your stereotypi-cal male: In other words, I didn't. And Gwen was happy to keep it that way. There were no arguments or deep discussions about whether we were progressing and what was next. We studied, we had sex, and our few conversations were restricted to the bar exam. Most nights we'd lie quietly in bed afterward, careful not to stir my parents. And with waves crashing on the Jersey shore, we'd bitch about BAR/BRI. Gwen, like David Markey, was much more at peace with the exam experience than I was.

"Did you know that there is no legal duty to save a dying room-mate?" I asked her one evening.

"No, I didn't. That would have come in handy in law school," she said. "Did you realize that you don't need *actual* damages to sue for in-tentional infliction of emotional distress when it involves the mishan-dling of a dead body?"

"That would have come in handy in law school," I said. "Actually, that's news to me. In my law school Torts class, we *never* discussed mis-handling dead bodies. Did yours?" I asked. She nodded no. For most law students, a Torts course covered car accidents, medical malprac-tice, and product defects. Tort lawyers were the ambulance chasers who advised you to get properly compensated for a slip-and-fall.

"Yeah, that keeps happening to me, too," Gwen said. "BAR/BRI re-views a course that I think I've taken before, and it turns out that I'm starting all over again."

"I guess I'm finding it hard to come to terms with the fact that law school law and bar-exam law don't have much in common with each other," I said.

All of a sudden I thought about Arjun's friend who had failed the exam, Harold Franklin. Had he done anything wrong in law school? No.

Even without knowing him I was sure he'd studied hard, taken challenging classes, and been before talented professors. It was just that the bar and law school were two completely different experiences.

The primary goal in law school was to learn to "think" like an attorney. Every professor told you this. I paid tens of thousands of dollars to learn how to write, speak, research, argue, and persuade like an attorney. I had to be prepared to argue both sides of a legal dilemma. And our exam format was aimed at honing these skills. Most exams were open book because good lawyering was always preferable to mass memorizing.

For the bar, there was no "thinking" like an attorney or arguing both sides. Instead, there were flat-out answers. For the bar, you needed to develop stamina, work quickly, and practice. Thinking like an attorney was replaced with memorizing, instinct, and reflexes. Your oral skills were irrelevant, and all your writing skills needed to be was satisfactory. It suddenly occurred to me that I was on familiar ground: The bar was engineering school all over again. There were answers, and instead of boxing them, I'd fill in an oval.

"Passing the bar has little to do with how you did in law school," Gwen concluded.

Lying there next to her, I thought about it. "And passing the bar has little to do with how you'll perform as an attorney."

A minute passed in silence. "I don't want to get dressed and I don't want to drive home," she said, nestling under my arm. "I wish we could just fall asleep here."

"Me, too."

CHAPTER 18

I'S TIME TO come clean. Two days after I took the SATs, I canceled my scores. Maybe I canceled a perfect sixteen hundred. Probably not—my retake was only slightly above average. Two weeks after I took the LSATs, I canceled my scores. The retake: again, average. Given my weak standardized scores over the years, I've tried to distract admissions committees with good grades, extracurricular activities, and innovative table-tennis paddles. Of course, the Child Prodigy was destined to pursue a simpler life. If you stood still and remained very quiet, you could spot him shuffling from room to room with an SAT prep book tucked under his arm.

The New York bar presented a challenge to my practice of canceling scores. For the bar, there would be no canceling. I could not pretend it hadn't happened. The results would be published in the *New York Law Journal,* and everyone would know whether I'd tested positive or negative. "Guilty" or "not guilty." You "passed" or . . . you "didn't pass." I avoided saying the f-word; simply thinking "failure" was taboo.

Every day BAR/BRI poured it on. And every day it got harder and harder to understand how the first-time pass rate, year after year, was about 78 percent. Could 78 percent of the people in my graduating class pass the bar? There was no doubt that some were destined to be great attorneys, but we had our share of dim ones, too. The fact that I'd graduated in the top 10 percent of my class somehow didn't convince me that I'd be among the lucky 78 percent.

By the time BAR/BRI finished teaching the six MBE courses and the ten NYLE primaries, my head was swimming. I was running out of memory addresses to deposit each and every element of each and every crime or cause of action. I had to start cleaning shop. My brain could store only so much. I purged memories of my seventh birthday party, my second kiss, my pizza-topping preferences, and my mother's maiden name.

Just short of dumping all the positive memories from my formative years, I had an epiphany. It hit me during BAR/BRI's secured-transactions lecture.

I'd taken Secured in law school. It dealt with the elaborate legal requirements associated with buying on credit and regulating secure credit transactions. The codebook that we used in law school was four inches thick and contained thousands of rules. For that very reason, my final, like most exams in law school, was open book. The final would have been impossible to complete without that codebook, my notes, and a series of handmade flowcharts.

The examiners penning the New York bar didn't care about any of this, of course. Of the twenty-five subjects we needed to know for the New York bar exam, secured was at the bottom of the list. Regardless, I suppose New York expected us to memorize the entire codebook. According to BAR/BRI's supercomputers, in the past twenty-two years, out of 249 essays, New York tested on secured transactions twice. That meant there was less than a 1 percent chance that I'd have to write out a New York secured-transactions essay.

That's when it finally hit me—there was simply too much information to memorize. No one could possibly memorize twenty-five codebooks' worth of material for twenty-five topics on the NYLE. So how *did* 78 percent of first-time test takers pass? Seventy-eight percent passed because you could pass the bar . . . with a failing grade. Crunching the relevant numbers set me free.

The way I figured it: The NYLE essays were worth 40 percent of my score, and according to BAR/BRI, I needed to score five out of ten on each essay. The NYLE multiple-choice questions were worth 10 percent, and I needed to get twenty-five out of fifty questions correct. The MPT was worth 10 percent, and I needed to get at least 50 percent correct. Finally, the MBE was worth 40 percent of my overall score, and according to BAR/BRI, I needed to get 125 out of 200 questions right. If you took a weighted average of those scores, the end result was 55 percent. Based on all the statistics, scores, and scaling, all I needed to do was get 55 percent of the exam correct. Anywhere else, 55 percent was a failing grade. Perhaps that was why some test takers were willing to disregard certain subjects altogether. It was a calculated risk.

I needed a D. I knew that if I got a D, I'd pass. How quickly I'd forgotten my days of engineering, where getting 55 percent right made you a genius. All I had to do was pass, and part of the test was surviving the prep. The bar course was a rite of passage. Surely my future clients were entitled to an attorney capable of withstanding extreme pressure and surviving six and a half weeks of intensive bar-review boot camp, and taking the bar was a good start.

This liberating revelation helped me feel less apocalyptic than usual. Being around the Optimist also helped. David Markey's mentality was truly starting to rub off—the bar was a job, and odds were, I'd pass. I began mentally phasing out all distractions. When I studied, the telephone didn't ring when it rang. The television was off when it was on. Even the jackhammering in the street became white noise. I began to concentrate, to Zen.

"You know if you use up the eraser before using up the pencil, you're making too many mistakes," I said to Mike, who was changing an answer on his Scantron sheet. It was nearly ten P.M. on a Friday night.

"Where'd you go?" Mike asked. He was surrounded by commonly tested SAT words and half a dozen number two pencils, midway through a practice exam.

"I jimmied my way up there and finally did it." I pulled out a can of WD-40 from my back pocket. My bedroom was located fifty yards from the beach and fifteen yards from the squeakiest beach swings I'd ever heard. It was summer on the Jersey shore. Between the hours of one and three A.M., teenagers came to the beach to drink beer, pontificate about current events, and squeak.

"It's late. Were you able to see anything?" Mike asked.

"Enough to make them *stealth* swings."

"Ah, congratulations. We'll all sleep better now."

"If only I could oil the teenagers."

"In all likelihood, I go to school with them. If you'd like, I can have a few words with them," Mike said jokingly.

"Choose them wisely. I'm not convinced their vocabulary extends much beyond 'motherfucker,' " I said. "I'll study with you. Make some room." I spread out some books next to Mike's and began reviewing New York trusts.

Our mother walked in. She'd been biding her time all night. We shared the same house but operated on our own train tracks. The family was trying to give me space. She had determined it was time to break the strict library-silence guidelines and socialize. Our family was best at night.

"How about I make some coffee?" she said. Coffee at ten P.M. was normal.

"How are you feeling?" I asked.

"I'm trying to fight this headache. I've had it for three days," she said.

"Oh, I'm sorry to hear that."

"Yeah, I'm in Migraine City."

"Migraine City, population one," I said. This made her laugh.

"Okay," the Optimist said, as if we'd just called out his name. He made his way up the split-level steps to the kitchen. He had heard all the commotion in the kitchen, turned off the television, and decided to join us.

"Tea?" my mother asked him.

"Sure. Thanks. So, what are we studying tonight?" he asked, clapping his hands. "We" never studied together.

"Come on. We'll help you pass the bar," my mother said. "Then you can write in your diary, 'Today my parents were nice to me.' " I smiled. When I was ten, my parents had bought me a diary. We found it years later. Paging through, it had one entry: "Today my parents were nice to me." Anthropologists would conclude that my parents tortured me as a child.

"I thought we'd start with 'pour-over gifts,' " I offered. I was trying to take time every day to memorize some remarkably obscure point that I assumed 90 percent of my colleagues ignored. I considered this legal minutiae "the edge." Each edge was a lottery ticket. Pour-over gifts were one of those tickets.

"What is a pour-over gift?" the Optimist said.

"Dad, really? Okay, fine." I read from the BAR/BRI definition: " 'A pour-over gift from a will to a revocable inter vivos trust is valid. And the trust to which a pour-over gift is made may be unfunded.' " The definition went on for another five sentences. Three long, hard years of law school still did not provide me with the skill set to comprehend that sentence. I didn't dare reveal this to my family.

"Maybe you can explain it to us with an illustration," my father said.

I looked at the first sentence again: A pour-over gift from a will to a revocable inter vivos trust was valid. I began working it out loud: "Okay. While you're alive, that's what 'inter vivos' means, you set up a trust for Mike. You put fifty thousand dollars in the bank, and under this trust, Mike gets one thousand dollars every month for fifty months." Mike raised his eyebrows. "The trust is revocable, meaning you can take it away at any time." Mike lowered his eyebrows.

"So I've set up a revocable inter vivos trust," the Optimist said. This was very logical to my father the engineer.

"Exactly. So a pour-over gift works like this: When you die, your will can instruct the executor to add more money to that trust and continue paying Mike one thousand dollars a month," I said.

"That's the pour-over part?" my brother asked. "The new money in the trust pours over the old money in the trust?"

"Precisely. Mom, do you have anything to add?" I asked.

"No, that sounds right to me," she said, handing me a cup of coffee and a bowl of sugar.

"Next sentence," I said. " 'The trust to which a pour-over gift was made may be unfunded.' Okay, this is also very straightforward. All this sentence says is that a trust is not necessarily dead just because there's no more money in it. Dad, let's say you set up that trust for Mike, but by the time you die, there's no money left in it. That means your existing trust was unfunded. It doesn't prevent you from writing a will that adds money to that unfunded trust."

"But then the new money isn't pouring over anything," Mike said.

"You're absolutely right. But I guess it's still considered a pour-over gift," I said.

"You see, now you won't be Joe Bloggs—that average student from the SATs," Mike said.

His ability to grasp the concept so quickly encouraged and worried me at the same time. "That's it. I'm ready for the exam," I said, closing the BAR/BRI book.

"Here, I circled a few promising leads for you," my father said, tossing me the *New York Times* travel section. "Tower Air seems to have
the best deals to Paris." The plan was for me to take the bar and then
get out of Dodge for four weeks. I planned to travel to Western Europe
with Arjun. Between the apartment in New York and this trip, we'd be
spending a lot of time together after three years apart. I hoped the trip
would help us get reacquainted. Plus, Arjun was the only person in the
world I considered traveling with across Europe. God forbid I went
with someone else who also just sat for the bar.

"I think you're overdoing it with this trip," my mother said.
"Backpacking across Europe? Why don't you take a break after the bar,
find a decent apartment? You're about to start a new job. Don't you
have enough on your plate?"

Yes, I thought to myself. "No. When am I ever going to get an entire month off to travel? I'm sticking to the plan: Europe in August. I'm
not crazy about the backpacking part, either, but Arjun won't go unless
we do it low-maintenance." Arjun's last year at NYU was about to cost
him another forty thousand dollars.

"Come on, it will be great," I said to my mother. "You should come."

"Okay, I'll come with you to Europe," she said flatly. Mike laughed.
The Oracle rarely ventured outside the two-mile radius of our home.

"We'll visit the Louvre in Paris, the Uffizi in Florence. We'll see
Picasso in Barcelona, Matisse in Nice," I said. The reference to art
was my last-ditch effort to convince her that the trip was a good idea.
"There's a great van Gogh exhibit in Amsterdam, Mike. Are you interested in seeing it?" I asked.

"Sure."

"Well, van Gogh."

"Ugh! That joke is terrible," my mother said.

"You know, if ain't baroque, don't fix it," Mike added.

"We can catch the latest Gauguin exhibit," I offered. "And *you* know
what you want to do after seeing a good Gauguin exhibit."

"Gauguin. And again, and again, and again," we all said in unison.

"So when do you leave?" Mom said, taking a more serious tone.

"Two days after the bar," I said, walking over to the calendar next to her. "Exactly one month from now." I'd never backpacked before and hadn't done anything to prepare for the trip. Making celebratory plans after the bar was the last thing I wanted to think about.

I picked up the travel section of the newspaper and scanned the airfares. Right about now a one-way ticket to Europe sounded pretty good.

CHAPTER 19

GWEN AND I had a wonderful Fourth of July weekend together. We walked on the beach, caught glimpses of the fireworks, and watched the submarine races. We'd promised each other that we'd take that weekend off from studying and enjoy ourselves, because the madness was close at hand.

Fourth of July was infamous as the moment everyone started to freak. The exam was only a couple of weeks away, and class was winding down. At that point, whatever you were going to know was whatever you were going to know. In preparation for this intense time, Gwen and I started to see less of each other. The pressure was getting to both of us. Correction: The pressure was getting to me.

"Why don't you ever invite me to study with you? I'm beginning to think those cadavers see more of you than I do," Gwen said. For the last two weeks I'd been trespassing into the nearby medical school to study across the hall from a freezer full of medical cadavers. I'd made the switch in locale after overhearing two BAR/BRI students bickering at the local library over some legal nuance that I'd never heard of before.

"I know. I'm just trying to zone. It has nothing to do with you, Gwen."

"How can you say it has nothing to do with me? I can't just sit there next to you and study on my own? This is ridiculous," she said. "I'm not going to beg."

"We have too much fun together. I can't concentrate," I said.

"You don't take me seriously," she said. "This is a bigger issue. You're driving yourself crazy with this exam."

She was right about me driving myself crazy, but she was wrong about me not taking her seriously. I'd been acting this way ever since receiving the results from the BAR/BRI practice MBE exam. What little confidence I'd gained from the Markey method was now gone. According to BAR/BRI's supercomputers, I was in the bottom 45 percent of the nation. On the practice exam, I answered 108 out of 200 multiple-choice questions correctly. Gwen had gotten 118 correct. Ten more questions correct increased her percentile by 30 percent. She was positioned just right of the New York pass rate, and I was positioned far left.

Unbeknownst to Gwen, the new scores were driving a wedge between us. I was insecure about telling her where I was in my studies, and I didn't want to know where she was in hers. I needed "me" time. In other words, I needed "memorizing" time. And that meant complete and utter seclusion.

So far I'd spent most of my time studying for the MBE, worth 40 percent of the exam, and I was in the lower 40 percent. Since I'd done minimal work toward the NYLE, I could only assume I was even worse off in that category. I hadn't taken any NYLE practice exams yet, because BAR/BRI was still piling on the courses. In the final ten days, BAR/BRI would review/teach thirteen of the twenty-five topics tested on the NYLE. For the first time ever, I'd learn about conflicts of law, no-fault insurance, worker's compensation, personal property, federal jurisdiction, income taxation, and domestic relations.

BAR/BRI was now employing desperate tactics to teach us the courses quickly enough. No more long lectures. Professors now spoke in bullet points, probabilities, and trends.

"Over the past ten years, the New York bar examiners have tested candidates on these thirty-seven no-fault insurance bullet points. Memorize them," a virtual BAR/BRI professor commanded. "You can expect at least one no-fault insurance multiple-choice question on the exam." I was struggling to type the information into my laptop fast enough. Recently I'd added carpal tunnel syndrome to my dental, visual, and gastronomic ailments.

It was time to take some drastic measures. BAR/BRI's various MBE workshops weren't working for me. Against my better judgment, I signed up for a separate, supplementary bar-review course focusing on the MBE. The course was called "Preparation for the Multistate Bar Review," or PMBR.

PMBR was the Tier 1 MBE prep course. I'd observed its followers all summer. They were the ones who came to BAR/BRI class sporting their newly acquired PMBR garb and acting as if they'd found a new religion. PMBR was like a secret society, offering its course in a different location every weekend. The final three-day crash course was being offered in Atlantic City, New Jersey, the weekend before the bar exam. It was time to join their cult. Nickel picked up the PMBR tab, of course—anything to ensure that its entire incoming class passed the bar.

PMBR did present a scheduling conflict, however. The last day of BAR/BRI class and the first day of PMBR fell on the same Friday. I picked PMBR. I'm sure it was going to be a very emotional day at BAR/BRI saying good-bye to the VCR and all, but I figured I'd get the notes from Gwen. PMBR was all of three days long and I couldn't miss the first day, the barometer reader, what they called the Trial Run. That day I'd take a six-hour MBE practice exam under simulated test-taking conditions and again find out where I stood. Then we'd spend the next two days in class reviewing the questions and answers. It was a good idea to take another MBE practice exam. I needed the endurance building, if not practice with the nausea-inducing state of mind.

"I noticed some PMBR materials in your bag. Are you taking the course in Atlantic City this weekend?" Sam asked me in BAR/BRI class.

"I am," I said, feeling violated.

"Check this out—my friend did this last year: You know the Trial Run? We should ask PMBR to FedEx it to us ahead of time. That way we can go to BAR/BRI's domestic-relations lecture on Friday, take the exam at home on our own time, and not miss anything. Multitasking. What do you think?"

It was psychotic. I liked it. Plus, I had no desire to drive an hour south to Atlantic City just to sit for a practice exam. "Okay," I said. "We'll kill one bird with two stones."

"What?"

"Nothing," I said. "PMBR will FedEx it?"

"Sure. PMBR will do anything for a fee. Just bill it to Nickel." Then Sam paused. "Which brings me to Saturday and Sunday—the Intensive Review of the Trial Run. Could I crash with you that weekend?" No. "The commute from Asbury Park to Atlantic City is like two hours, and you live so much closer." No. "We could even knock out some review together?" Good point. No.

Up until now Gwen had been the one exception to my no-study-group rule. And even now *she* was out. As the exam loomed, I needed my space more than ever. Studying with Sam frightened me. His personality was so in-your-face that I assumed bar prep with him would be like hard-core boot camp. A lot of yes sirs, no sirs, crying, drills, and P-A-I-N. Plus, what would Gwen say about Sam and I studying together? I'd rebuffed her. Could I cheat on her with Sam?

Sam continued to give me this desperate look, so I gave in. "Sure," I said. "I don't see why not." He would stay in my parents' guest room. Perhaps studying together was exactly what I needed. My laundry list of other study techniques had failed so far: Writing out rules at repetition—not helpful. Creating my own flash cards—not helpful. DAMP RIM—painful. Creating or adopting my own mnemonics, acronyms, and other word-association tricks—not helpful. Pour-over gift analyses with the family—hit or miss. Staring at the ceiling—remarkably helpful. Complaining, whining, and moaning—invaluable.

I couldn't lie to Gwen. I confessed later that day over the phone.

"Yeah. Good luck with that whole new overlapping bar review course," Gwen told me. Very little seemed to shake her. "You and Sam are made for each other."

CHAPTER 20

PMBR DIDN'T HESITATE to FedEx the Trial Run. Apparently, this was more common a request than I'd thought. The practice exam arrived the next day. Sam and I answered the first hundred questions on our own time. On Friday, following our last BAR/BRI lecture, we went back to my parents' house and, for the next three hours, took the second half of the exam. Sam wore earplugs. I still hadn't found a pair that didn't distract or hurt me.

PMBR's practice exam was brutal. What was I practicing for, failure? I couldn't even narrow it down to three out of four on more than sixty of the questions. All of those answers were blind guesses.

When the three-hour timer on the microwave oven went off, I'd gotten through only eighty-nine of the one hundred questions. Sam had five left. We took another fifteen minutes to finish up the questions that we skipped. Then we graded our Scantron sheets against the answer key in silence. It was a race to see who got more questions wrong. As in a sparring match, we exchanged soft jabs of pain: "Ugh. Cool. Ugh. Come on! Damn! Whew! Damn, damn!"

I was in phase three of classic trauma. Full-blown bargaining had set in. "Please let me get half the questions right," I chanted under my breath. "Please, please, please. I'll be so happy." It was looking close.

We finished correcting and just sat there, staring through each other. Sam spoke first. "So?" His facial tic kicked in.

"Out of a total of two hundred questions? One-oh-three," I confessed. Guilt jabbed me in the side. "But that includes the eleven questions I completed after the time was up." I braced myself for his response. What would he say? One-fifty? One-sixty?

"One-oh-five," he said.

We were both noticeably nervous. I turned back to my answer sheet. "What if I guessed 'B' for the eleven questions I'd done after time was up?" I whispered. "B" had always been my multiple-choice guessing letter. I knew it conflicted with the universally accepted "C," but history had demonstrated that I was better at the "A," "C," and "D" questions.

Six of the eleven correct answers to the eleven questions that I guessed on turned out to be "B."

"Sam, had I just guessed 'B' for these eleven, I would have gotten two more right. Two more right had I simply guessed." But Sam couldn't hear me. He was too busy slapping himself on the right side of his head to get his left earplug out.

I looked down again at my Scantron and then at the PMBR answer sheet. "Damn!" I said.

"What?" Sam said, relieved that he'd gotten the earplug out.

"Look at the answers to questions one-forty-five through one-forty-nine," I said.

"They're all 'C.' Five answers in a row, all 'C.' Dude, that's not cool," he said, shaking his head.

"Definitely not cool. You can't do that," I agreed. It was the unspoken multiple-choice law that no five answers in a row could be the same letter. That was about the only thing you could count on for a multiple-choice exam. If you answered five multiple-choice questions in a row with the same letter, at least one of the answers *had* to be wrong. The bar had no respect.

"I'm depressed," Sam said.

"Me, too," I said. "I've had enough PMBR for one night."

"It's almost nine-thirty. I'm reviewing New York wills, trusts, and commercial paper this evening. Interested?"

It was just as I'd feared. Sam was way ahead of me. I hadn't even started reviewing wills and commercial paper, and I wasn't much better off with trusts. Beyond pour-over gifts, I didn't know much. I definitely wasn't ready to start reviewing. My itinerary for the evening was much different. I'd allocated some quality time to sulk, followed by a short bout of complaining.

"Why don't we just stick to our own schedules," I said. "Maybe we can quiz each other later or tomorrow."

"Here, I made you two a couple of sandwiches," my mother came in and said, breaking the silence. "Eat," she kindly commanded. She seemed relieved. Finally she was allowed to talk following three hours of simulated test-taking conditions.

After the sandwiches, Sam and I regrouped and found a compromise. It turned out he wasn't reviewing New York wills at all—he was first learning it. In four hours we made it halfway through the course, reciting the key elements back and forth. It was intense.

"You have to be eighteen years old, sign the bottom of the document, do it in the presence of two witnesses, and both witnesses must sign it within thirty days of each other." Sam was repeating the elements needed to create an enforceable New York will.

"Right," I said. "And both witnesses have to know they're signing a will. I know, that sounds obvious. But it's the fifth requirement."

It was nearly two A.M. We were looking at about four and a half hours of sleep before we needed to depart for the Intensive Review in Atlantic City. After our pitiful practice scores, Sam and I had managed to rehabilitate the evening before we turned in. I lay in bed staring at the ceiling, anxious and overtired. I could hear Sam snoring in the guest room. I wished so much that I was done with this test. Seven days left. My stomach turned. I should have studied more.

CHAPTER 21

"I'LL DRIVE," SAM offered. I bought the coffee. We had an hour and a half to make a forty-minute trip from Toms River to Atlantic City.

Sam merged in to Garden State Parkway traffic with his left hand on the steering wheel and his left eye on the road. With his free eye and hand, he reached behind him to the backseat and began frantically patting it down for his knapsack, which was on the floor.

I was annoyed. "Can I help you?"

"Nah, I got it," he said, and at that very moment he swung his knapsack inches from my face and dropped it on his lap. While changing lanes, he began unzipping the bag with his elbow and free hand. Then he pulled out a loose-leaf binder. "I'm gonna study. Is that cool?"

I was at a loss for words. No, that is *not* cool, I thought, as he changed lanes again. I watched in awe as Sam proceeded to wedge the corners of his loose-leaf notebook between the spokes of the steering wheel. He seemed impressed with his improvised reading rack.

"You quiz me or I quiz you?" he said. That was my cue to lecture Sam on the cons of driving and reading. Instead, I offered to quiz *him* to minimize the risk of a fatal accident. I began where we'd left off the previous evening.

"Adopted children in New York. When it comes to their inheritance rights, what are the three rules?"

"That's easy," he said, clearly fighting the temptation to take his eyes off the road and read his notebook. "Adopted kids can inherit from their adopted parents. That's one." He gave up and began paging through his notes. "I have it here somewhere."

"Way-way-wait. Why don't I just tell you?" I read from my notebook: "First off, adopted children have no automatic inheritance rights from their *natural* parents. So once you're adopted, you're severed from your natural parents' will. There is an exception, though."

"Right, right," he said.

I began speaking more slowly. "A child adopted by the spouse of a natural parent can inherit from the adoptive spouse, the natural parent, both the adoptive spouse and natural parent's families, and the other natural parents' family. Got it?"

Sam began to rock back and forth in his seat. "No."

"I agree, that doesn't make sense. Let's see. If my mother became widowed and she remarried Winston, Winston could legally adopt me. At that point I could inherit from my mom and her family, Winston and his family, and my natural father's family."

"That makes sense," Sam said. "What about the third rule?"

"The third rule. When a *relative* adopts a child, the child may inherit from the natural parents' families, the adoptive relative, and the adoptive relative's family. So if my parents passed away and my aunt adopted me, I could inherit from my parents' families, my aunt, and my aunt's family. No problem?"

"No problem." He moved out of the passing lane. "Can I repeat it all back to you?"

"Sure." We did this for the next twenty minutes until we saw the exit ramp for the Atlantic City Expressway. "Sam, there's our exit!" He cut across three lanes and made the exit without receiving a single honk.

At that point we switched roles. I didn't drive because we were almost there, but Sam quizzed me from memory: "What are the four elements necessary for testamentary capacity?"

He was asking me what qualifies someone as sane enough to make a will. I covered my notebook with both hands and began reciting the requirements. "Well, the testator has to know he's writing a will. He has to understand the nature and approximate value of his property. The testator must also understand the disposition he's making, and finally . . ." I stared blankly down the highway. The fourth element escaped me as we passed underneath a sign for the Delaware Bridge Crossing.

"Sam, that's the second sign I've seen for the Delaware Bridge Crossing. How long have we been on this highway?"

"I'm not sure. Do you think we should get off and ask for directions?"

Traffic in the opposite direction was backed up for miles. "AC should have been just a few miles off the expressway," I said. "Do you remember seeing the skyline? We couldn't have missed *Atlantic City.*" Sure enough, five minutes later a gas-station attendant was telling us that we were going the wrong direction on the Atlantic City Expressway. Class was going to begin in ten minutes.

We crossed over the highway and pulled into Saturday-morning Atlantic City traffic. The sign on the right-hand side of the road read: GLASSBORO 6, HAMMONTON 18, ATLANTIC CITY 40.

"Forty miles?" I whispered in disbelief. "You must have been driving pretty fast." Sam tensed up. Two minutes passed in silence. We rolled forward another ten feet.

"I thought you knew how to get there?" he said.

I pressed my lips together and gritted my teeth for the next thirty-five miles. No radio, no small talk, and no studying. Eventually, Sam pulled his notebook out of the steering wheel and threw it on the backseat.

We arrived exactly one hour later. The PMBR class was on its first break.

"We're way late," Sam said to the proctor outside the conference room.

"Actually, we're late by more than a day," I added, referring to the fact that we'd both missed the Trial Run.

"You must be Wellen and Weaver. I'd just about given up on you guys." The proctor smiled. "If you'd like, I can replay the first hour of the videotaped lecture at the end of the day." We gladly accepted. Sam and I were friends again.

Like BAR/BRI, our lecturer was a twenty-seven-inch television and VCR. Unlike the BAR/BRI conference room, this one was sound-proofed to avoid the distraction of bells and coins crashing into the loud bowls of the slot machines on the Trump Plaza casino floor twenty yards away.

Professor Robert Feinberg, our virtual lecturer for the two-day in-tensive review, was a breath of fresh air. He was engaging, funny, sharp, and crass. "I know this sucks, but you don't want to *fail,* do you?" The f-word! He'd said it! "Stick with me, we'll get through this." And so the PMBR chanting began.

Feinberg had fourteen hours, spread out over two days, to review the two hundred questions from the Trial Run. It turned out that the questions had been carefully chosen to test us on a fair cross-section of the universe of information we might encounter. Each question was a springboard for a larger discussion on similar points of law. This was how we'd begin to understand the fine-line distinctions and nuances tested on the MBE.

Feinberg was a pro. Time passed quickly as he identified the im-portant distinctions unique to the MBE universe. "Hit it and move on" was the drill sergeant's advice on attacking each question. "Hit the question and move on. Time's a-wasting." Feinberg used charts, dia-grams, and timelines to simplify and condense convoluted legal con-cepts. BAR/BRI couldn't come close to PMBR on the MBE.

Throughout the day Feinberg would routinely ask the class a simple question, and many of us would mutter an answer in the general direction of the VCR. Feinberg would bark back, "Ruff-ruff! Wrong! Pavlov responses are wrong! I knew you'd say that answer. Snap out of it. Don't let them sucker-punch you!"

Feinberg said it, and we believed it. "There will be approximately seventeen questions on criminal search and seizures. Eight questions on mortgages." We faithfully wrote down his every word. He could have said, "Give up all your worldly possessions. Sever all ties with your loved ones," and we'd have obeyed. Finally we were getting the guidance we needed and the answers to the questions about the questions. I went to our lunch break with a better understanding of intentional, negligent, and reckless trespass, the Parol Evidence Rule, the admissibility of a written statement as a record of past recollection, public and private nuisances, criminal duress and necessity defenses, and when to apply the Rule Against Perpetuities. We spent the afternoon reviewing the next fifty questions, and I left the course a PMBR junkie.

That evening Sam and I drove carefully to Toms River, study-free. When we got back to my parents' place, we reviewed the second half of New York wills. The next day we attended the Intensive Review of the last hundred questions. Sam dropped me off at home on Sunday night, we wished each other tremendous luck in our final preparations, mentioned the possibility of meeting one last time before the exam, and never studied together again.

CHAPTER 22

THE MOTEL IN Albany where I had a reservation presumably had desk lamps, but I packed mine anyway. It wasn't a particularly special lamp—one of those cheap imitation banker's lamps with a green shield. I just needed to be surrounded by my own things.

I packed my most comfortable clothes, along with the lucky navy blue shirt that I was wearing when I was admitted to Temple Law, and the white Kenneth Cole shirt that I was wearing when I received my offer to work at Nickel. I didn't want to take any chances and I had to look good for the exam. That was one superstition I'd carried over from law school. The theory was: The better you looked, the better you felt, the better you did. I knew one guy in law school who took that routine to an extreme— he wore his best suit and tie to every final. He should have done pretty well. He was a buffoon. His grades were below average.

As for study materials, I took as few as possible. The art studio was papered with books, notes, practice exams and questions, outlines, and flash cards. I took the bar necessities. The exam was three days away. There wasn't much I could do if I didn't know it by now. I made the big decision to leave all of my MBE practice questions at home. Their time was over.

I was imprisoned. For the last week I'd been moved from general population to protective custody, studying nearly sixteen hours a day at the medical library. It was now time for solitary confinement. The plan was to drive to Albany and arrive two days before the exam. It was time to make my final arrangements. Never before had I even contemplated such extreme measures for "just a test." I'd never seen myself like this before.

"Okay," I yelled, standing in front of the door with my backpack slung over my left shoulder. "The car is loaded. I'll see you in a couple of days." I could hear the Oracle approaching.

"Oh, you're going? Good luck, sweetheart. Take care of yourself. Be careful driving, and call us when you can. Can we talk the day before the exam? Monday?"

"Sure. That's fine." I took a deep breath. "Okay." She walked over to me, gave me a hug, and handed me a sack containing a Diet Coke and a turkey sandwich. It was as if she were sending me off to my first day of kindergarten.

"I love you," she said as I walked out the door.

"I love you, too."

The six-hour ride to Albany went quickly. I kept my eyes pinned to the temperature gauge on the dashboard of my 1987 Renault Alliance.

I wasn't feeling too well lately, and neither was my car. What on earth had compelled me to buy a Renault? Oh, that's right, I was so distracted with the button for the moon roof that I missed the transmission skipping second gear. Its newest ailment was a propensity to overheat after an hour or two of driving. In my trunk I carried two jugs of water, just in case.

I spent the better part of the trip listening to the PMBR "Property" audiotape. It was far and away the best lecture on tape because it was the only one performed by none other than PMBR's own Bob Feinberg. I listened to the tapes and smiled. "Hit it and move on," he said. "Hit it and move on." Yes, O Great One. "No-starch diets don't work." But of course, Your Greatness.

The Howard Johnson Inn was about ten miles outside Albany. It was your run-of-the-mill Bates Motel. That Sunday afternoon I was one of two guests. But within twenty-four hours, the motel would be at full occupancy, with bar applicants in every room, performing final rituals. I spent the rest of the day pacing back and forth past my banker lamp, chanting laws to the ceiling.

On Monday morning, feeling somewhat batty, I took a practice drive downtown to the Empire State Plaza, where I'd sit for the exam. The exit off the highway led directly into the plaza. It was a dramatic building with a Gothic design. As I approached, I couldn't help but feel like I was entering Oz.

I drove around the city for another twenty minutes and then made my way back to the motel. Fiddling with my card key to the room, I could hear the phone ringing inside. I frantically opened the door and dashed for the phone. Who could it be? Wasn't I in complete seclusion?

"Alex? Is that you? I've been trying to reach you for like an hour now."

"Sam?" I couldn't believe it.

"Yeah, your mom told me you were here. How's it going? I'm staying here, too." There was nothing particularly strange about the fact that Sam was staying at this Howard Johnson; the motel had been recommended to all of us by Nickel. "Do you want to grab some dinner?" he asked.

It was a terrible idea. "I would, but I have to make a few phone calls, and I'm going to try to get to bed early tonight. Maybe we'll run into each other at the HoJo's restaurant later on."

Getting the point, Sam wrapped up the conversation. "Well, if we don't, good luck. And remember; 'Ruff-ruff.' "

I barked back. "Yep, I know, 'Pavlov responses are wrong. Hit it and move on. Hit it and move on.' Good luck to you, too, Sam."

With phone in hand, I decided to call my parents as I'd promised. Mom had looked worried when I left.

"It's your son," my father cheered over to my mother, and my mother echoed to my brother in succession, "It's Alex!" "So? Did your car hold up? You made it out there all right?"

"Yep. No problems."

"Good. It's getting late. Did you eat something yet?"

"Nah. I think I'm gonna do that now. I'll just go next door to the restaurant."

"Okay. Sounds good," the Optimist said. "Maybe you want to get those fried clams they have. I know you like them." I smiled. I hadn't had fried clams in ten years. They sounded pretty good.

"Are you crazy?" my mother yelled to my father as she lunged for the phone.

"Your-mother-wants-to-talk-to—" He trailed off as she grabbed the phone.

Then her voice came loud and clear over the phone: "Whatever you do, do NOT eat the fried clams."

Mike was in the background singing to the tune of "La Cucaracha": "Do-not-eat-the-FRIED-CLAMS. Do-not-eat-the-FRIED-CLAMS."

"Gotcha. Makes sense," I said.

"They-will-make-you-NAU-SEOUS. They-will-make-you-NAU-SEOUS," Mike added.

"Really, don't eat the fried clams," my mother said. "I'm not joking. That's all you need before this exam."

"Okay. No fried clams. Loud and clear." I laughed.

"So, are you ready?" she kidded me. By now that was a funny question.

"I dunno, Mom. I'm ready for it to be over. That's what I'm ready for. Anyway, I'm done talking to you," I kidded her back. "Put the Optimist back on. He always has better things to say." Mike's fried-clams chant began to die down.

"Your brother wants to tell you something *very, very* important. Hold on." She passed the phone to my brother.

Please, Mike, I thought to myself, avoid the obvious joke. "I just have one thing to tell you," he said, then waited for me to bait him. I didn't. "If the answer to the question seems too easy, remember: *Hay un gato encerrado.*" We both laughed. Our family had adopted the expression ever since Mike had inadvertently picked up the idiom from his Spanish teacher. On a field trip, Mike had overheard his teacher saying the expression. Apparently, the school bus had pulled up next to a car containing the Spanish teacher's husband and another woman. Loosely translated it meant, "Something fishy is going on here." *"Hay un gato encerrado,"* strictly translated, meant, "There is a locked-up cat." Mike had his own interpretation: "Look for the hidden cat."

"Good advice, Mike. Thanks."

"Good luck," he said. "And remember, you're no Joe Bloggs."

I went to the restaurant and had a grilled cheese and tomato sandwich and a black and white milk shake. No fried clams. Ice cream with dinner always made me feel at home. Before my brother came along, in those early experimental parenting days, my mother occasionally sat my father and me down to a hearty meal of waffles and ice cream. She'd serve us ice cream sandwiches, cut in half, no different than roast beef.

Afterward I went back to my room and refrained from studying. Half paying attention, I watched a couple of B movies, then turned off the lights and began trying to fall asleep.

This was it. Tomorrow was the NYLE. Was I ready? Did I know all twenty-five topics? Could I keep track of the MBE and NYLE distinctions?

I tossed and turned. Finally, lying on my back, I began the sleep therapy I'd done for years. It was a ritual I saved for emergency circumstances. Lying there, eyes closed, I began putting each part of my body
to sleep, starting with my toes. I mentally brushed each toe with a
soothing eggshell-colored paint. Once a body part was painted, it was
asleep, and I moved on. I took my time. This game usually worked, but
tonight I was particularly wound up. To increase the meditation's ef-
fectiveness, I slowed the process even more by imagining a smaller
brush. I'd never gotten past my waist before falling completely asleep.

Tonight was no different. Somewhere near my right knee, I drifted off.

CHAPTER 23

L YING ON MY stomach, both arms against my body and my face in
the pillow, I opened my right eye and took a long deep breath.

Beep. Beep. Beep. ". . . and it's another overcast day with a high
of . . ." Beep. Beep. Beep. ". . . and we can expect thunderstorms late
this afternoon . . ." The clock and radio alarms were going off at the
same time.

It was six-fifteen A.M. on July 30. I'd been doing that lately—waking up seconds before the alarm went off. I hit the snooze button, took
another deep breath, rolled over on my back, and stared at the ceiling.
Suddenly the phone rang. Sam? No, it had to be my wake-up call. Like
the remote control to the bed, the phone was hard-bolted to the desk
across from my bed. Leaning out of bed, I reached over to the phone
and, in one quick motion, lifted and dropped the handset. If it was
Sam, he'd have to call another time.

The room was freezing. I'd left the air conditioner on high
overnight. I pulled the covers up to my chin. They were still tucked
tightly into the foot of the bed.

"What am I doing?" I whispered. Who memorizes twenty-five volumes of New York practice? Could I really identify a no-fault insur-

ance problem if I saw one? Under New York domestic relations law, first cousins may marry, but a brother may not marry a sister's illegitimate daughter. For whatever reason, sort of like a favorite song, my mind defaulted to that rule of law. It was indelibly marked in my memory, thanks to my study sessions with Sam.

I boosted myself out of bed, threw on sweats, and walked over to the restaurant for breakfast. I wasn't even hungry. I barely ate anymore, but I knew I had to have something this morning. I passed on the breakfast buffet—it was gross—and had a cup of coffee, a muffin, and a banana: brain food. The woman in the booth in front of me and the man in the booth behind me were looking over their BAR/BRI notes. I kept my head down, finished my meal as quickly as possible, and went to pay my bill. In front of the cash register was a tip bowl that said, "Tip for good karma." The nerve! I dropped in a dollar bill. There was too much at stake. I handed the woman behind the register my bill and some cash. Without covering her mouth, she coughed in my face. That had to be bad luck somewhere in the world.

Back at the room, I shaved for the first time in two weeks. No cuts—a good sign. Then I put on my now slightly stained navy blue button-down shirt, grabbed a half-dozen presharpened number two pencils, and headed for the exam. I expected traffic. I parked in the underground lot of the Empire State Plaza and made my way to the sign-in location.

The main auditorium housed more than two thousand applicants, two to a table. Just as Hayley had predicted, power red was everywhere. I was assigned to take the exam in one of the smaller testing rooms nearby. My last name put me in the art museum. Another good sign, since I'd done most of my studying in my mother's art studio.

I found the museum across the street. My seat was on the ground level with two hundred other students. The room was spectacular. Even though the walls were bare—either because there wasn't an exhibit in session or they were dismantled for the exam—the floor-to-ceiling windows were dramatic, with a perfect view of the Empire State Plaza complex. A gigantic water fountain sat about a hundred yards from the window. I couldn't hear the water running; the room was soundproofed. On either side of the water fountain was a series of light-colored buildings, each about twenty stories high. All things considered, the testing conditions were serene, scenic, and nondistracting.

As the clock radio had predicted, the sky was overcast. It was going to pour. I sat down at my table and thought, God help me if I have to go through all of this again. "This" meaning everything. The studying, the drive, the motel, everything. At that particular moment I really didn't want to fail.

As in the main auditorium, we were seated two to a table. I arrived first. Taped to my designated table was a red label with my name and seat number. The seat number, selected at random, would preserve my anonymity for the examiners grading my paper. There was nothing anonymous about the results.

My tablemate or bar buddy arrived silently, sat down, and said nothing. Twice I tried to offer her a smile. She may have tried to smile back, but if so, our timing was off.

At precisely nine A.M. the proctors began painstakingly walking us through registration. First they checked our IDs. Anytime we left the building, the proctors would recheck our IDs. Fifteen minutes of "darken in this oval and darken in that one," then they handed out the morning section of the NYLE, along with a couple of flimsy blue books for our essay answers. A tab in the center of the exam booklet sealed the pages.

"Please take your pencil and place it in between the pages of the exam and against the tab," the proctor commanded the room. "You may break the tab and begin."

I hit the top left button on the digital watch I'd borrowed from Mike. It began counting down from three hours and fifteen minutes. "Here goes," I whispered to myself and, taking a deep breath, broke the tab. I had just over three hours to complete three essays and fifty multiple-choice questions on New York law. Then lunch.

As I paged through the exam for the first time, the New York multiple-choice questions took me by surprise. I hadn't devoted an ounce of energy preparing for them. Those questions were always considered the black sheep of the NYLE; even BAR/BRI didn't bring them up much. On the few occasions they did, the professors joked that the questions were "too hard." I needed to get about twenty-five out of fifty correct just to be considered average. Fifty percent, I reassured myself. Ten percent of my overall score would be attributed to my performance on these questions. BAR/BRI's frank advice—don't get yourself too crazy; concentrate on the twenty-five New York topics and the five essays. If I could do that, I'd be fine.

So there I was, staring down these multiple-choice questions for the first time, and I was about to find out firsthand whether BAR/BRI was right. Wouldn't it be a shame if these miserable multiple-choice questions ended up being the deciding factor?

I'd made a conscious decision in advance to do the multiple choice last. I planned to put aside an hour and fifteen minutes to complete them. BAR/BRI recommended spending approximately one and a half minutes per question. The first order of business was the essays. Just coming off my second cup of coffee, I was ready. I scanned each of the three essays and hoped the fact patterns bought me a clue. Which of the twenty-five topics had the bar examiners settled on? One essay could test on two, three, even four different areas of New York law.

From what I could tell initially, the first essay dealt with criminal law and criminal procedure; the second with corporations and New York practice; and the third with wills and trusts. Your standard topics; your standard combinations. All fair game. Whew. No outlandish questions on conflicts of law or estate tax. Or at least it didn't appear that way.

I skipped to the end of the first essay to confirm that it was in fact a criminal law and procedure question. There were three questions associated with the essay:

1. Will Bill's motion to suppress his confession be granted?
2. What crimes can Al be charged with?
3. What crimes can Bill be charged with?

Strange that the examiners would end the last two questions with a preposition, I thought. I did what I'd done dozens of times before in law school: I slowly read the essay, made notes in the margins, and circled the obvious legal issues or dilemmas.

Starting with the criminal law and procedure essay was a good call. Criminal Law fact patterns were always interesting, and this one was no different. It dealt with an armed robbery.

Al ("A") takes his gun from the glove compartment and goes into a bank. Bill ("B") sits in the car and is instructed to honk if the police arrive. Al robs the bank and, while exiting, ends up in a shoot-out with the police. A random bullet ricochets off the wall, hits and kills Officer Cal ("C"). But the shoot-out is enough of a distraction to enable Bill to sneak away. Al is arrested and rats out Bill.

So the cops pay Bill a little visit and politely ask him to come to the police station so they can ask him a couple of questions. Bill complies. At this point the fact pattern got more complicated.

Shortly thereafter, Bill's mother, Dot ["D"], returned home and learned that Bill had been taken to the police station for questioning. Dot went to the police station and asked to see Bill, saying, "He's only fourteen, you know." The police officer told Dot she could see him "in a little while." While his mother waited, Bill was informed of his rights, including to counsel. Bill responded that he did not want a lawyer, but he did want to talk with his mother. Although the police knew that Dot was at the police station, they told Bill that they would try to locate his mother. The police then questioned Bill. Soon Bill signed a written confession admitting that he acted as a lookout for Al. The police then allowed Dot to see him.

I glanced at the first question again: "Should the court grant Bill's motion to suppress the confession?"

It was criminal procedure: In other words, did the police properly elicit a confession from Bill? If they didn't, it should be inadmissible against Bill at trial, and suppressed under the Fourth Amendment and the common-law doctrine, called the "exclusionary rule."

Of course the confession should be suppressed. I could have told them that without reading the fact pattern. The bar examiners weren't about to give me all those details so I could write, "Looks good. What the police did was fine by me."

I circled what seemed like the important details: 1) Bill was fourteen years old, a minor; 2) Bill was informed of his rights; 3) Bill's mother was at the police station and wished to speak with him; and 4) Bill requested his mother *after* she arrived at the station.

Before writing out the essay, I took some notes. I needed to go through certain analyses and plot out my answers to the question. Only then could I write my answers in CIRAC form (conclusion, issue, rule, analysis, and conclusion).

Nearly every criminal procedure question implicated the Fourth, Fifth, Six, or Fourteenth Amendment. I eliminated the ones that didn't apply. Here, the Sixth Amendment's right to counsel wasn't relevant. That right attached only after formal proceedings have begun, and despite his confession, Bill hadn't been charged with anything yet. I crossed off "Sixth Amendment" on my notes.

The Fifth Amendment's right against compelled self-incrimination definitely applied, since that was exactly what the confession was. I began moving through the analysis. First of all, the police had "informed him of his rights." That just meant Bill was read his Miranda warnings: "You have the right to remain silent. Anything you say can and will be used against you in a court of law. You have the right to speak to an attorney, and to have an attorney present during any questioning. If you cannot afford a lawyer, one will be provided for you at government expense."

For Bill to receive Miranda warnings, he needed to be "in custody" and "under interrogation." He seemed to be both. It didn't appear that he felt free to leave, and the police station was synonymous with custody. When the police started questioning Bill was when the interrogation began. Okay. He was in custody and under interrogation, so it *was* appropriate for the police to read him his Miranda warnings. So far, so good.

At that point Bill could have waived his rights. When you waive your rights, it has to be "voluntary." If it's not, the court can exclude the confession. It appeared Bill had voluntarily waived his rights. He said straight out that he didn't want an attorney.

There was one problem, though. Bill was a minor. Or, as they say under New York law, an "infant." Not only that, but being fourteen years old put him in the "juvenile delinquent" category. Because of his inexperience and youth, New York offered Bill even more protection against potential constitutional violations than your normal run-of-the-mill infant.

The fact that the police interrogated a juvenile delinquent without the presence of a guardian or parent—especially with his mother outside the door—was definitely a problem. I guessed that Bill wasn't old enough to answer questions under police interrogation, and he wasn't old enough to waive his Miranda rights. Did that make his confession involuntary? I wasn't sure, but something wasn't right. I mentioned the possibility that his confession was involuntary based on his age for fear of missing something.

I moved on, assuming his confession was voluntary. The next inquiry: Was Bill's confession made "knowingly" and "intelligently," as required under the Fifth Amendment? Again, his status as an infant threatened both elements.

What exactly did Bill waive? He waived his right to an attorney. But he asked for his mommy in the same breath. Did these two actions somehow conflict? That was the essence of the question. The analysis on *this* issue would make the difference between an average and above-average answer. I thought of Mike and the SATs. This was the difference between the good student and Joe Bloggs. Did an infant in police custody have a legal right to talk with his mother before spilling his guts? Furthermore, did it matter that Bill's mother had asked for him before he confessed? Yes to both.

Here was where memorizing and recall on demand made all the difference. Under New York law, Bill's mother could be considered a youth adviser, and Bill was entitled to see her before he gave his confession. When Bill asked for his mother, it was as if he'd asked for an attorney. It wasn't enough that the police would "try to locate" her. In fact, they were perfectly aware that she was sitting just outside. Damn those cops.

The police were dead either way. They knew that if they let his mother in, Bill wouldn't confess. So they picked the lesser of two evils. They elicited the confession and hoped someone like me wouldn't know any better. Sorry, boys, a motion to suppress would likely be granted, the confession would be ruled a violation of Bill's rights under the Fifth Amendment, and it would be inadmissible in a court of law under the Fourth Amendment and the exclusionary rule.

I began detailing all of this in the blue book. I carefully described each of the legal issues in rigid CIRAC form—conclusion, issue one, rule, analysis, conclusion . . . conclusion, issue two . . .

Then I moved on to the remaining two questions associated with the essay: What crimes could Al and Bill be charged with?

Al was clearly in deep trouble. He was looking at first-degree robbery for using a gun, and second-degree murder under what was known as New York's "felony-murder rule." Officer Cal was killed during an armed robbery. Armed robbery was a felony under New York law. First came the felony, the armed robbery; then came the murder: thus, the felony-murder rule. The law stated that it was foreseeable that an officer might be killed in an armed robbery, and it didn't matter that a *random* bullet had killed Cal. (Had Al intended to kill Cal and succeeded, I could have charged him with first-degree murder under New York criminal law.)

Bill wasn't much better off. He was an accomplice to both first-degree robbery and second-degree murder, and that meant he could be charged with exactly the same crimes as Al. Bill took steps to further both crimes, even if all that meant was sitting in the car with his hand hovering over the horn. New York viewed Bill as if he himself had run into the bank with the gun, then pulled the trigger.

Maybe Bill could raise a defense to either crime. Maybe Bill didn't know an armed robbery was about to occur, and could argue that he didn't know what he was getting himself into and that he could not have possibly foreseen Cal's death.

I looked at the fact pattern again. Bill had watched Al take the gun from the glove compartment. The bar was like the movies—the examiners never added a prop unless they were going to use it. In other words, the fact that Bill watched *mattered*, since he obviously knew an *armed* robbery was about to occur. It also meant Bill was screwed. He could be charged with the same crimes as Al.

I was lucky to have gotten an entire question devoted to criminal law and procedure. Usually the essays included at least one other topic. For example, most questions on criminal law and procedure included something about evidence. Since it wasn't part of this question, it was unlikely that I'd see an evidence essay question on the exam. That was a shame. I hoped I would have a chance to show off my familiarity with hearsay. And after that phone conversation with David Markey, I was ready for DAMP RIM. The "I" in DAMP RIM stood for "Inability to physically testify." Come on. Just ask me.

Midway through writing out my criminal-law analysis on Al and Bill's crimes, the room got slightly darker. Deep thunder and hard rain followed flashes of lightning. Despite the museum's soundproofed walls, I could hear the rain crashing on the cement outside. I waited for the lights to flicker. They didn't.

After regaining my train of thought, I regrouped and took an accounting of my time. It had taken me just over an hour to complete the first essay. The essay questions were completely reasonable, and my answers were satisfactory, but I was running at least twenty minutes behind schedule. According to my watch, I had a little over two hours left to complete the rest of the morning section—about thirty-five minutes for each remaining essay and an hour for the fifty multiple-choice questions.

Back to the essays. I had to choose—corporations or wills and trusts? I went with wills and trusts. I read the fact pattern slowly and circled the legal issues that jumped off the page. I identified two. Too few: There were always at least three. I was missing something. I scanned the first two paragraphs twice more. There was something unmistakably familiar about them. It's here somewhere, I thought to myself. I could hear the Child Prodigy now: *"Hay un gato encerrado."* Where was that damn hidden cat?

Then it dawned on me—the first two paragraphs appeared to be de-scribing a *pour-over gift*. Woo-hoo, a pour-over gift! Could it be? Could I really be that lucky? Pooh-pooh on DAMP RIM, but hooray for the edge and pour-over gifts.

I read the fact pattern for a fourth time to be sure. I wasn't. I'd never seen a pour-over gift contained within a fact pattern before. Time was running out. I had to make a decision: Spend a precious thirty-plus minutes writing out a pour-over gift analysis or mention it in passing. It's got to be a pour-over gift. Only then did I realize that I might have said that out loud. No one seemed to notice. My bar buddy was fran-tically finishing up her first essay. Unless she'd done the multiple-choice questions first, she was *way* behind schedule. She was perspiring. I could relate.

It was decided. I'd write one bad-ass pour-over gift analysis. As I wrote, the silence in the room was deafening, the low hum of scrib-bling interrupted only by the sound of someone bolting down the hall for a quick bathroom break. It never occurred to me to use the bath-room.

With only an hour and a half left, I had to revise my plan again. There wasn't nearly enough time to complete the final essay and all fifty multiple-choice questions. One of the two would have to take a hit. The corporations essay became my sacrificial lamb. I just didn't have the recommended fifty minutes to complete the last essay. To some extent, I split the baby, apportioning thirty minutes for the essay and a little under an hour for the multiple-choice questions. This meant reducing my time per question from one and a half minutes to one. I tried to think of what my father would say to me given the cir-cumstances. The Optimist would likely advise me that between my solid criminal procedure and pour-over gift analyses, I was in fine shape. I hoped he was right.

The Corporations essay. It was a perfect example of how taking the course in law school actually crippled you for the bar. In law school, I had studied general corporate law, which gave me an overview of things like how to incorporate, electing and removing directors, shareholder rights and responsibilities, fiduciary duties, and mergers and acquisitions. Thanks to the law school course, I could spot the issues. Then again, thanks to the course, I couldn't easily apply the appropriate rule of law on the bar exam. I couldn't remember, for example, whether New York applied the general rule to shareholder voting, as I'd learned it in law school, or adopted the minority rule.

For corporations there were very strict rules. You needed a majority vote for this, and a two-thirds vote for that. You needed two days' notice for this, and one week's notice for that. There was very little legal reasoning. It was a matter of memorizing as much of New York's business corporation law, or BCL, as possible. You'd think that because corporations was a lot like engineering, it would have come naturally to me. But I didn't do exceptionally well on it in school and wasn't about to get very far on the bar exam, probably because I'd always found the subject so painfully boring.

I spent the next thirty minutes spastically deciding whether corporate directors Mark and Mindy breached their fiduciary duties to shareholder Mike when they held an unannounced meeting. I evaluated whether Mike waived his right to object to the meeting by attending and voting at the unannounced meeting. And I determined whether Mark and Mindy could terminate Mike without cause. My essay was weak, to say the least.

With about forty-five minutes remaining, I began the fifty NYLE multiple-choice questions. They turned out to be much more brutal than I'd anticipated, each successively more difficult than the next. At least 60 percent of my answers were educated guesses.

No sooner did the proctor announce "Time's up" than I finished randomly filling in the last five ovals with the letter "B."

"Please STOP writing. Place your pencils down on your desks. Please stand to the left of your desk. Lean over, close your test booklets, and place your Scantron sheets in the test booklets. A proctor will come by to collect your materials. Please be patient."

I scanned the room to get a sense of how my colleagues might be feeling. Everyone seemed antsy. *Get me out of here*, their faces screamed. Mine, too. We filed out of the building with nobody saying much. The day was still overcast, but at least the rain had stopped. We had an hour for lunch.

Everyone taking the bar had the same idea—find something quick and get back to the cockpit for the afternoon ride. We were competing with the local businessmen. I passed a few cafés. The lines were out the door. The farther I got from the museum, the more nervous I became that I'd bump into someone I knew. I ducked a few familiar faces. I was in no mood to make small talk or, God forbid, discuss the exam.

Any way I cut it, I considered the morning a loss. I did the percentages in my head. Last summer's first-time pass rate was 78 percent. Had I just performed in the top 78 percent of all candidates taking the exam? It was dicey.

I began breaking down the day in my head. Today represented 60 percent of my overall score. The morning section accounted for 34 percent—the essays were worth 24 percent, and the multiple-choice questions 10 percent. The New York essays were graded on a zero-to-ten-point scale, depending on your issue-spotting and analytical skills. According to BAR/BRI, a five was considered passing. I gave myself a seven on the criminal procedure essay. Given that it might not be pour-over gift, I gave myself a four on will and trusts. And a two on the corporations essay. So I'd averaged a 4.3 on the essays. Not good.

The average passing grade on the multiple-choice questions was about twenty-five out of fifty questions correct. Did I get half of them right? Not likely. The test was a third of the way over, and I was already in the hole.

After walking past the same vending cart three times, I settled on a hot dog and a Diet Coke. Before I knew it, I was back at the table, staring down two new essays and the Multistate Performance Test. Each essay was worth 8 percent of my overall score, and the MPT was worth 10 percent.

I read my assignment. My boss was asking me to draft an "in camera brief in support of a motion to quash a subpoena." It sounded much worse than it was. All "in camera" meant was that the brief would be reviewed by the judge in private and would not be available to the public. The subpoena was from a prosecutor who wanted access to a report summarizing a conversation between a social worker and my client, James White. My job: Write a brief in support of voiding, or quashing, the subpoena. I had to prevent the prosecutor from viewing the potentially damaging report.

Because the MPT didn't test us on our knowledge of the law, the bar examiners provided us with the universe of what we needed to know. In fact, we were given too much law. It was then our responsibility to apply the appropriate authorities and precedents. My library of materials included two cases and a portion of the Franklin evidence code. Franklin was the imaginary jurisdiction where I practiced. I liked Franklin. Franklin was a lovely place where justice prevailed. In Franklin attorneys could do their job. They could look up the law and not commit malpractice by applying legal precedent based on recollection. If only the entire bar exam was like this. I wondered what the cost of living was in Franklin. Maybe I'd move there.

Once my stomach settled from my delightful lunch, I began drafting my motion. Citing the relevant precedent, I argued that the communications between my client and the social worker were privileged under both the social worker–client and the attorney-client privilege provisions of the Franklin evidence code. The memorandum took me an hour and a half to complete, and I was satisfied with my final brief. The MPT counted 10 percent toward my overall score. I hoped a good MPT score would offset the 10 percent from this morning's pitiful multiple-choice questions.

I had an hour and a half to do the remaining two essays. The best I could tell, one of them dealt with New York practice and contracts, and the other with New York real property and domestic relations. Again, standard topics, fair game. I was lucky. I was grateful.

But the issues were very complex. Of the five essays tested on the NYLE, these two were the most difficult. Perhaps this was the bar examiners' way of evening up the score following a straightforward MPT.

As my watch counted down the final minutes of the afternoon session, I could feel my hand beginning to cramp. I was writing drastically faster and faster, and both my handwriting and content were beginning to suffer. My legal analyses and conclusions began to read more like an outline than a series of reasoned sentences.

There was little time left to think. Damn it, I thought, staring three-quarters of the way down the real property essay, is it or isn't it a covenant running with the land? In CIRAC form, I began writing the conclusion.

"Mildred is prevented," I wrote. No, no, no. I crossed out that part of the sentence and began over on the next line. "The covenant running with the land prevents Mildred from—"

"Time's up. Please STOP writing." The same routine; pencils down, stand up, lean over, et cetera. No one dared to write a single word after the time was up—there was too much hanging in the balance.

Shit, I thought. Now they'll never know what the covenant running with the land prevented Mildred from doing. What a freaking shame. Then again, maybe it wasn't a covenant running with the land at all. In any event, it would have been nice to finish my essay, or at least my sentence.

That was it. It was over. Hundreds and hundreds of hours of studying for the NYLE, and all I had to show for it was a decent MPT, two well-written essays, two panicked ones, three paragraphs about Mildred and her respective covenants, and fifty arbitrary multiple-choice ovals. I knew so much more about New York law than my essays suggested. I'd been positive there would be a question on commercial paper. I'd spent nearly three straight days memorizing hundreds of nuances about negotiable instruments, holders in due course, and endorsements.

Had anyone asked me to predict how I might have felt after finishing the NYLE, I probably would have said relieved or depressed. I never expected to feel angry and gypped.

I stepped in line with the other zombies and exited the building. Back at the motel room, NYLE law outlines were scattered everywhere. I walked around the room tossing books into a pile near the nightstand. It was liberating—perhaps I would never have to study them again. Maybe not. I sat at the corner of the bed, swinging my legs, zoning. Feeling claustrophobic and anxious, I decided to take a swim in the motel pool.

I wasn't thinking "bathing suit" when I packed, so I slipped on a pair of shorts and made for the pool. Standing in the pool was a familiar figure. Sam had his eyes closed and his face pointed up toward the sky. The clouds had finally cleared, and here he was, basking in the last few minutes of summer sun. He didn't seem to have a worry in the world. A thin, attractive woman with blue eyes and blond hair sat near him on the side of the pool, her feet dangling in the water. She wore a tank top and shorts.

"Counselor," I greeted Sam.

"Is that a question or a statement?" he asked, squinting at me with the sun in his eyes and a smile. "Fancy meeting you here."

"On vacation?" I asked.

"No, I'm here for the bar. But just, you know, as an observer. Or at least that's what I spent most of today doing."

"I agree, Sam. Today was tough."

"Alex, this is Diane. I'm glad you guys finally get to meet."

I extended my hand and said, "Nice to meet you." She smiled. I was shocked that Sam had brought Diane to the exam. I knew nothing about their relationship, but I couldn't fathom bringing a date to the exam. Gwen was taking the bar exam in New York City, but even if she were here with me in Albany, surely we would have had our own rooms and a no-hanky-panky rule in effect. Who knows? Maybe Sam and Diane had also decided "no sex before the big game." I simply wasn't capable of having anyone around me these days. My God, there was a reason why I'd locked myself up in a motel room for three days in solitude. The bar was something I had to do alone, and I couldn't have anyone see me like this.

Diane put her hand on Sam's shoulder, and he gave her a warm smile. At that moment I envied them. I missed Gwen.

"Let me ask you something," Sam said. "Have you ever heard of banking your score?"

"I've never heard of such a thing."

"I heard that in some states, you can save a good score on one part of the exam and just retake the part you failed. So, hypothetically speaking, if I failed the NYLE today but nailed the MBE tomorrow, maybe I could bank my MBE score and only retake the NYLE in February."

"I don't think New York subscribes to that. BAR/BRI would have mentioned it. Geez, the peace of mind banking would have given me over the last six weeks. Anyway, tomorrow you and I will be back here in the pool, pondering whether we can drop the MBE and bank today's performance."

We both started laughing. "Yeah, I don't know about that," Sam said. "Well, Nickel can't be mad at all sixteen of us if we all fail, can they?"

"Well, I guess so, but what if it's just you and me?"

He suddenly became serious. "Margaret Denton says nobody's failed the bar at Nickel in six years."

"Sam, that's a load of shit. I'm sure people have failed in the last six years. The firm's just not saying."

"I dunno. I wish she'd never said that. I hate that she said it to *me*. Did she say it to you?"

"No. But now that *you've* said it to me, I hate that *you've* said it to me. I'm sure people have failed. How's the water?"

"Nice. Warm. It feels good. Jump in."

I slipped into the pool, Sam and I made small talk without mentioning the bar again, and we wished each other good luck. Back at the room, I called Gwen on her cell phone.

"Hey! I bet I did better than you today!" she said jokingly.

"Remind me again. Is the bar scored like golf? I was thinking of you. What's going on?"

"I'm okay. I'm hungry. I wish you could come eat with me. I want fries."

"That sounds *so* good right now. Where did you end up staying?" Even though Gwen was also an out-of-state resident, she was entitled

to take the exam in New York City by virtue of her choice to take both
the New York and the New Jersey bar exams. Days one and two she'd
take the NYLE and MBE in New York. Then she'd drive to Trenton,
New Jersey, and sit for the NJLE on day three. The MBE would count
toward both the New York and New Jersey exams. The New York bar
examiners had determined that the alternative—driving six hours from
Albany to Trenton—would be a hardship too grueling to endure.

"I'm staying at the Paramount Hotel. It's a short walk to the Javits
Center, and I have a huge feather bed with down pillows." I looked
over at the six-by-four piece of plywood that I called a bed. Why did I
choose Howard Johnson's? With Nickel picking up the bill, I should
have at least gone with a *hotel*. I admired Gwen for springing for the
chic hotel. Her clerkship with a state judge, while highly coveted, was
a no-frills, modestly salaried job.

"I leave on Saturday for Europe. I need your schedule so we can
rendezvous," I said.

"Okay, I'll e-mail it before you leave. But when we meet in Europe,
promise me you won't talk about the exam. Promise?"

"I promise. I promise-promise."

"I'm gonna go eat now," Gwen said.

"All right. Tomorrow's the MBE. Finally, after all those flash-card
sessions at your place. Wink-wink. Nudge-nudge. You made this whole
process so much more bearable. You'll do great tomorrow. Good luck.
Oh yeah, good luck with New Jersey on Thursday, too. You're a mad-
woman."

"But of course. I'll tawk to you lata," she said with an exaggerated
New Jersey accent in an effort to be cute.

The next twelve hours were hell. I couldn't fall asleep. And no form
of therapy was going to do it, no matter how small the paintbrush or
how soothing the paint.

I had to purge myself of the New York distinctions and shift into
MBE mode. Many of the exceptions, and the exceptions to the exceptions, were now reversed. It was time to forget that in New York,
under the rules of evidence, a document was considered ancient after
thirty years. For the MBE, documents hit ancient after twenty years.

It was also time to forget that in New York, before using deadly force as a form of self-defense, you must retreat unless one of three conditions is met: One, you're in your own dwelling and didn't instigate the aggression. Two, you're a peace officer or acting at the direction of a peace officer. Three, you're attempting to prevent a kidnapping, rape, robbery, arson, or burglary. For the MBE, you could use deadly self-defense under any condition. For the MBE, you could take out your aggressor with your trusty double-barrel shotgun, no ifs-ands-or-buts about it.

A tinge of horror hit me. Was I supposed to consider self-defense in the criminal law question today? Oh, wait, hadn't I? I couldn't remember. Could Al or Bill have claimed self-defense? Don't be stupid. Of course not. Perpetrators of an armed robbery can't claim self-defense.

But that moment of panic got my mind racing. What else did I miss? I must have missed something. Did I miss something big?

CHAPTER 24

WAS SURE I'D failed the first half of the New York bar exam. It now seemed pointless to show up for Day two, since I'd have to do something extraordinary to rehabilitate my chances of passing. The very thought of starting the whole process over again sickened me. Could I really dedicate another thousand hours to studying, only to drag my sorry ass back to Albany, don my lucky navy blue button-down shirt, and take the exam again next February? I made a mental note: Burn this shirt if I fail.

Like the day before, I arrived at the testing center before my bar buddy. I took the time to lay out my seven neatly resharpened pencils and focus my attention on the small tab holding the pages together on the exam booklet.

My bar buddy arrived after a few minutes and, like the day before, quietly slipped into her seat staring straight ahead, clearly consumed by the experience. I refused to spend another eight hours sitting next to this woman in silence. We were going to bond. It was a time of tragedy. I tried to snap her out of her trance with a curt "Hey."

"Oh, hello. I'm Mary, hello," she said with an unrecognizably thick European accent.

"Nice to meet you. I'm Alex."

Staring at my army of pencils: "Would it be okay if I borrowed one of those?" She had only one.

I hesitated. "Sure, of course. Here, take this one. Keep it." She smiled. More silence. "We're almost done. That's a good thing, right?" I said.

"Who knows? This is my second time with bar exam." My God, this woman's English was broken. A guilty surge of confidence overcame me. Maybe I *could* pass this thing.

At the proctor's direction, we began filling in ovals with our name, address, and other bar-related information. The proctor gave us five minutes to do something that took two. Could I bank the extra three minutes for the end of the exam? I wondered. I tried to keep it together and wait patiently for the exam to begin. Let's go, let's go, let's go. Come-on, come-on, come-on.

Then Mary turned to me in slow motion, as if we were in a dream. Her accent miraculously disappeared, and she spoke to me in the most lucid, cogent voice I'd ever heard. "Excuse me," she said politely, "I don't mean to make you more nervous than you already are, but . . ."

Time slowed some more. I took a deep breath and began to feel light-headed. What could she *possibly* say to make me feel more nervous? What is it? Am I on fire? Is my head on fire? My head's on fire, isn't it? Just tell me—it's okay.

"Alex, your head's on fire," she said calmly.

"What?" I blinked hard.

She repeated herself, but this time the words were different. "I know the exam is to start right away, but I'm terrifically nervous," she whispered. "I cannot remember the names of the specific-intent crimes. Do you remember what they are? Please tell me. Quickly—before the exam starts."

Wait a minute! You can't do that. You can't ask me a substantive question seconds before the exam is about to start. Isn't that cheating? No, I guess not, but still. Mary was breaking one of the most sacred test-taking rules: Once everyone has blackened in the name and address ovals, no talking allowed.

A bead of sweat formed over my left eye. What the hell was she asking me, anyway? I repeated the question to myself: What are the specific-intent crimes? Crimes. Criminal law. Of course, the specific-intent crimes.

I turned to her and began whispering: "You must have specific intent to commit . . . first-degree murder and property crimes like larceny and robbery." She stared at me, captivated. "Oh yeah, rape, too."

"Please break the tab with your pencil and begin," the proctor said. Huh? What? The room filled with the sound of hundreds of tabs breaking and pencils scribbling. Mary was already hard at work. I regrouped, broke my tab, and began reading MBE question #1.

CHAPTER 25

QUESTION 121: B. Question 149: B. Questions 199 and 200: B. Okay, that about does it. Two hundred ovals for two hundred questions.

"Time's up. Please STOP writing. Place your pencils down on your desks. Please stand to the left of your desk."

The room remained just as quiet as it had been for the last three hours. I propped myself up next to the desk with my right hand. It was really over . . . for now. I was numb, tired, annoyed, and, how do you like that, hungry.

I made a beeline through the Empire State Plaza underground for the parking garage. Midway through my brisk walk, I found myself heading directly toward Sam and another incoming Nickel associate, Morgan Pitts, a lanky nervous man in his mid-thirties. He looked disheveled. Sam caught a glimpse of me and waved.

"We're going to Down-It, a bar a few blocks from here. BAR/BRI is hosting a party. Isn't that thoughtful?" Sam said.

"Free pizza and beer," Morgan added.

"I dunno," I said. I usually passed on free stuff. Besides, I was too tired to interact. And sulking was no fun in company. I stood there deliberating. Suddenly friends and acquaintances began popping out of the woodwork. First someone from law school, then someone from BAR/BRI. In a matter of minutes, we had a posse of twelve. We collectively decided to Down-It after all.

Thousands of students with the same blank expressions poured into the streets of Albany. More than one in four had failed the bar. Maybe I was one of them. Many seemed to be heading toward the same bar we were. I wondered what their motivation for drinking might be. Perhaps they were flooding the streets to celebrate the easiest exam in bar history.

I didn't feel relieved at all. That was the very moment it occurred to me that the exam *wasn't* over. There were still four more months. Four more months of *waiting*.

It was time to wait for the results. Time to try and avoid overhearing something about the bar that might haunt me for months. I couldn't bear learning that it wasn't in fact a pour-over gift, or that it wasn't a covenant running with the land. I didn't want to know whether the MBE property or contract questions had been especially easy this year. I wanted to shut out all the people who had taken the bar. "La-la-la-la-la," I'd say repeatedly, as I had at *The Shining*. "I can't hear you."

The twelve of us made our way to the bar in silence, only occasionally making small talk. We were trying to feel one another out. After about ten minutes of "You okay?" "How's it going?" "It's over, huh?" and "Crazy few days," the battle of the failures began.

"Dude, I think I failed," someone said.

"I'm telling you that if you failed, then I definitely failed," said another.

"How could you fail? You finished," said a third.

"I'm sure I failed. I skipped like ten MBE questions."

"I didn't even see the New York practice part in that contracts essay."

"I analyzed the property question like it was a constitutional law question."

"Give me a break, I didn't even do two of the essays." Actually, that guy probably did fail.

As on the first day of BAR/BRI class, everyone started unloading their best excuses. We became a walking support group, prepping one another for the possibility of grim results. Undoubtedly, this would be the first of many stressful conversations between now and November or December.

What was my excuse? I wondered. All I'd done that summer was study for the bar in near-complete seclusion, seeing only good family and good friends and having good sex. Did I have any excuses? No. The exam was difficult. There was no way to get around that. In the end, two of my essays were good, two were average at best, and two were pitiful, most of my NYLE multiple-choice answers were guesses, and I was lucky if I got half the MBE questions right. Suffice it to say that I was banking on a disproportionate number of the multiple-choice answers being the multiple-choice answer "B."

Twenty minutes into our sojourn to Down-It, it occurred to all of us that we were lost. Sam ducked into a convenience store and asked for directions. We arrived at Down-It just as BAR/BRI began laying out the second round of pizzas.

"Beer?" asked a BAR/BRI rep. I accepted and smiled. Still working off that bar-review course, huh?

The party was lame. But there was plenty of beer and pizza, and everyone was remarkably nice to one another, though none of us had any social skills left. There was nothing to talk about, and the one topic we had in common remained off-limits.

My original plan had been to take the exam and drive directly home.

I had already checked out. But after a couple of beers and some pizza, I wasn't up for the six-hour trek home. I left a message on my family's answering machine saying that I was fine and would be home the following afternoon. After drinks, the twelve of us moved the party to the Hyatt in downtown Albany, where most of them were staying, including Morgan. By our third drink, all of us were bashing the exam every way we could. If it wasn't the format and content, it was the bad instructors, the inadequate preparation, and the lack of time. We did shots, we laughed, and we whined. Every last one of us let on that we failed. But the chances of all twelve of us failing was statistically impossible. It would be more like three.

Sam and I stayed in Morgan's room. I curled up in a hotel armchair and slept wonderfully. I woke up the next morning, surprised not to feel as if I'd been drinking all night and slept in a hotel armchair. Then it occurred to me that today was the Day After. My stomach dropped. Wow, the bar was over, and I didn't feel relieved at all. I had very little to show for all of that work. Tequila began creeping its way up my throat. Did I fail? I wondered. Geez. Was this the way I was going to feel every morning until the results arrived?

The six-hour drive home was a blur. When I realized I'd been driving in silence for nearly an hour, I flipped on the car stereo. Professor Bob Feinberg was midsentence, describing the legal distinction between covenants running with the land and equitable servitudes. Ugh. I ejected the tape, threw it on the backseat, and stuck in the Dave Matthews Band, the only band that mattered.

By the time I got home, it was late afternoon. Both cars were in the garage. Everyone was home. Walking up the steps, I could see my mother in the kitchen.

"Hi, darling," my mother greeted me. "I'm *so* glad you're home."

My father and brother approached from downstairs.

"You're done!" my dad cheered.

"Yay! You're done. You're done with the bar," Mike repeated with similar vigor.

"I dunno. I'm done. I guess I'm done. For now."

The four of us walked into the living room. "Sit down," my mother said, excited. Beaming, she handed me a large white envelope and three wrapped presents. I got nervous.

"What's this? What are all these? Why did you guys buy me gifts?"

"Because you're done. You did it," Mike said. He looked confused.

"But I don't want gifts." My eyes began to well up. "I don't think . . . I don't think I passed. I don't . . . deserve . . . gifts." Two tears rolled down my left cheek.

"You did it," the Optimist said. He sat down next to me on the couch and patted my back softly. "Come on, you did it. You're done. You did it."

"But I'm so upset." I was completely drained. I put my face in my hands and began to cry. "You shouldn't have gotten me these gifts."

My mother stood over me and began rubbing my head. "Come on, open these up. They're good ones. They're all neon." I smiled. The Oracle had never been forgiven for buying me an ungodly neon shirt for my sixteenth birthday. "I even kept all the receipts. Wasn't that smart?" Returning gifts was a long family tradition.

I shook my head, wiped away the tears, partially regained my composure, and opened the card. My mother's cards were always handmade. This one resembled a medical form. My mother had drawn a Blue Cross Blue Shield logo in the top left corner. Copyright infringement, I thought to myself. I'd let it slide. The card read:

CONFIDENTIAL MEDICAL INFORMATION

Patient's Last Name:	Wellen
First Name:	Alexander
Middle Initial:	B.
Diagnosis:	Suffers from Severe Brain Overload
Rx:	3Rs: Rest, Relaxation, and Recreation
Signature of Doctors	
Primary Physician:	Carole Wellen
Second Opinion:	Lester Wellen
Third Opinion:	Michael Wellen

Have a great trip! We love you.

On the back of the card, she'd drawn a picture of a duck with the tag line: "A Quack Card." I was touched.

Inside the boxes were two Europe travel books, six hundred dollars in traveler's checks, two pair of khaki shorts with plenty of pockets, a rain jacket that you could store in a tiny plastic tube, and a blue hooded sweatshirt. Everything was perfect, even the clothes. No returns necessary.

"My wrist is killing me," I said to my father as I rubbed my right wrist with my left hand. Pure adrenaline had enabled me to overcome the pain during the exam. But now my carpal tunnel syndrome was beginning to act up.

"Can you do this?" the Optimist asked, tipping his hand toward and away from his lips. I nodded. "Then you're in good shape. You can drink some beers, read your new books, wear your new clothes, and enjoy yourself in Europe." He was right. I was off in forty-eight hours.

SECOND TRIMESTER

CHAPTER 26

'M AN IDIOT. I must have been delusional when I agreed to go on this trip. You'd think "backpacking" would be self-explanatory. It's not. For some reason, when Arjun said "backpack," I was thinking "book bag." I was mortified when I saw the actual size of the pack.

"You have to roll up each piece of clothing tightly, like this." Arjun showed me the evening before we left. "That's how you keep them wrinkle-free." After that I went through my big suitcase, picking and choosing what to take. Fully loaded, my backpack was the size and weight of an adolescent boy. I called him Pierre.

I had four weeks to travel. Because classes started early for Arjun, he had only three. We began in Paris. The plan from there was to spend some time in France, then make our way through Switzerland, Greece, and Italy. At that point Arjun would take a plane home from Paris, and I'd spend the extra week exploring Spain. Per Arjun's demands, we were on a student budget. That meant inexpensive meals, youth hostels, bunk beds and bedbugs, and, of course, Pierre ("Where do we go next, Papa?").

The flight to Paris from Newark was remarkably effortless. Effortless, that is, except for the pretzels—or rather, the pretzel. There

I was, halfway across the Atlantic Ocean, reclined the full four degrees in seat 14C, pondering my potential future as an attorney or grocer, and it happened. In a split second I went from vacation mode to emergency dental surgery. I popped a stale pretzel in my mouth, bit down, and hit the airplane roof in excruciating pain. Something was now wrong with the second-to-last molar on the upper left side of my mouth. Since then, with the aid of heavy doses of ibuprofen, I was doing my best to ignore the pain, though it had only intensified.

For Arjun and me, the honeymoon was already over. Arjun was already sick and tired of hearing about how I failed the bar. At first he kindly tried to convince me that perhaps the results weren't so dire, but I used my best lawyering skills to persuade him otherwise. He also wasn't so thrilled with my packing. We spent the morning of our second day in France looking for an electrical transformer.

"You left your sleeping bag in New Jersey but you brought your hair dryer?" Arjun said as we walked the streets of Paris, looking for an electronics store.

"It's just one of those luxuries I've grown accustomed to having," I said. "Let me have this one thing. Here, this place may have one."

"Are you a woman? You've been using a hair dryer ever since college. Why? Your hair is like two inches long." This was the fifth store that didn't have the proper transformer.

In the end I wound up buying a new hair dryer with the proper European plug. But I couldn't just throw away my trusty American dryer. So now I was carrying two dryers across Europe.

Arjun wasn't exactly without his own travel quirks. Besides imposing strict expense rules, he believed in "speed-seeing." In four days we saw countless churches, monuments, arcs, gardens, and museums. I thought if I saw one more masterpiece, I'd heave. We speed-saw nearly half of the Louvre in one afternoon. The museum, set in the heart of Paris, is nearly 650,000 square feet and covers one hundred acres of land. We skipped straight to Leonardo da Vinci's *Mona Lisa,* and from there we averaged about a century's worth of artwork every half an hour. We took in artifacts from the Bronze Age, sculptures from the Middle Ages, and paintings from the Renaissance. I was in the middle of surveying a tablet from Mesopotamia when Arjun said, "Before we grab postcards, what do you say we swing by the *Venus de Milo?*"

"When you go to a museum, don't try to take in the whole exhibit. Select a few pieces to appreciate, then leave." This was one of the Oracle's life instructions. I passed along this wise advice to Arjun, but he wasn't having it.

Between speed-seeing and our student-budget diet of French bread and cheese, I was beginning to lose some weight. Pierre, on the other hand, seemed to be getting heavier. Each successive hostel smelled worse than the last. After just one week I was tired and ready to go home. What saved me was the TGV—France's "train of great velocity." Here, Arjun had done well. He'd scored us first-class tickets from a friend in New York City.

So here we were traveling to Switzerland at 186 miles per hour in meat-locker paradise. The chilly air was a rare treat: Most of Europe wasn't hip to air-conditioning, and I'd been going through heavy withdrawal since leaving New Jersey, the air-conditioning-mall capital of the world.

With Pierre quietly asleep in the overhead storage container, I had an opportunity to enjoy the cool air and reclining seats and do some thinking. Arjun was asleep. Over the years Arjun had demonstrated an ability to sleep anywhere, in any position.

I turned off my Walkman, opened my journal, and wrote the question that had been on my mind for days; the answer still escaped me. "Why are you allowing the bar to define who you are?"

Next to it I began listing the problems with the bar: "Too much content, too much memorizing, too impractical, too late, too important, too public." I scanned the list. The content, the memorizing, the fact that I'd had to learn all the information only *after* completing law school, and the likelihood that I'd never use any of it again—all of this I was slowly coming to terms with. But it still didn't address the true question.

I circled the word "public." No test I'd ever taken before was quite so public. SATs, LSATs, college and law school exams, blood tests, urine samples—none was published in the newspaper next to my name. But everyone knew I'd studied for the bar. Everyone knew I'd taken it. And everyone would ultimately know whether or not I passed. In fact, if they got a subscription to the *New York Law Journal,* they might even learn before me. It was a violating feeling. If I failed, I'd be humiliated. Even worse, I'd be pitied.

Who was it then that I was so afraid might see this insignificant publication? Again I wrote the universe of options: "Family, friends, law school colleagues, Nickel." I crossed off "law school colleagues." It was unlikely I'd bump into any of them in the near future. Family and friends—I'd hate to be embarrassed in front of them, but they'd always be there regardless. What about Nickel? Yeah, Nickel was a problem. It didn't help that Margaret Denton claimed that no one at the firm had failed the bar in the last six years. If I failed, everyone at the firm would know. I'd have to face them every day. I'd have to walk through the halls in my faker suit and pretend to be a faker lawyer.

"People don't care as much about you and your problems as you might think," the Oracle always told me. "You may be the topic for the moment, but then they're on to someone else and his problems. And trust me on this one, they're much more concerned with their own problems." Perhaps she was right. Then it occurred to me as we pulled up to the Interlaken train station in Switzerland. There was *one* person I was worried about disappointing. I wrote "me," circled it, and closed the journal.

Arjun and I exited the train and began following signs to Balmer's. Fellow packers described it as the ultimate in youth hostels. Countless travelers recommended it. Located in the Swiss Alps, it was literally a good jumping-off point for amateur cliff diving, kayaking, ice climbing, rappelling, and what's known as "canyoning": sliding face forward down a white-water river on your stomach.

The Balmer's hostel turned out to be one of the largest I'd ever seen. It had a huge kitchen where packers could prepare food. There were a few Ping-Pong tables, a fully stocked bar, movies, and dozens of hammocks that looked out on a breathtaking view of the snowcapped mountains. But the most exciting thing to me about Balmer's were the two washing machines and two dryers located on the first floor. I was already out of clean clothes.

There's nothing simple about washing your clothes in Europe. Balmer's was only the second youth hostel we'd found so far that had working machines. At the hostel we'd stayed at in Paris, tons of people were waiting for the machines; apparently they were a big draw. But even when the mad rush of filthy Parisian backpackers died down, I didn't end up having the right coin denominations.

This time was going to be different. I put my name on the laundry list, and Arjun and I went upstairs to drop off our packs in what appeared to be army barracks. I took the bottom bunk. Arjun took the top. The remaining nine bunk beds were occupied. I went downstairs to wait. I allotted two to three hours for the laundry process. You had to be Johnny-on-the-spot when it came your turn, and then you had to baby-sit your wash or risk having your clothes stolen.

One wash, two dry cycles, and three hours later, my clothes were clean. Once I finished rolling up my clothes and putting them in my backpack, I decided to reward myself with a shower and clean underwear. Ahh, the thrill of clean underwear. I laid them on my bunk bed and went to the communal bathroom to stake out some space. I hung my towel on the hook behind me and positioned my toiletries around one of the unoccupied sinks. First a nice clean shave, then a long hot shower. I hadn't shaved since we arrived in Europe. Slowly, I pulled the blade across my face. The dirt was ground into my whiskers. The shave felt so good. I wiped the steamy mirror to inspect myself and reached behind me for my towel. It wasn't on the hook. I whipped around. It wasn't on the floor. Then I found it. It was between the legs of an anonymous pudgy Japanese man. He had one hand clamped around either end of my towel and was doing this grotesque towel-floss between his legs. I was mortified.

"What are you doing?" I said in disbelief.

"What am I doing," he repeated flatly.

"I can't believe you're doing this."

"What am I doing."

"That's my towel. My towel, my towel, my towel," I said as he stood there naked and unsure what to do with his hands. I turned away from him slightly and pointed toward my towel. "That's, my, towel!"

"Your towel," he said in the same monotone.

"Yes, yes. My towel," I said, poking the center of my chest with my forefinger. "My towel, you have my *only* towel. You've used my towel."

"*Your* towel. I thought this was from here. I thought they give it to you. I thought—"

"You thought what? You thought the youth hostel gives you a towel? Are you on crack? What kind of youth hostel gives you a towel? What are you talking about? I can't believe you've used my towel . . . oh-my-God, you don't understand, do you? That's my towel. You're using it. Do-you-understand? Just finish getting dressed," I said, throwing my hands in the air and walking back into the bunk-bedroom.

He followed me. I sat on my bunk bed staring at my clean boxers and T-shirt and facing away from him to give him privacy while he finished drying off.

"Here," he said, offering me back my own damp towel.

"I don't want it. You should—"

"Here," he said, offering his washcloth as an additional peace offering.

"No," I said, shaking my head. "You should *wash* my towel." He didn't understand and just kept staring at me apologetically. "Look, don't worry about it," I told him.

It was getting late. I didn't shower. Instead, I went downstairs, put my name back on the laundry list, and met Arjun in the bar. I kept checking the list. It was midnight before one of the washing machines freed up. Forty-five minutes later, I moved my precious towel into a dryer. When Arjun and I closed the bar at two A.M., I went to the laundry room to retrieve it.

"Shhhhh," said a man's voice.

"But you're not doing it the right way," a woman pleaded. By then it was too late. I had walked in on a couple screwing on the dryer—cushioned, of course, by my towel. They must have seen it lying in the dryer and thought, Perfect. Frankly, there weren't too many private places at the youth hostel. And after all, why shouldn't they be comfortable?

"It's yours," I said to them, doing an about-face.

In the morning a Balmer's staff member took pity on me. "You might be surprised to learn how often backpackers lose their towels," she said as she unlocked a secret room. She opened the door, and I half expected to hear a church choir singing. Stacked inside were piles and piles of clean, folded towels. I picked a nice designer one, thanked her, and took a shower. I would have dried my hair, but the plug on the French hair dryer didn't work in Switzerland. I'd have to find an adapter.

CHAPTER 27

I N THE MORNING Arjun and I went to the train station. Our next destination was Greece. As we arrived, our train pulled away.

"I can't take it. This keeps happening. We've lost two or three full days of traveling to poor planning. The next train to Athens is in three hours," Arjun said, reading the schedule. "I'm off in search of a battery-operated alarm clock."

I stayed with the backpacks. According to standard operating procedure, I sat on the train platform with Arjun's pack strapped to my left foot and my pack strapped to my right. Somebody would have to drag me through the Swiss train station if he really wanted to steal them. Over the past week I'd heard horror stories in which travelers— usually Americans—were distracted for seconds and then suddenly their packs were gone. Game over and thank you for playing. Please proceed to the closest American consulate, have your family wire you some money, and fly home. To minimize the risk of a catastrophe, Arjun and I each kept our passports, tickets, and cash in a belt underneath our clothes. Depending on the country and youth hostel we sometimes even slept with the dirty, sweaty pouches buckled to our waists.

Mission accomplished. Arjun secured a clock, and three trains later, we were in a youth hostel in Athens, Greece. We spent the morning speed-seeing the Parthenon, the Temple of Zeus, and too many ancient walls, monuments, arcs, and towers to remember. By midafternoon we were purchasing ferry tickets to the Greek Islands. The name of the ship was the *Santorini Express*. As its name suggested, our destination was Santorini, the most beautiful island, and the most distant from the mainland. For ten times the price of the ferry ticket, we could have flown and saved a full day of travel, but that didn't jive with our established expense policies. The window where we purchased our tickets was about a half mile from the port. Pierre was getting a bit grouchy, so halfway there, I let him rest on a bench. By the time we got to the port, thousands of people were standing around waiting for their ships. August was a crazy month for Greece. We were competing with not only all the other packers but also all the Europeans who took August off for holiday.

For the next six hours we watched boatloads of people leave for and arrive from the Greek Islands with no sign of our ship. Every boat was oversold. The problem was, you could buy your tickets from any of a dozen independent travel agents around the city, and none of them knew what the other ones were doing. Arjun and I were sure that our ship was oversold, so we made a point of standing as close to the docking area as possible. The *Santorini Express* finally arrived. It was four hours late. We boarded at ten-fifteen P.M. It was a mob scene. By the time we got on the ship, we were already exhausted.

Arjun and I were lucky to get on board. In a matter of minutes, every backpacker had staked out floor space. By the time we got our bearings, all the coveted cabin floor space was already taken. Like the majority of packers, we grabbed some real estate on the deck. We carved out a four-by-six space in the back of the ship, next to the boat railing.

I threw up during the first, third, and fifth hours of the trip, and the nausea remained well into the sixth. I'd always had a weak stomach.

One time I actually vomited on an amusement-park ride before it began moving. (It was the combination of two semesters of physics—that is, appreciating what was about to happen—and the fact that I'd just eaten a corn dog and ridden the spinning-teacup ride.) I never lasted very long as the navigator in a moving car, either. By the time I'd found the start and end points on the map, I'd be nauseated, with my head out the window like a dog, gulping air and staring at the horizon. Maybe it was the boat, the bad weather, or the fact that there was no horizon to concentrate on in the pitch dark, but I couldn't even keep water down. Lying there, shivering in the soot, high winds, heavy waves, and forty-degree temperature, I wished I had my sleeping bag and not two hair dryers. The inflatable blue mattress I had purchased in Interlaken was deflating underneath me after being punctured by some tiny sharp object protruding from the deck of the ship.

Arjun was asleep. His miraculous ability to sleep under any and all conditions had reached new heights. He'd phased out not only the adverse weather conditions but also the six Greek teenagers blaring their techno music next to us, the Italian family arguing behind us, and the cat meowing incessantly in its cage in front of us. Arjun slept faceup, with one shoulder against two ship railings spaced about a foot and a half apart. Fearing that there was just enough room for him to slip between the railings I occasionally propped him up, remembering the promise I'd sort of made to his mother before we left. Her request went something along the lines of "Make sure Arjun doesn't get killed or maimed in Europe." I could hear myself now: "You know, it was the craziest thing. I got distracted for all of two seconds, and I think that's when Arjun slipped into the Mediterranean." People die on vacations all the time, I reminded myself. I propped Arjun up again.

For hours I sat there on my deflated blue air mattress, hugging my backpack. Even if it were stolen, where would the thief go? By hour nine, I'd had enough.

"Arjun," I said. Without moving an inch, he opened his eyes slightly. "I can't take it. I have to get off this ship. Between the nausea, my toothache, and a cold, I'm losing my mind."

"I agree," he said slowly. "Let's get off at the next island. Do you know where we are?" I hadn't a clue. It was pitch-dark. The sea and sky were indistinguishable from each other. The ship was pushing through a black void.

It turned out that for us, the *Santorini Express* was neither express nor destined for Santorini. We got off at the island of Naxos. Neither of us had ever heard of it, and we were among very few people who got off there. It was five-thirty A.M. Aside from quite a few cats wandering the streets, there were no signs of life. We found a couple of benches near a closed café and made our beds. Clutching Pierre in my arms, I quickly fell asleep. In a few hours we'd find a place to crash for a few days before taking the accursed ferry back to Athens and then another two ferries to Italy.

CHAPTER 28

THE NEXT TIME you're in Tuscany, I recommend the tomatoes, olive oil, pasta, and dental work.

Naxos was beautiful, but what little recuperating we did there was defeated in Corfu. That was the small island where Arjun and I stopped on our way to Italy. We stayed at the world-famous back-packer hotel the Pink Palace. The hotel's slogan: "We drink more ouzo before eight A.M. than most people drink all day." Bad slogan. Ouzo, this awful licorice-favored Greek drink, reminded me of grain alcohol—clear and extremely potent. That night we partied with the people of the Pink Palace. We threw back shots of ouzo and watched as a street performer smashed clay plates over people's heads.

"Opa," the Greek performer said each time he shattered a plate over another eager backpacker's head. At one point Arjun grabbed one of the unbroken plates off the ground and cracked it over the back of my head. "Opa," he screamed. I don't think he did it right. After that I don't remember too much of the evening.

Between the boat incident in Greece, the towel incident in

Interlaken, and the plate incident in Corfu, Arjun agreed to indulge me a little. We'd taken our last ferry, and now we were at the tip of Italy, traveling north. We went to an Internet café, and I punched "villa" and "Tuscany" into a search engine. Surely adding those words to my experience portfolio would accentuate my new cosmopolitan image back in New York City. The Internet gave us "Villa di Piazzano."

Villa di Piazzano was a recently restored sixteenth-century villa, originally used by Cardinal Silvio Passerini as his manor to hunt wild boar and pheasant. Though the villa had been abandoned for years, a family had recently taken to renovating it. The website said it was "ideal for relaxing." The rooms were "spacious and elegant." Every room had a bathroom, air-conditioning, satellite television, and yes, a hair dryer. For the common traveler, the price was extremely reasonable. For the frugal student traveler, it was unconscionable. We'd spend more in two nights than we'd spent on every hostel put together.

We took the train to the nearby city of Cortona and then a fifteen-minute taxi ride to the villa. It was late afternoon, and the sun was setting. The taxi turned onto the country road and revealed a dramatic approach. Chestnut trees lined the road like soldiers. Arjun and I were silent as the taxi slowly rolled forward. Then we took another turn, which revealed an even more extraordinary path lined with linden and oak trees leading directly to the gated villa.

The villa itself was set in the middle of rolling green hills. On every side were crops like tobacco, sunflowers, and corn. At the reception desk was a woman in her late fifties. She had dark Italian skin and short brown-reddish hair. She wore a white button-down shirt and a black skirt.

"*Buon giorno,*" Arjun said to her. We introduced ourselves. Her name was Adriana. She, along with her daughter and husband, owned the villa.

"This is our first villa in Tuscany," I confessed, putting down my backpack.

"Actually, you're no longer in Tuscany," Adriana said stiffly. "The road to the villa is in Tuscany, but the villa itself is across the border, in Umbria." Arjun and I quickly agreed that we'd still tell everyone we'd stayed in a villa in Tuscany. Adriana then gave us a tour, pointing out all the restorations and explaining the painstaking eighteen-month renovation process they'd just undergone. This was a place for lovers, families, and weddings, not backpackers.

I wished Gwen was here. Our master plan to meet in Europe had fallen apart over a week ago. Our original itineraries had put us both in Rome by mid-August. The plan was, once in Rome, to agree on a rendezvous point using our e-mail accounts at Internet cafés. We both knew it was a long shot, but we promised to try. By the third day, I'd realized it wasn't going to happen. Arjun and I had missed some key trains, extended our visit in Interlaken, and taken those nightmare ferries, and Gwen and I were gradually growing farther apart in proximity. By the time Arjun and I set foot in Italy, Gwen was long gone.

"Arrivederci," she wrote in an e-mail. "We'll always have the bar."

Adriana escorted Arjun and me through the villa's exquisite garden. We stopped at the pool.

"I have a request," I said to her. She nodded. "I'm having this terrible toothache." The pain was full-blown and throbbing, and my cheek was swollen. There was no way to ignore it and nothing in my near future that suggested it would get any better. I wasn't sure what I intended to gain by telling Adriana this. I wasn't prepared to go to an Italian dentist.

"Let me see what I can do," she told me. The next twenty-four hours were filled with comfort food like homemade chicken-noodle soup, fruit, and lemon juice. She took Arjun and me to the center of town, where we bought antibiotics and a powerful powdered painkiller. But in spite of her efforts, my one slice of luxury was filled with angst, agony, and pain. By the time we were ready to leave the villa, two days later, my toothache was out of control. The antibiotics hadn't worked. I still had a mind-splitting headache, and I couldn't tell whether it was due to my toothache or the clay plate that Arjun had broken over my head.

"I've made an appointment for you with a local dentist," Adriana said.

"Oh, that wasn't necessary," I told her, thrilled and terrified at the same time.

"Soon you will fly home, and the pressure in the airplane will only aggravate your tooth," she told me. "What if you need a root canal? What if it's an abscess?" I was impressed by her familiarity with dentistry. I'd been trying not to think about those potential problems. "We must take a taxi now. You will take a different train to your next location."

The dentist's office was located in a small outdoor shopping mall in Camucia, a tiny town fifteen minutes from the villa. The buzzer on the door said "Dr. Giovanni Alberto." In the waiting room were a mother and daughter pacing back and forth. Adriana spoke quickly in Italian to the receptionist who was also one of the dental hygienists. The office was remarkably clean. All the magazines were in Italian and outdated.

"You're next," Adriana told me. I took a seat across from Arjun and her.

"Do you go to this dentist?" I asked Adriana. In a neighboring room, a small child was wailing to the sound of a dental drill.

"I do not go to the dentist, Alex. I do not have time to have problems with my teeth. There is too much to do at the villa," she said. It was getting more and more difficult to ignore the tortured child in the background. Arjun shook his head with a smirk. He could see the terror in my face. He tried to advance the conversation.

"But you know this dentist?" Arjun asked her.

"No. The dentist we know is out of town. His office recommended this one." Even Adriana was having trouble pretending not to hear the alternating shrills and drills. At that moment another hygienist led Adriana and me to a room away from the screaming. The hygienist spoke no English. She simply pointed me to the normal-looking dental chair set amid the normal-looking dental equipment. Adriana sat across from me. She would serve as my translator.

After a few minutes Hygienist Number One and a man entered the room. This was presumably Dr. Giovanni Alberto. He was short with dark olive skin, bushy dark hair, and wire-rimmed glasses. He wore a smock and a mask. Giovanni and Adriana began speaking Italian. I was not invited to participate. By this point Adriana was intimately familiar with all of my symptoms and the spectrum of failed remedies.

Giovanni indicated that I should open my mouth. He began poking around. The smell of the plastic gloves made me gag. He stuffed a piece of cotton between my upper left molar and my severely swollen gum. He then took a hooked metal rod and began picking at the tooth. He spun the instrument around and used the blunt end to tap on the bad tooth and the two teeth surrounding it. He hit each tooth so hard I thought one might shatter. Tap, tap, tap, and then he'd say something in Italian. He stared at me.

"He wants to know if that hurts," Adriana said.

I lifted my head slightly and looked at her. I gave a muffled "A little," along with the corresponding hand gesture with my thumb and forefinger. Giovanni didn't understand. Adriana translated "a little" to Giovanni. Back and forth he went, banging away on each of the three teeth. He'd hit a tooth, and I'd tell Adriana, who would then tell Giovanni whether it hurt, and if so, how much. He'd narrowed it down to two teeth. Then he swung his deadly elbow inches from my sore cheek as he swiveled in his chair to get another dental tool. More poking, more conversation with Adriana, and then it was decided. Giovanni reached for a syringe and began stripping off the clear plastic covering the needle.

"Wait," I said to Adriana. "What's going on?"

"He has to take out your filling and see what is happening inside," Adriana said.

"So we definitely have to take out my original filling?" I said. "No X rays?"

"No. He doesn't have his own X-ray machine."

"Without an X ray, how will he know whether it's the tooth or the root?" I knew this much from my last root canal. Adriana translated my question. Giovanni and the hygienist were dumbfounded.

"He has to take out the filling," Adriana said. "This is the only way he is going to know what is going on inside your tooth. His goal is to temporarily relieve the pain. Your dentist at home can then fix it up and make it look nice." Giovanni gently injected me with the needle and began drilling and scraping for the next twenty minutes. I didn't cry. When the pain occasionally spiked, I squeezed the armrests of the dental chair, hit the moon, informed Adriana, and she translated.

Afterward, Adriana translated the total cost. I paid Hygienist Number One the equivalent of forty-six U.S. dollars. I handed her fifty Euros. She scrambled to make change from the large bill.

"He took out two fillings and found one cavity. So he drilled that one, too," Adriana said in the car. I now had a major crater in my mouth. "Then he put something temporary inside until you can see your dentist in the United States."

"He put in a temporary filling?"

"No. They don't have that. Something else."

"Thank you again," I said to Adriana through the Novocain. "You're my Italian angel. Thank you so much."

"You went through all this unnecessary pain. We should have gone to the dentist two days ago," she muttered. She kissed me on both cheeks and dropped Arjun and me off at the train station.

CHAPTER 29

PISA WAS OUR last destination together. By late afternoon Arjun and I found the center of town only to be greeted by a mob scene. Tickets to go inside the leaning tower were sold out. We walked along the neighboring street, where vendors sold everything imaginable, either stamped with or in the shape of the tower.

"Are you going to buy any of this crap?" Arjun asked.

"You mean this 'Pisa' crap?"

Arjun smiled. "That's good. I like that. That's good stuff." We laughed and made our way to our final train, or rather the final series of trains. It would take us three trains and one full day to get to Nice, France. From there Arjun would head back to Paris and catch his plane home, and I'd go to Barcelona, Spain, to do some last-minute speed-seeing. We planned to meet back in New York in a week and nail down an apartment.

After three adventurous weeks traveling through Western Europe together, we were getting along famously. Arjun got the award for patience. The bar was always my subject of conversation. But if anyone could make me relax and sometimes even forget, it was Arjun. He'd stopped trying to convince me that I passed, yet he refused to acknowledge that I failed. And he kindly entertained my every hypothetical.

"Let's say I fail, Nickel lets me go, and I can't afford the rent for our apartment," I said midway through our trip.

"Then you'll get another job. Kinko's is hiring," he said. "Or you'll move, and I'll get a new roommate—someone who *can* pass the bar. Everything can be fixed." I appreciated the jab, or as we called it, "jack." By the time Arjun and I were ready to go our separate ways, I believe he truly understood that the bar exam was not a direct measure of one's ability to practice law. Arjun and I had endured engineering school together, and maintaining his respect was important to me. Plus, just talking through the worst case scenarios was liberating. The trip was a good opportunity for Arjun and me to rekindle our friendship and to see how we'd grown and changed. After everything that we endured over the last few weeks, we were ready to be roommates again. Living together now would be a cinch.

I spent four days alone in Barcelona. I toured the Gothic Quarter and took in the Olympic stadium and some spectacular buildings designed by Modernist architect Antoni Gaudi. The youth hostel was located on Las Ramblas, the main artery of the city, lined with galleries, restaurants, and theaters. At this point I could have coughed up the big bucks to stay in luxurious accommodations, but I'd grown accustomed to the backpacker lifestyle. Flower and vegetable vendors, shoe-shine boys, and street performers also populated the boulevard. One afternoon I even managed to take in some sun at Barceloneta Beach. Fellow backpackers claimed that a sewer flood had forced some dead rats into the water, so I didn't swim.

After Barcelona I began the two-day trek back to Paris. It was time to fly home. I arrived in Cerbere, France, and spent a few hours in a small café, waiting for my connecting train. Cerbere was a travel hub. The city was very plain, with few residents. The waitress and the small dog by my leg continued to give me dirty looks: I'd been milking my cup of coffee for over an hour. I poured a little more cream into my coffee to give the impression that "things were happening" at my table. The cream was still lukewarm. Why didn't they warm up the cream back in the United States? I'd miss that. The café overlooked the blue-blue Mediterranean. I'd miss that, too.

Barcelona and the pilgrimage back to Paris had given me time to get some perspective and reflect on my future. I was ready to start my life in New York. And I was ready to face the bar results, whatever they were, even if they were three months away.

All my life the Optimist had told me: "There's nothing you can do about it now, so why bother worrying?" He was right. If I had to take the bar again, I would. In the end no one would care but me. Somehow I had thought my trip would help me forget about the bar, yet not a day passed when I didn't think about it. Every enjoyable moment was immediately followed by a pang of guilt that I wasn't entitled to happiness because I might be a failure. I had learned that you can't run away from yourself, no matter how much physical distance you put between yourself and those Scantron sheets and blue books in Albany, New York.

CHAPTER 30

MY FIRST TWO days back in Toms River, New Jersey, I managed to stay clear of the art studio. When I finally did break through the yellow police tape, the crime scene was untouched. Books, hand-written practice essays, outlines, and notes were sprawled everywhere.

I felt bad—it had been months since my mother had stepped into her own art studio. For the summer I'd banished her to the garage, where she chiseled away at a new alabaster stone.

Sitting on the stool in the middle of the room was a legal pad with handwritten notes. The title made me smile: "Things Alex Keeps Getting Wrong." On it were more than a hundred different rules of law that I was incapable of memorizing no matter how hard I tried. Stuff like:

Rule 4: "A school principal must have a reasonable basis for a warrantless search of a locker. If the principal is acting as an agent of the police, however, a warrant and probable cause are also required."

Rule 35: "When the doctor misdiagnoses a patient and an unwanted birth is the result, the doctor's liability is limited to the costs associated with the birth."

Rule 36: "An overhang is a property encroachment."

Rule 42: "Observations made in a low-flying airplane or through a telescopic lens violate your right to privacy."

Rule 51: "Intentional infliction of emotional distress must be *extreme* and *outrageous.*"

Rule 73: "The police may follow someone in hot pursuit into another country under the border exception to search warrants."

Rule 88: "Natural catastrophes are foreseeable."

Rule 104: "Evidence elicited from an undercover police officer in jail is not admissible because the waiver was not voluntary, known, or intelligent."

Thankfully, the list didn't instill horror in me. There were dozens of points I should have known for the exam but didn't. Overall, maybe two or three of the rules had been on the exam. Thank God for Europe. The test seemed so far away.

What I really wanted to do was dump everything into one of those toxic waste barrels and set it on fire. I knew I couldn't do that. I took out a small moving box and began dumping everything into it, then I taped it up twenty different ways. With a fat red indelible marker, I wrote PANDORA'S BOX on every side.

"Alex, phone for you," my mother yelled from the kitchen. Only then did I realize that I'd shut off the ringer on the studio phone. I picked up.

"Glad to see you made it back safely," Arjun said. "How's your tooth?"

"I went to the dentist yesterday. It appears Giovanni took out the wrong fillings, and I need a root canal after all. The dentist needs to take out the roots of the tooth, put in a supporting post, build up the tooth, put on a temporary crown, and then a permanent one. I think all he did was put my mind at ease so I could fly home. Maybe, just maybe, he relieved some pressure in the upper left area of my gum. It's hard to say."

"Actually, I was just being polite. I wasn't looking for an education in dentistry. I'm starting to have sympathy pains. My mother suggested that maybe it was some form of karma. Not that you did something wrong, but Buddhism teaches, for every event that occurs, another event will follow whose existence was caused by the first. You pushed yourself so hard studying for the bar. It's possible your body was trying to tell you something. Or perhaps there was a reason you had to go all the way to Italy to have a toothache."

"First off, I take issue with your characterization of the last four weeks as a 'vacation.' And second, perhaps it was cosmic, or post-traumatic stress disorder, or maybe it was just that stale pretzel I bit into on the flight to Paris."

"Well, I need you and all of your original teeth to come to New York. We have an apartment."

"We do?"

"We do. It's in a great location and in our price range. But let me start off by saying it doesn't have air-conditioning. You'll just have to stop carrying that torch. There are a few other issues, too."

"Issues?"

"First off, it's a walk-up," he said.

"Okay. How high?"

"Four flights, and they're steep. There's no denying that. But it's a loft, a big space, and it's in Tribeca. That's a very chic part of town. It'll also need a couple of walls, but that's just a matter of some strapping and Sheetrock."

"It needs walls? With all of the apartments in Manhattan, we're getting one without walls? I thought walls were implied. I didn't even think to request them."

"Don't give it another thought. It's just some strapping and Sheetrock. Really, no problem," Arjun repeated.

"Where and when do I sign?"

"Manhattan and tomorrow. I've fronted the deposit, but we've got to sign the lease right away or we'll lose it."

Arjun was speaking another language: "strapping and Sheetrock"; "loft." Wasn't "loft" code for "bunk beds"? I didn't understand but didn't ask. I was just happy we had a potential abode.

CHAPTER 31

MET ARJUN IN New York at the original Coffee Shop restaurant near Union Square Park. After lunch we took the A train to Chambers Street and walked a block to the apartment. Lined with dollar clothing stores, fast-food restaurants, and seedy bars, the area by the subway worried me at first, but one block north was a major improvement.

I scanned the buildings in Tribeca and finally understood what "loft" meant. It was New York–speak for a large open space with high ceilings and windows at either end. Nearly every five-story building on the street had a single loft dominating each floor.

I recognized our building without even knowing the address. It was the most dilapidated one on the street. According to Arjun, it was the second–oldest cast-iron building in New York City. I was sure it could have passed as the oldest. A dozen shades of gray paint were chipping off every part of the rusty exterior. There was no apartment at street level, just an abandoned storefront with a metal garage door pulled shut.

Directly across the street was a store that sold lighting equipment. A gigantic electric sign over the storefront said ELECTRIC OUTLET in big, bold red and white lightbulbs. The sign was so bright in the daylight that I could only imagine how blinding it might be at night. Would I ever fall asleep?

A man paced back and forth in front of the entrance to the building. He saw us approaching and deliberately looked at his watch. "That's Richard, the landlord," Arjun whispered to me. "He's not particularly pleasant."

As we got closer, Richard feigned a smile and then began to drool. We were his next victims. Arjun and I followed him up the steps. The climb was brutal—far worse than I'd anticipated, far worse than the walk-up in my Philadelphia apartment. Off the heels of a major trek across Europe, I didn't expect to feel physically expended after just four flights, but I was. Arjun, also out of breath, was half laughing. Richard turned away from us to unlock the door and disguise his own heavy breathing.

This was Arjun's second visit to the apartment. He was ready to commit and sign the contract. Barring something extraordinary, I was expected to do the same.

The apartment was bigger than I'd expected. According to Richard, we were standing in an eighteen-hundred-square-foot space. The shape of the apartment was one long rectangle, stretching from one end of the building to the other, with gorgeous oak windows at either end. One end looked out over Reade Street, the other over an alley and directly into a neighboring loft twenty feet away. The space was divided into two bedrooms, one living room, a kitchen, and a bathroom. The hardwood floors had deep cracks and divots, and in opposite corners of the apartment, two industrial-size heaters hung from the ceiling.

The bedrooms were far too small and the living room too large. Each bedroom, no larger than a prison cell, had a ladder that led to a mini-loft for sleeping. Arjun was right. The mini-lofts had to be eliminated, and every wall needed to be shifted out by about ten feet, which would probably mean leveling every wall and rebuilding both bedrooms. "Some strapping and Sheetrock," Arjun assured me again.

Richard handed me the five-page lease and a pen. He should have known better. Early on Arjun had made the mistake of mentioning to Richard that I was an attorney. No one—repeat, no one—in New York City wanted to rent an apartment to a lawyer, especially someone only *purporting* to be a lawyer. Lucky for me, Arjun had neglected to mention the part about the pending bar results. I paged through the lease. The first three pages were photocopies of a standardized lease form with the appropriate blanks filled in. The lease outlined our responsibilities and his. The last two pages comprised a rider outlining the amount of rent due each month and the terms for renewal.

"I've already read it," Arjun said to me quickly. Richard stood over me as I tried to focus on the language of the contract. Hey, Rick, you're crowding me. Coercion, duress, I thought. You *do* want this contract to be enforceable, don't you? Back off.

The three of us knew it was a done deal, but I tried to bluff anyway. I began surveying the apartment. I walked over to the corner of the living room and indicated the fuse box. It was missing a cover plate. "That's very dangerous," I said to Richard, pointing to the exposed switches and wires.

"I don't know where that cover went. We'll get you another one. That's not a problem."

"The walls are filthy. You do plan to repaint them?"

This was the first of three times Richard would refer to Section III, subsection (d), of the contract: "The lease says you accept the premises as is. That's our policy."

"But New York residents are entitled to new locks and a new paint job," I said, reciting New York landlord-tenant law.

"Actually, lofts are treated differently than residential premises. You're taking a commercial space. A paint job isn't included." But if this was a commercial space, then how could Richard rent it for residential purposes?

Arjun interjected, fearing the deal might go sour. "New paint will just get ruined when we change the walls," he said to me. I gave him an annoyed glance. He gave me a desperate look. I walked over to the wall opposite the fuse box.

"What's on the other side of this wall?" I asked Richard.

"Oh, that's the elevator." The elevator! "All of the machinery is also behind this wall. That stuff just happens to be on this floor. About forty years ago the elevator stopped working, and it was never repaired." I peered through a small hole in the wall. I could make out a huge wheel with steel cable wrapped around it.

"We boxed in the elevator behind this wall," Richard said, tapping on it. "It will never work again. Theoretically, if it were to go up, the elevator would crash into the kitchen on the fifth floor. And if it went down, it would break through the ceiling on the third floor. You know what I'm saying?"

I know what you're saying—you're saying we got the shaft. Actually, we got the shaft, a stationary elevator, and the accompanying equipment. "In the apartment directly above us and the apartment directly below us, the area where the elevator is supposed to stop is now an open space, is that what you're saying? That would make their apartments bigger, right?"

"Yeah, they pay more."

"I see." I walked into the kitchen and opened the refrigerator. The light came on. "Uh-huh." I walked over to the kitchen sink and turned on the faucet. Water came out. "Uh-huh."

Finally Arjun spoke up. "What's this tube and bucket behind the washing machine?"

"Sometimes extra dirty water empties into the bucket. Just keep an eye on it. It's not something to worry about." Arjun nodded in agreement. "Guys, this is getting silly," Richard said impatiently. "At this point I'm going to have to say take it or leave it. We've got at least four other potential tenants interested in this space."

We took it.

Before we signed, Richard responded to two more improvement requests with "as is" and "as is." He added a note to the bottom of the contract indicating any improvements could be made only at our own expense.

"This place is great," Satan said as he threw the signed contract into his briefcase. "It used to be an underwear factory, then a bakery. Four models lived here, a rap artist soundproofed the living room once to mix records, and a famous photographer, I forget his name, made this his studio. This place has lots of character." We were in trouble—we sensed it but didn't realize how deep.

CHAPTER 32

I T WAS OUR first Saturday morning in the apartment, and it was time to level it. We measured out the entire space and sketched a new configuration for the two bedrooms and living room. The original bedrooms had mini-lofts. Neither of us was about to climb a ladder to get into bed every night. Plus, when we brought women back to the ultimate bachelor pad, the mini-lofts would surely inhibit our ability to be spontaneous. "Darling, have I shown you my sleeping space?"

The mini-lofts had to go, and that meant destroying every wall in the apartment.

"I've been giving it a lot of thought. We can still do the demolition, but we're going to need a building contractor," Arjun said. "We're running out of time. I start b-school on Thursday, and you start work next week. Plus, my lease uptown is almost up. Once we knock these walls down, I'll move in." I was living on Arjun's floor, with an occasional commute to Toms River.

"How difficult is it to build a wall?" I asked.

"First you lay down a track on the floor and ceiling, outlining the boundaries of each bedroom. Then you place studs or strapping every four feet, from the ceiling to the floor. After that, you Sheetrock all the walls." Arjun paused. "Oh, I forgot. If we want soundproofing, we have to do that before we put up the Sheetrock. I assume you want soundproofing."

I nodded. "Do we order all the supplies, or does the contractor bring them?"

"It depends." Arjun began pacing. "It would be a lot less expensive if we ordered that stuff ahead of time. That way it's waiting for the contractor when he gets here. Oh, I also forgot about electricity. Before we cover the walls with soundproofing and Sheetrock, we have to wire them with power outlets, switches, and probably wires for ceiling lights. That means we'll also need an electrician. Which reminds me—we should pick up ceiling fans."

"You're kidding."

"And if we don't get that electrician set up now, he'll be the bottleneck." "Bottleneck"—Arjun was throwing around industrial-engineering terms of art. "We can't put up the Sheetrock if the electricity isn't in place." He looked down at the ground to find his place. "Okay, so as I was saying, once the walls go up, the creases where the Sheetrock meet must be taped, so when you paint them, the cracks are gone and it looks smooth."

This was all very educational. "Can we do that part?" I asked.

"Not really. Taping is probably harder than cutting the Sheetrock to fit the walls. It's an art to measure and cut Sheetrock so it lines up perfectly with the outlets and switches. There's nothing like destroying a perfectly good piece of Sheetrock by putting the hole for the light switch in the wrong spot.

"Anyhow, the walls, the strapping, the electricity," Arjun continued, "it's all going to be twice as much work and money because we have such high ceilings." You could see it on his face. His mind was racing. He began to pick up speed. Now he was whispering to himself. "And we can't order pieces of Sheetrock that are too large, because they won't fit up the stairwell, they're too heavy, they'll break too easily, and they're impossible to handle. We're going to need a lot of Sheetrock."

"So, an electrician, a building contractor, and a taper. Can the building contractor do the taping?" I asked.

"It's hard to say. Taping is also sort of an art. It's not easy to tape the creases between Sheetrock without leaving bumps or wrinkles."

"I dunno, Arjun. Maybe this is too much."

"Wait, the doors!" Arjun said, ignoring me. "The building contractor will have to leave spaces for the doors to our bedrooms. And we'll need someone to come in and install them. It's not as easy as you might think—they've got to be hung just right. Oh yeah, there's also the transom window. We promised Richard transom windows."

"Again, you've lost me," I said, shaking my head.

"Transoms. Transoms are just bedroom windows. We'll want a couple of them high up on the walls. For example, one of mine will open up to the kitchen. One of yours will open to the living room. That way we can both get some natural sunlight and ventilation. Plus, that's the only way we'll get heat into our rooms, thanks to those industrial heating fans in the kitchen and living room. Remind me to tell the building contractor to leave space for transoms."

"We can do the painting, right?" I said, desperate.

"Absolutely. We can do the painting, and we can do the demolition."

"The mini-lofts are built into all the walls. So we'll have to destroy all five bordering walls."

"Five seventeen-foot walls," he added. "Thus the collapsible ladders." He pointed to our newest four-hundred-dollar purchase. Our beautiful high ceilings were proving to be the bane of our existence. "Between the mini-lofts and the high ceilings, it's going to feel like we're knocking down a dozen standard-height walls."

Arjun put down his coffee and walked up to the wall that separated the living room from my future bedroom. He put his ear up to the wall like a doctor listening for a heartbeat and began frantically tapping the wall.

"There," he said, holding the space with his index finger. "Hand me a nail." He marked the spot with the end of the nail. Then he pulled up the goggles hanging from his neck, grabbed a crowbar, and swung it at the nail hole as hard as he could. Missing the mark by a few inches, he still managed to make a significant puncture in the Sheetrock. Then he twisted the crowbar ninety degrees and pulled off a good chunk of wall.

"See, that's what you're looking for—a hollow space, the space between two studs, the space between the strapping." Then he backed away from the wall. "You can also do this," he said, and took the heel of his right boot and jammed it into the wall below the crowbar hole. "It's fun. Come on, pick a wall."

And it was fun. Invigorating, even. Until, of course, it became impossible to breathe from all the Sheetrock dust. We wore face masks and used floor fans to help circulate the air. By the second day of demolition, every muscle in my body ached, and I was a chronically itchy zombie. For hours at a time, I'd stand in front of the same wall, zoning out to the Dave Matthews Band on my Walkman and swinging ever more wildly with my crowbar.

"Whoa," I screamed as my crowbar hit something inside the wall that divided my future room from the living room. The two-foot blue and white electrical arc threw me backward five feet.

"That was awesome. Are you okay?" Arjun asked.

"Yeah, I think so," I said, inspecting myself. My hands were shaking.

"We should probably label the switches in the fuse box with the corresponding outlets in the apartment," he said. "Then we should shut them off."

It took us four days to dismantle all five seventeen-foot walls and both mini-lofts. I spent the evenings on Arjun's couch in his studio apartment in Chelsea. Arjun had four more days left on his lease. I was nervous for both of us. There was no way we could move into our new apartment. It was a war zone. There was nowhere to walk. What had we done?

Two days later, a truck dropped off a twenty-cubic-yard Dumpster. The rental company charged us fifteen hundred dollars, cash only. That Sunday morning friends began to trickle in around ten A.M. Arjun and I had cashed in every outstanding favor, and the rest of the people we enticed with a keg of imported beer.

We set up assembly lines and routinely changed positions. Position one broke the Sheetrock into smaller pieces. Position two bagged the pieces in exorbitantly expensive heavy-duty black plastic bags. Position three carried—usually dragged—the bags down the steps to the Dumpster. Up and down those unbearable four flights of steps, the twelve of us brought nearly one hundred ninety-pound bags of broken Sheetrock, nail-infested two-by-fours, and mangled metal studs or strapping.

Frequently the bags were packed too heavily, carried wrong, or ripped due to a protruding nail or piece of metal. The bag would break open, and all the contents, along with millions of dust particles, would roll down the steps toward friends approaching for another load. At different points in the day I'd be in position one or two and hear victims shrilling in the stairwell.

By late afternoon the apartment was completely cleared out, and the keg was completely tapped. We needed a bigger Dumpster. It was quite a balancing trick to get the last ten bags in. I hoped the rental place would accept the overflowing Dumpster. After everyone left, Arjun and I grabbed dinner. Then I kindly refused an offer to sleep on his couch again. The ride home to Toms River was . . . itchy.

I walked in the door around eleven-thirty P.M. My mother was in the kitchen, a cigarette in one hand, drawing something. The air-conditioning revived me.

"Hey," I said, walking up the stairs of the blessedly well-walled split-level. My God, our walls were beautiful. "It looks like your stone sculpture in the garage is almost done."

"Funny you should say that. There was always so much to do, then today I realized there was nothing left to do—so it was done."

"What are you doing now?" I asked, looking at the sketches.

"They're interesting, huh?" On her paper were six silver-dollar-size drawings of abstract shapes. "The first one here is the sculpture in the garage, the rest are different possibilities. How's the apartment coming?"

"Wall-less," I said. "Take a look at this." I stretched the collar of my T-shirt over my left shoulder. It was blotchy. "Does that look normal to you?"

"No, you have something. It's on your neck, too. Take off your shirt." My back, shoulders, and chest were also blotchy. "You're breaking out. I don't know what it is. I'll put some calamine lotion on. Take some Benadryl, and go see Dr. Tan in the morning."

"I start work next week."

She was distracted by my spots. "Doesn't look like hives. It's not impetigo. Maybe it's an allergic reaction? Hmmmm. I don't know what you've got, but it's weird."

"I must have unleashed some rare virus buried in the walls of my apartment. Great, now I'm the host. The itching started about five hours ago," I said, dancing around. "Ooch, ooch, ouch, I wanna scratch."

"Don't scratch," she warned, and we both started laughing.

It took most of the bottle of calamine lotion and about thirty cotton balls to cover the mystery skin disorder. I carefully climbed into bed and, lying on my back, stretched my arms and legs out so as not to smudge the protective coating. Twenty minutes later, the Benadryl kicked in and I fell asleep. Overnight the rash spread to the rest of my body. When I woke up in the morning, I looked down at my mentally detached right hand scratching my left thigh. I stopped scratching, jumped out of bed, threw on some loose clothes, and went directly to the doctor's office.

"It's a nonspecific epidermal abnormality," he diagnosed quickly.

"In other words, it's weird," I said.

"Take these steroids for ten days," he said, ripping the prescription from his pad.

"I start work in a week," I said.

"Your face should be fine by Friday."

CHAPTER 33

SMACKED HER IN the boob.

I was illustrating how small the room was with my hands, and I inadvertently smacked her in the boob. First there was this awkward silence, then her facetious question: "So what did you think?"

"I'm so sorry about that, Hayley. And yes, they're very nice."

Hayley was a good sport, seeing that we were now officemates. The firm knew that we were friends, so they squeezed us in the same ten-by-fifteen-foot office. It didn't matter that I was slated to work in the patent-litigation department and Hayley in the trademark-prosecution department. All the first-year associates were sharing offices. In fact, so were most of the second-years.

To be frank, I was worried about shacking up with Hayley. We'd recently stepped up our level of flirting (I'm on record that she purposely stood too close to me during the notorious brush), and I knew that it would be a terrible mistake for me to mess around with my officemate. "You're better off keeping away from temptation rather than trying to fight it," the Oracle told me. Yet now Hayley was within striking distance.

"Maybe we should set up some ground rules?" she said.

"You mean like college, where you hang a sock on the doorknob to say that you want privacy?"

"You did that?"

"No," I said.

"Let's agree to show some respect for each other when we're on the phone."

"Okay, but I don't want to hear about the guys you're dating," I said. "Try to remember, this is a place of business."

"That's fine, if you agree not to date women like that girl Molly from last summer. She made you miserable."

"Why, do you have someone else in mind?"

"Maybe," she said. "I know plenty of eligible women. The same goes for you. If you know someone I should meet, bring him in." I was familiar with this sort of dance. To deflect a potentially complicated romance, we were going to take care of each other's love lives.

"Let's pick out some office furniture. Unless, of course, you'd like to register with Home Depot?" she said. We then strategized about the size, color, and location for two small bookcases.

Aside from the office furniture and the boob incident, which I would keep to myself, my first day at Nickel was nothing to write home about. But with the apartment in limbo, I'd promised to come home instead of crashing on Arjun's floor. On the drive, I checked my voice mail at the apartment. There was a message from the Oracle.

"Hi, it's Mom. I won't leave you a long message, because I don't want to use up all your tape." She hadn't yet grasped the concept that she was in a computerized voice-mail system. There was no machine. There was no tape. "I hope you had a wonderful first day. The thought of seeing you tonight helped me get through the day. When you get home, talk to your dad."

That wasn't good. It was commonly known that the Oracle shamelessly monopolized my time, whether in person or on the phone. If she was punting to Dad, something was wrong.

As I pulled up to the house, I could see my father sitting in his usual position on the outside upper deck, overlooking the bay. As I walked up the driveway, I could hear him yell to my mother in the kitchen: "It's your son."

If my father had something to say, I was glad he'd tell me in person. He and I were always better in person. Our phone conversations rarely lasted longer than five minutes and only occasionally evolved past simple small talk. The key to talking to my father was rhythm and pacing, and they were much easier to get a handle on in person. Once we got on a roll—and it was sporadic—we'd launch right into something substantial. Whether it was about love, sex, money, fear, anger, or despair, no subject was off-limits with my father, much like the Oracle.

I said hello to Mom. She gave me a kiss. "What's with all the drama?" I said.

"No drama," she said, pretending. I opened the sliding glass door to the deck. My father was smoking his pipe and reading a quarterly report on one of the companies in which he owned stock. There was no better place to set the pace for a good (or bad) conversation than on our deck.

"Alex! How was your first day?" I gave him a kiss on the cheek. He wore shorts, a short-sleeved button-down shirt, and sandals. Dad had recently started shaving the little hair that he had left on his head. It was dark tan, from a summer of sunning sessions on the deck. He never looked better.

"Pretty uneventful. Just some orientation and new office supplies. I have a secretary. I'm not exactly sure what she's supposed to do. She's about ten years older than I am, and I don't think she's thrilled about the assignment. What's happening with you?"

"Not too much. Today was your first day of work and my last. We had more layoffs. Instead of delivering the bad news, I received it." At that moment I regretted capriciously mentioning my secretary. I knew that I'd started at a salary that my father wasn't likely to make, but I never expected the gap to widen so quickly.

The whole family had known the layoff was coming. Over the last year his engineering company had lost several big bids on U.S. military aircraft projects. For the past two weeks my dad was charged with the unenviable task of laying people off. By the time he received the news, there was virtually no one left to lay off.

"This is the way it goes. On to bigger and better things," the Optimist said. "I'm ready for a change. I'm ready for a raise." He took a draw from his pipe.

I considered agreeing that he was underpaid. I considered saying that I was sorry, or that he was brilliant. That he could do anything— he had a nuclear physicist's brain and a doctor's bedside manner. But it was too late for those careers, and I started to worry. I wondered how difficult it might be for a forty-eight-year-old unemployed engineer to find good work. Three years back, I'd watched my engineering friends compete for entry-level jobs. I didn't have the foggiest idea what the market was like for senior managers. I'd never seen my father unemployed. But for the moment my father seemed truly at peace.

He suddenly changed the topic. "Tell me more about today. Assigned to any big cases yet?"

"I was told that I was assigned to some big ridiculous litigation, and that I'd learn more about it when my mentor gets back in the office tomorrow. He's a seventh year. His name is Aaron Reinstein, University of Michigan, Tier One," I said. My family understood me.

"Yeah, but that Tier One, Tier Two stuff is over now. Everyone in your firm is Tier One." He took another long draw from his pipe. We were both staring out at some Jet Skiers.

"Sort of. Now it has less to do with what school you went to and more to do with your engineering or technical discipline. Dad, it's like engineering school all over again. Everyone in the building has a law degree, but the same old engineering hierarchy still exists. The Tier Ones are still the electrical, mechanical, chemical, and biotechnology engineers." This was intended as a subtle compliment to my father, who held a master's in electrical engineering.

"After them come the Tier Twos—the civil, ceramic, and industrial engineers—me."

"You all get paid the same, don't you?" he said kindheartedly. I was losing track. Who was comforting whom?

I wasn't in the mood for a salary conversation. Size mattered when it came to a man's salary. It was the simplest way to define success in society, yet it was antithetical to everything that my father had taught me. The family considered my father a huge success regardless of whether he'd ever make six figures, and that type of environment always helped keep money issues in perspective. Money changed people, but not my family.

That said, there was no denying that somehow our employment status complicated things for me. I'd never made anything. My father had always made everything. I needed to get used to the new dynamic, even if it was temporary. As for the Optimist, today was no different than yesterday. There had never been any competition between my father and me, and for him, that wasn't about to change. He'd always been proud, supportive, and encouraging, which was exactly what he needed to be right now.

"Will you set up a Roth IRA? Do they have a 401(k) plan? You should put as much money into that as you can," he said. His financial advice had nothing to do with being laid off. Dad wasn't particularly worried about my financial future; he just wanted to help, and this was his way of saying "I love you." These were the moments when my father truly shone. Faced with struggles, he couldn't keep himself from focusing on someone else's success.

I listened as he enthusiastically planned the shortest path to my retirement and financial freedom. I was happy to let him talk.

CHAPTER 34

A
S MUCH AS I loved my parents' central air-conditioning, it was time to bite the bullet and move in to the apartment. Over the last two weeks I'd occasionally slept in the apartment, but most days I commuted back and forth between Toms River and Manhattan, and the two-hour commute each way was just too much. Because I planned to do the move in phases, I extended the rental on my storage unit for three weeks. That was how long I estimated it would take before the apartment had walls. Arjun and I estimated that renovations were going to cost us about $5,500 each. For the time being I'd bring the bare essentials to the apartment and sleep on a mattress next to Arjun's on the living room floor.

I drove into the city, pulled up to the corner of Church and Reade Streets, and quickly surveyed whether my car could stay there for ten minutes while I unloaded. The corner, the fire hydrant, and the COM-MERCIAL PARKING ONLY sign all suggested that my hazard lights weren't going to cut it. I got a flash of my car being lowered into a police lot with a parking ticket on the windshield that included three or four independent violations.

My best shot at hedging was the man and woman chatting on the stoop in front of the apartment. These were either my new neighbors or patrons of the store on the street level of the building. The heavy metal garage door that ordinarily covered the storefront was up, and I realized it wasn't abandoned after all. I could now read the name of the store in the window: THE TRIBECA MAD HATTER. This was a place the Oracle would call a tchotchkes shop. Nothing inside was bigger than a hatbox. The store seemed to sell odd jewelry, soaps, doilies, figurines, and, of course, hats, tons of hats. There were no customers inside.

I turned on my hazards, confirmed in the rearview mirror that I was wearing my most hopeless expression, and approached my potential guardians. "Do you think you'll be here for a while?"

The couple immediately broke off their conversation. The man wasn't having any of it. He kept his back turned away from me and waited a few moments, clearly hoping that I would buzz away.

"I'm sure we'll be here for at least another ten minutes. I don't know whether that helps," the woman volunteered. That was the man's cue to pick up the conversation where he'd left off. He cheated his body away from me some more and elevated his voice to secure her undivided attention. She was striking, with long brown hair and light blue eyes. She stood up to show off her long legs and sexy hip-hugger bell-bottom jeans. He remained seated, and she continued to look at him while occasionally eyeing me.

I threw a duffel bag over my shoulder and grabbed my two suitcases from the backseat. Hands full, I began fumbling with my keys.

"Tony, help him. Open the door," she nudged. He begrudgingly did so while she and I exchanged a glance for a smile.

On my second camel-packed trip up those abominable steps, I started considering my options. Did I really need walls, furniture, and groceries? I dropped my stuff in the apartment, caught my breath, grabbed a beer from the fridge, stepped over some drop cloths, and began surveying the war zone of an apartment.

The law considers termites a "latent" defect. A loose or rotted floorboard is also a latent defect. Latent defects, by their very definition, are hidden and sometimes difficult to ferret out. The latent defects I could forgive myself for, but the blatant ones haunted me.

For example, I'd recently tried to reheat some leftovers. With pasta in one hand, I opened the oven door with the other. The door, of course, was missing the precious spring that would have enabled me to crack it open slightly. I dropped the pasta when the ten-pound, 350-degree preheated door crashed onto my left foot. The pain was so intense and came as such a surprise that all I could utter was a high-pitched squeak. Dogs were tipping over in Brooklyn.

The makeshift washing machine would require baby-sitting. Duct-taped to the back of the machine was a plastic pipe that emptied into a large bucket, the very same bucket Arjun had noticed the day we signed the lease. By the second or third load, it was clear that the bucketful of grimy water needed to be emptied. The washing machine was tucked away in the corner of the kitchen, so emptying the bucket meant kneeling on top of the washing machine, reaching behind the machine, and steadying the heavy bucket up and over. It was a potentially disgusting job that was beginning to cause a rift between Arjun and me. Each of us was waiting for the other one to empty it for the first time. Ultimately, the brown water overflowed onto the kitchen floor and caused a twenty-minute ordeal. The bucket was so heavy that it took both of us to lift it. Then we'd carry it into the bathroom, where I held the pail while Arjun siphoned off the dirty water. Then we dumped the solid crud in the garbage.

The kitchen in general was in bad shape. Somehow we both missed the fact that there were no cabinets. There were just a few glass shelves collecting dust over the sink. Since there was no place to put Arjun's dishes, glasses, bowls, cooking equipment, or eating utensils, we left all of them in cardboard moving boxes.

The bathroom was tiny, and there was nothing we could do about it. The floor was wooden and warped and needed tiling. The wall needed a medicine cabinet.

"Ow!" Arjun screamed during his first shower in the apartment.

"What?" I yelled from the other side of the apartment.

"I'm showering, I've got my eyes closed, my face to the water, and the fucking showerhead flies off and hits me right between the eyes," he yelled back. Apparently the threading on the showerhead was worn. It became a daily ritual to secure it with rounds of duct tape.

I made a list of these latent defects. Had this apartment been the subject of a contracts or property essay on the bar, I would have missed all the critical issues and failed miserably.

On the plus side, our rennovations were coming along nicely. The place was definitely beginning to take shape—both bedrooms were framed out. I could see where the doors, transoms, and closets would go. The walls were wired with outlets and switches, and the sound-proofing on the wall separating my room from the living room was nearly complete. I leaned against one of the brick walls, took a mournful swig of beer, and aired out the place by opening all three of the gigantic wooden windows that overlooked Reade Street.

The buzzer rang. Peeking through the peephole, I recognized the man from the stoop. What was his problem? I smiled at his girlfriend, BFD.

"Hold on," I said, and unlocked the door. "What's up?"

"Just so you know, I'm gay. Are you dating anyone?" I noticed from his accent that he was British.

"Well, I date. I'm not dating someone special right now. I mean, I'm always dating, but I'm—"

"My friend, the one you were hitting on outside? She told me to give you her number in some sort of subtle way. Here." He handed me a small piece of paper.

I took it, and before I could thank him, he was headed down the steps. "I'm Tony," he said without turning around. "By the way, the store downstairs—the one you were giving such a snooty look—it's mine." I looked at the piece of paper. The woman's name was Margo.

Downstairs I was relieved to see my car hadn't been ticketed or towed. I popped the trunk to grab my last few items. It was empty. I stared inside, trying to figure out whether I'd already brought my suits and laptop computer upstairs. I hadn't.

"Oh-my-God," I whispered. "Oh-my-God, oh-my-God, oh-my-God." Inside the shop, I could see Tony rearranging doilies.

"Tony!" I said, blasting through the front door.

"What? She's not here." The bell on the door was still jingling.

"Tell me you saw something—anything. All my stuff is gone from my trunk."

"Oh, that's rich." He chuckled. "Brilliant. What's wrong with you? This is New York." I ran out to the car and popped the trunk again. The lock didn't appear to be tampered with. Had I locked the car? Of course I had.

I stared incredulously into my empty trunk, then plopped down on the hood of the car parked behind mine, scanning the neighborhood for clues. The city continued about its business. Someone must have been staking out the car. In those precious few minutes that I was jabbering away with Tony in the apartment, some thief must have jimmied the car door, popped the trunk from the inside, and cleaned me out.

"Oh-my-God," I repeated as New Yorkers walked past me, occa-sionally shaking their heads in disapproval.

CHAPTER 35

T HE Q TRAIN to Ocean Parkway in Brooklyn let out two blocks from Grandma Mary's apartment. My mother's family met there once a month, and I'd missed quite a few visits lately. I was looking forward to seeing everyone, especially Grandma Mary, who was more than the matriarch of the family; she was grandmother to the world. She welcomed anyone and everyone into her home and treated each and every one of them like a member of the family.

The core group at these gatherings consisted of my parents and Mike; Aunt Greta and Uncle Stephen; Cousin Jayne, her husband, Danny, and their twins. Other relatives and friends occasionally dropped by, so there was never a fixed number of people in attendance.

I pressed the intercom button and heard Grandma's familiar "Okaaay" as she buzzed me in. I took the elevator to her apartment and rang her extraordinarily loud doorbell. Another "Okaaay," and I was in. So much for security. She gave me a big hug and kiss.

"Why did you let me in?" I asked.

"Why? Because I love you, Alexander," she said, confused.

"But you didn't know it was me. You let me into the building without asking. Then you opened the door without asking."

"But darling, I was waiting for you." What more could I say?

Grandma Mary looked wonderfully primped. Her reddish hair was beauty-parlor bouffanted and lacquered. She wore a silky patterned blouse with typical stretchy brown polyester pants. The accessories were heavy tan orthopedic shoes and her signature dangling earrings. Whenever you saw Grandma Mary, she was smiling or laughing. She said "whoopee" when she was surprised. Mary was normal grandma height and enjoyed classic grandma pastimes like saving things and knitting. When I was a child, she knit me a series of sweaters that unfortunately were too scratchy to wear. Once, when I was about ten, she knit a sweater for my two-inch Yoda *Star Wars* action figure. When it came in the mail, my mom and I laughed to tears.

My parents and Mike were next to arrive. Their chore today was to pick up the deli. They started arranging the folding tables in the living room and putting it out. Mike and I began picking from the platter of corned beef, pastrami, rye bread, mustard, and pickles. I took a Dr. Brown's cream soda. Family and friends would stagger their arrivals due to distance, traffic, and general tardiness. We were a loud, rowdy bunch. The laughter was easy, and twenty conversations would be started and interrupted at once. We were vocal and opinionated, and God have mercy on anyone who brought up politics. We were close enough to step metaphorically on each other's toes. What we all had in common was our genuine devotion to Grandma and one another.

The hoopla was about to begin, but I was glad to have a chance to talk to Grandma, Mom, Dad, and Mike.

"Mike is so excited about staying with you tonight," my mother said, as if he weren't in the room. With a mouthful of pastrami, Mike nodded in agreement.

"This came for you today," my father said, handing me an envelope from BAR/BRI. It read like a waiver of liability and warranted nothing.

TO: All July BAR/BRI New York Candidates

This letter is to thank you *(for your $2,500)*, especially those who took the time to fill out course evaluations and to send us issues from the summer exam *(BAR/BRI received a total of three course evaluations—the rest of the feedback didn't actually qualify as constructive criticism)*. While we are sure you may feel this was the most difficult bar exam ever administered *(it wasn't, you're just being a baby)*, based upon on our extensive debriefing *(we asked a couple of people around the office)*, it was very much in keeping with prior administrations, and again we covered all issues tested *(so if you fail, don't come crying to us)*.

Many of your suggestions are now being implemented *(that should be very helpful for the retake)*. Although these changes do not work to your benefit *(unless, of course . . .)*, evaluations from prior years improved the quality of the course you took *(yeah, I noticed that*). Your evaluation will have a similar effect. Based upon your suggestions, the following will occur:

1) Many of you noted how pleased you were with the constant availability of BAR/BRI's attorney staff (*yeah, right, I'm sure most of our evaluations indicated that many of us were "pleased"*). Therefore, we will introduce P.A.C.E.™—Personalized Attorney Counseling and Evaluation. During the bar-review course, at selected locations, BAR/BRI attorneys will meet with students, one-on-one or in small group sessions, to address related concerns. (*My first concern is this PACE program. Tell me again why I need personalized counseling from an attorney?*)

2) Some of you recommended particular professors and other attorneys as possible BAR/BRI lecturers. We are committed to a diversified faculty and are now speaking with several recommended lecturers (*in other words, we've fired our current staff*).

3) Some of you requested that we include our Gilbert New York Essay Advantage free to all BAR/BRI enrollees. We agree. (*The word "free" offends me in this context.*)

To each of you, the best of luck with the results (*sentence fragment*). If we can assist you in any further way (*presumptuous*), please feel free to call.

Sincerely,

Steven R. Rubin

"So what does it say? It says 'do nothing,' right?" my father asked.

I nodded. "It says the waiting is half over. I think we spend most of our lives in some mode of waiting."

"Well, darling, I wish you the best of everything on the answer to the lawyer's degree," Grandma Mary said. She kissed me on both cheeks. Then she went back to preparing dessert, vanilla pudding with melted marshmallows. When I was ten, I'd told her I liked it, and she'd been making it ever since.

The doorbell rang, and Jayne and Danny came in with the twins.

Soon the place was packed. When we were stuffed and talked out, we left, and our parents dropped Mike and me off in the city.

I did the standard things you do with a fourteen-year-old brother in New York City after eight P.M. We went to Times Square and bought some music at Virgin Records. Then we grabbed some overpriced burgers at Planet Hollywood. At about eleven P.M., we made our way downtown and played some pool at SoHo Billiards. Music, pool, burgers—these things were all fine and good, but I wasn't delivering anything particularly chic or cool. He wasn't saying it, but the pressure of being a cool New York City big brother was excruciating. I couldn't possibly reveal that I was square.

"I'd say we go to a bar, but I don't know if I could get you in."

"I don't mind," Mike said. Code for "Please, for the love of God, can we go?"

"You don't have a fake ID, do you?" Mike shook his head. "I never had one, either. I'm a terrible brother. All this time I should have given you one of my IDs. I could give you one tonight," I said hesitantly.

"I don't mind."

The plan that could jeopardize my yet-to-be-legal career, I thought. "Okay. We'll try the Screening Room." We took a cab to Canal and Greenwich and stepped into the short line outside the bar. I gave Mike my license and began quizzing him on being me. I planned to talk my way in using my Nickel identification. Four models, dressed to kill, latched on to Mike right away.

"You are so precious." The leader of the pack patted Mike on the head. "You guys are such brothers. Isn't that cute—your big brother is sneaking you into a bar." The fact that we hadn't duped these girls was not encouraging.

"This isn't going to work, is it?" I said to them.

"Of course it's going to work," the leader said as the group stepped to the front of the line. "Come on, ladies." On their looks alone, the bouncer waved the four of them in and with that, the scantily clad foursome engulfed and clandestinely escorted Mike into the bar. To my knowledge, this was the furthest Mike had ever gotten with a woman, not to mention four of them.

"ID," the bouncer commanded. I handed him my Nickel identification. "Yeah, I'm gonna need something else."

"I'm with *that* group," I said, pointing to the women dancing around
Mike. "This is my work ID. I'm an attorney."

"Fine. Do you have a business card?"

"It doesn't look like I have one here," I said, picking through my wallet in search of a card that didn't exist. "I have a Sears credit card," I
offered jokingly. Nothing. *Nada.* Zilch. He was a tough crowd. "I have
a twenty-dollar bill." Finally a smile.

Inside, Mike was already sipping a drink. "Hey, you made it," he
said. "Annie bought this for me. It's rum and Coke. I've never had rum
and Coke. It's terrible."

"No straws," I said, throwing his on the floor. "Real men don't drink
through straws."

"Thanks. I appreciate that. If I want to go home with any of these
women, can I? I mean, I don't know. Yeah, sure, it's a long shot, but I
think I've got this younger-guy thing going. Am I being stupid?"

"Of course not. You can go home with them, Mike," I said opti-
mistically. I considered asking him to put in a good word for me. "I'll
pick you up in the morning."

"Thanks. If I do, don't tell Mom," he said. Mike was the life of the
party. Together we had a synergistic effect with the four models.
Without him, these girls wouldn't have given me the time of day, and
without me, Mike couldn't have played the cute little brother role.
Either these women were truly entertained by Mike's stories, jokes,
and miscellaneous facts, or they genuinely related to a fourteen-year-
old boy. He was using the same material being rejected by high school
girls every day in Toms River. At about two A.M., the girls called it a
night, and Mike and I went home—alone.

In the morning I took Mike to Laverne's, the local diner that served
great brunch and comfort food like fried chicken, meat loaf, and potato pancakes with sour cream. I introduced Mike to Linda, the head
pie maker. Laverne's baked all types of desserts, but pies were its bread
and butter. Linda was a curmudgeonly, overweight woman somewhere in her late forties, responsible for overseeing a dozen bakers

who produced tens of thousands of award-winning pies every year. Aside from her staff, Linda wanted nothing to do with anyone. For weeks I'd watched her go up and down the basement steps, carefully balancing stacks and stacks of pies and restocking the display case. Then one day I complimented her on her key-lime pie—by chance her favorite—and suddenly we were friends.

"My brother tells me that your chocolate-peanut-butter pie is to die for," Mike said to Linda.

"Yeah, I'm experimenting. When you finish your breakfast, you can test the new lemon meringue that I'm working on."

Mike's eyes lit up. As if he needed dessert after dining on sourdough French toast with whipped cream and strawberries. "I read somewhere that Granny Smiths are the best for apple pies because they're not too tart, they aren't too sweet, and they cook without quickly turning to applesauce." It was common for him to toss out gems like this.

"That's very impressive," Linda said. "If you'd like, sometime I can show you how to cut air vents in a pie and make the crust shiny." Later Linda brought Mike a sampler that included rhubarb crunch, apple, sour cherry, banana cream, and, of course, the new lemon meringue.

After brunch I took Mike to Port Authority. A few feet inside the terminal, he stopped me.

"How much time do we have until the bus leaves?"

"I dunno," I said. "Ten minutes, maybe."

"Do you remember what I asked you about before?" Mike was nervous. "It's totally no problem if we don't have time. But if we do, do you think, maybe—"

"Oh yeah, of course," I said, remembering. "Stay here. I'll be right back. Don't move a muscle. Do you have any preferences? Forget it. I'll be right back." I ran out of the bus terminal, jaywalked across Eighth Avenue, and made a beeline into one of the triple-X stores. The adult-entertainment center promised the largest selection of magazines, videos, and novelty items. The area around Port Authority was one of the few remaining red-light districts in Manhattan.

Inside were rows and rows of pornography. Video viewing booths were available in the back. Girls, girls, girls were upstairs. The place made me nervous. What if someone from my firm had seen me go in? What if ten guys jumped me inside? What if I bumped into a browsing senior partner?

"Right now, on the upper level, hot wet pussy in your face," a man's voice announced over the intercom system.

I began scanning the titles. Now, I liked porn as much as the next guy—well, maybe not that guy over there—it was just that I didn't have a lot of experience buying it. Magazines, yes, videos, no. It also occurred to me that I didn't know what Mike liked. He probably didn't even know what he liked. It was a lot of pressure. I could end up responsible for starting him on a lifelong obsession with big boobs, foot fetishes, or something really outlandish, like crushing—men aroused by women who crush bugs with their high heels. Probably not. I selected *Hardcore Hotties #39*. It was midrange in price, and the cover displayed a nice variety of women in both standard and nontraditional positions; plus, it promised over twenty-five hard-core scenes with "real" sorority girls. Perhaps I was setting Mike up for some disappointment when he got to college, but for the time being, he could dream.

The attractive but used-up woman behind the elevated counter wrapped the video in a brown paper bag, and I delivered it to Mike, who stood just where I'd left him. He hadn't moved a muscle.

"Thank you so much," he said. "Really, thank you. I really appreciate it."

I jammed the package into the side pocket of his duffel bag. "I hope it's a good one, Mike. The box has a good cover. Put away your money, but give me back my license. Come on, we can't miss this bus. Dad'll be annoyed."

CHAPTER 36

NICKEL ATTORNEYS REFERRED to the case as the "Rufus matter." The full caption of the lawsuit was *Bullock, Inc. v. Rufus Ltd.* Because Nickel represented Bullock in this suit and at least a dozen others, the shorthand convention (standard law-firm practice) was to refer to each case by the opposing party's name. Perhaps I wasn't getting into the spirit of things, but what little I knew about the Rufus matter already bored me.

"Bullock sued Rufus," Aaron Reinstein said, distracted by something on his computer screen. "The lawsuit involves Bullock's computer printers. We've sued Rufus because their printer cartridges infringe on Bullock's patented ink-jet technology and trademarks. Here's the complaint, the answer, and the countercomplaint." He handed me a pile of briefs.

Aaron, my designated mentor, had been practicing intellectual property law for nine years, but since he'd "lateraled over" from a competing firm, Nickel was willing to recognize only seven years. With all that experience, I figured, Aaron had to be at least thirty-four. Aside from his receding hairline, he looked more like twenty-five.

Aaron was the only attorney assigned to the Rufus matter. Even though Bullock was claiming billions in damages, the case hadn't gotten any further than the pleadings stage. "Everyone thought this suit would eventually go away," he said. "Nothing happened since we filed the lawsuit and they sued us back."

"What do you mean, 'go away'?" I asked.

"Settle," he said, only half paying attention. "Sooner or later these suits usually settle. There's too much at stake for a jury to decide. Even a bench trial is usually too risky. For the time being, it looks like a settlement is off the table.

"Oh, and take these," he said, handing me two small boxes. I already had my hands full. I put down the court documents. "Tell me what these are," he said.

"They say 'Bullock cartridge refills,' " I said.

"Who makes them?" I started studying the package. "No, quick, who makes them?" He grabbed both packages and held them up.

"I dunno, Bullock?"

"Exactly! Rufus makes them, but you can hardly tell, with Bullock's name in such large yellow lettering. You see here," he said, "the blue lettering of Rufus's name is hardly readable."

I took the package. "There's a small disclaimer here. I guess that doesn't cut the bread?"

"Do you mean mustard?"

"Yeah."

"Bullock is alleging that this packaging amounts to trademark infringement and trademark dilution. Essentially, we argue that Rufus has sullied Bullock's reputation. These packages," he said, waving them, "give the appearance that Bullock has 'approved, licensed, or authorized' the refill products. They haven't." He put the two packages back down on his desk.

"Sounds like a slam dunk," I said.

"Pretty much. We even have some examples of actual confusion in the marketplace. That's prima facie evidence that Rufus will lose on the trademark issues. We can point to hundreds of angry complaints from customers who were under the mistaken belief that Bullock manufactured these refills."

"And the patent issues?" I asked.

"To protect Bullock's billions, the company patented every element of its ink-jet technology. We also allege that the Rufus products *inside* these packages infringe on a dozen of Bullock's patents."

Aaron could tell that I was getting overwhelmed. "We might as well do this now." He grabbed one of the Rufus products. "Rufus basically has two products that they use to refill Bullock cartridges. The first is this syringe full of ink." He pulled it out of the package and handed it to me. The sharp needle had a piece of protective plastic on the tip and a "handle with care" warning label.

"That's exactly what it looks like," Aaron said. "It's a quick fix. A shot of instant gratification. Tempting, isn't it? Sure, why not, go ahead. Puncture our cartridge. Inject this poison."

"What's this?" I asked, picking up a small screw that had fallen out of the package.

"You use that doohickey to drill a hole in the top of the cartridge. Then you have to use brute force to inject the ink. And while you're doing that, make sure you don't destroy your clothes or couch with ink splatters. Also, be careful not to get any contaminants inside the cartridge and clog it up. If you can manage to do all that, then you take this little cork and plug the hole you drilled."

"And this?" I said, picking up the other Rufus package.

"This is new," Aaron said. "This is Rufus's other, more popular, snap-in ink refill. Rufus takes new and used Bullock cartridges, guts them, then manufactures these snap-in ink tanks.

"We say Rufus can't manufacture these refill products. Rufus says we're trying to bully them out of the business. Go to Walla Walla— Bullock's headquarters—and start piecing together the story. The story that supports the briefs . . . the *Bullock* story." As I turned to head out of his office with the armful of documents and the Rufus products, Aaron became very serious. "And remember, this is a Madison case." I didn't have a clue what he meant.

There was nothing sexy about computer printers, but the incredible opportunity wasn't lost on me. None of my other fellow first years was traveling, even if it was only to Walla Walla. Where was Walla Walla, anyway?

It turned out that Walla Walla was a small city in the southern part of Washington State. But Nickel's travel agent revealed to me that I wasn't actually going to Walla Walla. I was off to Helix, Oregon, a tiny town across the Washington–Oregon border, and getting there from New York would be no easy task. The circuitous path required me to fly to Seattle, Washington, change planes, then take a propeller plane to Walla Walla, rent a car, and drive about an hour southwest to Helix. If everything went according to schedule, fifteen hours later, I'd roll into the three-star Helix Ramada in my Ford Taurus rental.

CHAPTER 37

THE LONG COMMUTE to Helix, Oregon, meant leaving on a Saturday. This would give me a full day to adjust to the time change and prepare for my very first Monday-morning business meeting. The A train dropped me off in Times Square, and I rolled my travel bag to my usual deli for a cup of "coffee regular"—extra cream, extra sugar. The man ahead of me in line looked familiar. He was thin, young, about six feet tall, in his mid-twenties, with short, dark, receding hair. He wore a flannel shirt and jeans. I couldn't pinpoint how we knew each other. I began mentally age-progressing pictures of high school and college friends. As he walked out of the deli, the bell on the door gave a light jingle, and it hit me. I threw down two dollars and ran after him.

"Excuse me," I said, tapping him lightly on the shoulder. "I'm sorry to disturb you. Is your name Dave?"

He smiled. "Yes." He was Dave Matthews, of the Dave Matthews Band. Only in a place like New York City could you bump into your all-time music hero.

"Man, you are the best. You really are something else. I can't tell you how much I enjoy your music. I must have listened to your *Crash* album a thousand times," I gushed. "I tried to get tickets to your concert in Madison Square Garden last night, but it was sold out."

"I appreciate that. If we'd met yesterday, maybe I could have been some help."

"Thanks," I said. Standing there on the Forty-fourth Street sidewalk, I began to panic. I couldn't think of anything to say.

"Coffee for the guys," he said, holding up the bag. The coffee was getting cold.

"How cool. Tell me this." We started walking away from Nickel and back toward Times Square. "You guys have such a unique sound, how did you assemble the band?"

"Well, I'd always admired each of the band members individually," he said humbly. "I used to watch Carter Beauford and LeRoi Moore

play in a jazz group called the Secrets. They eventually became available, and we began recording together. I stumbled upon Stefan
through a friend when he was just a kid. Then Boyd joined later."

Caught up in the moment, I followed with a non sequitur: "So, do
you get recognized much?"

"No, not really." He graciously spent another couple of minutes answering my wide-eyed questions. Then he signed the front page of my
Bullock legal brief—it was the only paper I had—and I wished him
great success in his career. I ran up the block to the Town Car idling
outside of my building and knocked on the window displaying a sign
that said WELLEN.

"You're here for me. I'm Wellen. I just have to run upstairs and get
a few things. Can I put this bag in the trunk?" The driver popped the
trunk and got out of the car. "Sorry I'm late. It's the craziest thing. I
just bumped into Dave Matthews."

"Great. Who's dat?" he said.

I took the elevator to the twentieth floor to reprint my legal brief
and grab my litigation bag—a big heavy pleather-wrapped cardboard
box stuffed with hundreds of pages of documents. We arrived at JFK
forty-five minutes later.

"You're going to have to stow that," Roger, the man behind the ticket
counter, insisted. He was referring to my rolling bag.

"But this fits in the overhead space. I always take it on planes."

"Yes, but you're entitled to one carry-on and one personal item. Your
black box there is a second carry-on," he said.

"My litigation bag isn't a personal item?"

"It's too big. Pick one to be stowed, please." In determining what
constituted a personal item, Roger was borrowing from the U.S.
Supreme Court's definition of obscenity: the "I know it when I see it"
standard.

On the upside, he assured me that I had a roomy window seat in an
exit row. An hour later, I took my seat next to a normal-sized woman.
The exit row proved disappointing. The chairs didn't recline, and we
were located at the bulkhead, so the place where I'd ordinarily put my

feet was a wall. On the other side of the bulkhead was the bathroom. That meant a six-hour flight filled with lines of squirming passengers and the accompanying smells.

During takeoff, I noticed that the woman beside me was wearing a shirt with the Bullock trademark embroidered on the pocket. She had long dark hair, appeared to be in her mid-forties, and was very involved in her romance novel.

"Do you work for Bullock?" I asked. She nodded. "Me, too—sort of. I'm an attorney. I'm working on the case against Rufus." What was meant to be simple bravado suddenly induced panic. What had I done? I realized that I shouldn't be disclosing Bullock's legal business. Attorney-client privilege, I repeated to myself. What was I doing? I was discussing my client's business openly in public. Your Honor, I'd like the last sentence stricken from the record.

"You never know who's listening," Aaron Reinstein had reminded me in the hours leading up to this business trip. He had successfully whipped me into a full-fledged state of paranoia by telling me devastating stories in which attorneys recklessly discussed client matters in the bathroom and/or in a restaurant only to find opposing counsel using that information in court later the same day. I was instructed to keep my clients' business private at all costs.

In fact, that's how I'd always lived my life—fanatically private. Lately, it seemed I was prefacing everything I said with "The following is not for public consumption."

"I wouldn't worry," my mother had told me recently. "Your secret's safe with me. I know nothing, and I tell no one. I can't even remember what I'm not supposed to tell people, so my default is to deny everything unless you earmark it."

"I don't even tell people that I know you," Arjun had said to me the other day. "Just give me a sense of where I am on the hierarchy. How tapped in am I?"

"My life is a jigsaw puzzle," I told him. "No one has all the pieces. Think about it like the McDonald's Monopoly game. You have some of the most common pieces, plus a few of the rarely dispensed pieces, like Baltic Avenue and Park Place."

Given my obsession with privacy, I had always figured the law and lawyering were a natural fit. Everything in my life was attorney-client privileged. Yet here I was, five minutes into my first solo assignment, and I'd already blown my cover. I'd disclosed that Bullock was embroiled in a big litigation with Rufus.

"I'm just an attorney," I said, hoping to erase my last response.

"That's nice," the woman said, and went back to her novel.

When lunch arrived an hour later, she finally put down her book, but still made no effort to engage me in any conversation. There was apparently a mix-up in the airline food delivery. Our options were chicken or chicken. The salad came with a sealed small plastic cup of Italian dressing. I'd already learned the hard way that wherever this particular airline kept its Italian dressing, the storage conditions created a great deal of pressure inside the dressing containers. On a flight to visit friends in California, I had blithely opened a similar container, and a small dab of salad dressing jettisoned out, landing on and ruining my favorite navy blue button-down shirt. This time I gingerly opened the very corner of the container and heard a small hiss. I began seasoning my salad with the dressing, applying more and more pressure, squeezing the remaining dressing out of the tiny aperture. Suddenly, the peel-away top exploded, and the dressing shot out. I quickly surveyed my shirt, pants, salad, chicken—nothing. No dressing anywhere. Strange.

I turned to my left to see my Bullock colleague covered in Italian dressing. I don't think either of us realized how much was in one of those things. It was dripping down her face, fingers, and shirt. She continued to face forward, frozen, with her hands in midair and her fingers curled like claws.

"Oh my God, I'm so sorry." I grabbed the tissue-thin paper napkin from my lap and began dabbing her petrified fingers.

"Stop. Don't touch me. Do-not-touch-me. Take this," she said, handing me her lunch. She flipped up her tray table. "Move!" she told the man on the aisle, then bolted for the bathroom. When she returned ten minutes later, her hair was tied back, her shirt was drenched with water, and she smelled like Italian dressing.

"I'm so sorry. Here's your lunch. I don't know if you like vodka, but I bought you these," I said, handing her three tiny plastic bottles. She took them and silently stuck them in the seat-back pocket. "If there's anything I can do," I begged.

The pilot came on the loudspeaker. "For those of you sitting on the right side of the plane, you can see a breathtaking view of Lake Michigan, the third largest of the five Great Lakes. The name is derived from the Algonquin word 'michigami,' or 'misschiganin,' meaning 'big lake.' And for those of you on the left side, you have a clear shot of the people on the right side of the plane who can see Lake Michigan." I smiled at my garden salad, hoping that she and I could share this moment of good humor together. Nothing.

Then the plane was hit by lightning. The way I retell the story to friends is that it was a near-death experience. It was as if a bomb went off: The plane flipped upside down, and we dove ten thousand feet. Then, by the sheer grace of God, the pilot recovered the plane and safely escorted us to Seattle with one remaining engine. The way it really happened was a blinding flash of light darted through the aisle like a ghost. It was over in an instant. Like thunder, the passenger gasps lagged by two seconds. None of us was exactly sure what had happened. A minute passed before the pilot came on the loudspeaker.

"Okay"—he paused—"so we were just hit by lightning. That's what happens when you put a huge metal object between rain clouds. Everything seems to be in order," he said, as if looking himself over for lint balls. "This is not so uncommon an occurrence, actually. Most of the time you won't even notice that anything happened—the plane is designed to conduct electricity. The lightning hits the tip of the plane and travels along the outside of the aircraft and off into the air. For us up in the cockpit, it's like God took an impromptu snapshot. The flight attendants tell me you also got the rare opportunity to see it move through one of the aisles. How nice."

A few of the passengers laughed uneasily. I turned to my seatmate, who was now sucking on one of the plastic vodka bottles I'd given her. She said nothing. We nearly died together, yet she wasn't willing to let bygones be bygones.

The murmurs in the fuselage indicated that everyone was still feeling pretty shaken up. The pilot's tone—"nothing to see here"—didn't
instill much confidence. I assumed he was now inspecting the plane
to reconfirm that it was intact. Perhaps the lightning had destroyed
some of the electrical equipment, one of the engines, or the luggage
unit. Maybe my rolling bag was now drifting toward Lake Michigan.
Damn that Roger and his callous definition of "personal items."

Then, as I feared, the pilot spoke again. "Ladies and gentlemen," he
said somberly. My stomach dropped. Then, in an upbeat tone:
"Shortly, we will be serving a complimentary round of beverages in the
main cabin. Soft drinks, coffee, and tea are available at no charge.
Alcoholic beverages can be purchased. Please have exact change.
Thank you muchly." In unison, we let out a sigh of relief.

I soon fell asleep. Suddenly, someone in the bathroom on the other
side of the wall flushed the toilet. Startled by the sound of air being
sucked out of the plane, and thinking that I'd inadvertently leaned on
the emergency-exit door handle, I leaped from my seat, knocking over
my dime-novel-reading, salad-dressing-smelling neighbor's glass of
water.

"I apologize," I said desperately. Water dripped down her pant leg. I
offered her the paper napkin from underneath my glass. "I know this
sounds crazy, but I was half asleep, and I thought that somehow I'd
flipped the latch on the emergency-exit door." At this point she
couldn't even look at me. "Look, I'm really sorry."

When we landed in Seattle, I apologized again, then again as we
took the same connecting flight to Walla Walla, and once more as we
waited at the luggage carousel. By the time we bumped into each
other at the Avis counter, I'd given up. She got her car and gave me a
dismissive wave as she walked away. I stepped up to the counter.

"Where ya headed?" the Avis representative asked me.

"Helix, Oregon."

"All you have to do is follow that woman down Highway 335. She's
also headed to Helix. And by the way, it's said Or-uh-gun, not Ore-
gone. Think of it this way: Do you want to buy a rifle *or-a-gun*, get it?
Or-a-gun?"

CHAPTER 38

THERE'S NOTHING TO do in Helix, Oregon, on a Sunday. The entire city is built around Bullock. The woman at the Ramada front desk encouraged me to go to the corner deli. "They have real New York bagels," she said cheerfully. I was skeptical, but I found the bagel shop and, chewing on my tasteless bagel, strolled next door into the Back Store, devoted to devices meant to temporarily alleviate back pain. I scanned the neck pillows, lumbar supports, seat cushions, shoe inserts, and Goosebumps massage balls. Huddled in the corner were the only three customers. They were gathered around the Holy Grail of back therapy. There, at the focal point of three spotlights, was The Chair.

A man was fully reclined in the massage chair, eyes shut, letting out a vibrating "feels so good" moan as his wife and son anxiously looked on. "Just leave me here. You can pick me up after you finish food shopping," he said as his voice oscillated in time with the mechanical rollers tapping the center of his back.

I hovered near The Chair, perusing the ergonomically designed business chairs, desks, mattresses, and beds.

"I'm Sally," the salesclerk said to me. Sally was an attractive, busty blonde in her mid-twenties. "Those are the Baileys," she whispered, pointing to the woman and boy pulling at the man lounging in the chair. He was deadweight. "They're regulars. Do you want to try it?"

"Oh, no rush," I lied. "Is that the Sharper Image chair?"

"Actually, it's the new version of the very same chair that they carry—it's called the EMS Get-A-Way massage chair. You just *have* to try it." She leaned against an inversion table. "It's got dual massage rollers, nine different functions, and three programmed settings. It's the ultimate in relaxation. Imagine getting a massage whenever you want one."

Sally gave the Baileys a sweet but firm "Hi guys," and with that, they parted. I took a seat in the cockpit.

"I gotta watch this," Mr. Bailey said to his wife. "The first time in the EMS. I envy you, kid." The truth was that I'd tried the Sharper Image chair in New York and briefly considered buying it, but the cost was astronomical.

Sally bent down. Brushing up against me, with her face two inches from mine, she gave me a tender "hello." In one jerking motion, she used her left hand to recline me backward, and the right hand to prop my feet up. I was now lying parallel to the ground.

"Let's start with some full-range kneading," she said as she took hold of the programmable keyboard. Two rolling balls began to travel down the length of my back in small circular motions. It hurt. It was neither a good nor a bad hurt; all I could say was it was an artificial hurt. It didn't feel anything like a person massaging my back. "Now the feet," she said, and with that, my calves began vibrating. I instantly had to pee.

"We have a special going on today. The machine comes with a separate complimentary foot massager. The EMS Get-A-Way massage chair does kneading, tapping"—she hit a different key on the pad—"and rolling." The two mechanical balls rolling up and down my back felt good. "Then there's pointing." The rollers stopped at the small of my back and began rotating counterclockwise. "You can get the EMS chair in black or taupe leatherlike material."

"How much?" I asked curiously.

"Three nine-hundred-dollar payments. But we won't charge for tax or delivery."

"I live in Manhattan."

"Lemme ask my manager." Mr. Bailey was biding his time in the ergonomically sound business-furniture section. He yelled over to Sally, "If that fella buys this chair, he's not going to buy *this* chair. *This* chair will stay in the store, right, Sally Ann?"

"I wouldn't think of taking your chair," I said to him as the two rollers pounded my L4 and L5 vertebrae.

Aside from my education, $2,700 was more money than I'd ever spent on anything for myself—particularly a luxury item. In fact, the most expensive used car I'd ever driven cost no more than $2,500. Lately, I'd been disposing my income at breakneck speed. I'd quickly gotten comfortable with my comfortable salary. That is, until I received my first credit-card bill, followed closely by my first paycheck. After taxes, insurance, and my 401(k) contribution, it sure didn't feel like a six-figure salary. For now I'd pay the minimum fee and continue to spend.

It started with expensive ties. In law school I'd wince at a forty-dollar price tag. But over the last week I'd bought five hundred-dollar ties from Barney's. Another impulse purchase was a $250 solid brass, nickel-plated shaving kit, complete with a shaving brush composed of pure badger hair. Then I moved on to five-, six-, and seven-hundred-dollar suits to replace the ones stolen from my car. I was reminded of my mother's theory: Most of our purchases are about reinventing ourselves. The way I figured it, I was slowly satisfying certain lifelong needs. I'd locked up my shaving, tie, and suit needs, and here was an opportunity to satisfy massage requirements for the rest of my life, or for at least the life of those mechanical rolling balls. The Chair would be an investment, I reasoned. Over time the cash I'd save from getting massages—and the emotional baggage saved from owing girlfriends back massages—would easily pay for The Chair.

Sally returned too quickly to have consulted with anyone and reported that if I bought The Chair *right now,* they would waive the delivery costs to New York.

"I have four flights of steps," I told her.

"Not a problem," she snapped.

"Okay, I'll take it," I said, surprising myself.

Then buyer's remorse began to set in. I was embarrassed by how much I was spending on myself. I wouldn't dare tell anyone how much I'd spent, especially my parents. They hadn't raised me to spend money so recklessly.

I'd adhered to the Oracle's general rule on money and salaries: "Don't tell people how much money you earn. If you earn more than they do, they feel jealous. If you earn less, they feel smug. It doesn't help either of you."

"What if they ask?"

"You don't have to say 'Mind your own business.' It's so simple: All you have to do is make the decision, then say, 'I'm sorry, I've made a decision not to talk about my finances.' If you mean it, they won't ask again. If they do, repeat your answer. There's no need to be rude about it, even if they're rude enough to pry." Over time I'd applied this rule to all things money-related. What I earned and how much I spent were no one's business. Not even my parents, God, they'd kill me if they knew how much I'd spent on this ridiculous chair.

I gave Sally my credit card and signed the proper paperwork. "You'll have it in eight to ten weeks," Sally reported.

"I like a guy who can plop down three grand before noon on Sunday," Mr. Bailey said to Sally. Ten minutes later I walked out of the store waving my credit-card receipt good-bye. The Baileys sent me off like a war hero. Then they resumed their original positions.

CHAPTER 39

FOR ALL INTENTS and purposes, I was an attorney in Helix, Oregon. Even though I didn't possess a license to practice, I wore a suit, and I said and did lawyerly things. I arrived at Bullock's offices, ready for my first meeting with Roddy Helm, one of the pioneers of ink-jet technology. Roddy had rock-star status at Bullock. Employees lined up to meet Roddy and hear him lecture about the early advances in ink-jet technology. Aaron Reinstein said I was lucky to get a one-on-one hour with him.

Roddy met me at reception with a briefcase tucked under his arm. He was a tall, lanky black man with an impressive shaved head. Between his big goggle glasses and his unkempt beard and mustache, it was tough to get a sense of how old he was. My guess, mid-forties. He gave me a firm handshake and said, "Let's go into one of the conference rooms where we can talk and use a whiteboard."

From the outside, I could tell Bullock's facilities were immense. The building housed manufacturing plants, research and develop-

ment, and business offices. I was swiftly escorted into a nearby conference room.

"Let me start off by saying it was a gamble," Roddy said before I
could even sit down. He'd switched on his lecture-hall voice. "And it
was Bullock's foresight and the right managers at the right time that
allowed us to experiment with the technology, to invest billions of dollars in research and development, and to spend years devising and perfecting a new method of communication." I was already enamored.

"The moment of conception hit us in 1978. One of the engineers
was a big coffee drinker, so he always kept a coffeemaker brewing on
his desk. There he is, just staring at his percolator one morning, and it
hits him: Why can't we do that with a printer? A coffee percolator
heats the water, forming bubbles of steam that push the water up a
tube and over coffee grounds. He theorized that the same principle
could be applied to ink. We called it drop-on-demand ink-jet technology because, unlike dot-matrix printers that stamped dots onto paper
using a ribbon, or laser printers that roll charged particles onto paper
line by line, an ink-jet printer would fire, or *jet,* ink onto paper. It was
an extraordinary concept. It took us six years and millions to bring our
first cartridge to market."

Ink-jet cartridges and table-tennis paddles. Patent law was the perfect crossover between science and art. Much like engineering, the
law could be very impersonal. But stories like Bullock's attracted me
to it.

Roddy began walking around the room. "Eventually, we were able to
boil ink and fire it through a series of holes that were smaller than the
diameter of a human hair, and get it onto paper in a coherent form to
generate letters and graphics. The end result was a printing method
faster than dot-matrix, less expensive than laser, and perfect for printing color."

Roddy walked over to the whiteboard. "The heart of the technology
is in the cartridge, not the printer. All the printer does is transport the
magic cartridge back and forth across the page." He diagrammed the
chambers of a cartridge. "It's the cartridge that actually generates letters and graphics.

"The first ones were a joke—they were terribly slow, large and clunky, expensive, and exhibited poor print quality. But we've come a long way in twenty years. Our cartridges are ten times as fast as our first ones and can hold one hundred times as much ink. Bullock's new cartridges are truly breathtaking." He pulled out of his briefcase a small ink-jet cartridge, no larger than a bar of soap, and held it close to his face. "This 'pen' can generate inexpensive photograph-quality color pictures in seconds." I couldn't tell whether he was staring at the cartridge or out the window. It was raining. It hadn't stopped raining since I'd arrived in Helix.

I liked Roddy. We had a lot in common. We were both inventors. It's true, he'd figured out how to fire hundreds of thousands of droplets of ink through pinholes to generate letters and pictures, and I'd fastened two table-tennis paddles together with a few toy blocks. But we both could appreciate a novel, highly marketable idea when we saw one. I could use a guy like Roddy to help launch my double-sided paddle.

"How many ink-jet cartridges do you manufacture?" I asked.

"This plant produces tens of millions every year. Bullock manufactures thousands of different products, but this is our cash cow."

"So you give away the printers and sell the cartridges," I said.

"Exactly. It's the classic razor-blade business model. All the technology is contained in the cartridge. That *is* what consumers are paying for." He handed me the cartridge. "Look at it. It exhibits the elegance of what we call the disposable unit, which is hundreds of tiny components pulled together in a single self-contained system that doesn't leak. The disposable unit snaps directly into your printer. When the ink supply is gone, you just throw it away and buy a new one."

Roddy sat down next to me. "There are basically three parts to the cartridge: the ink, the front end, and the back end. Bullock's patented chemical compositions are very specific. It's taken us years, but our inks are formulated so they don't smear, streak with water, fade with sunlight, bleed with other colors, or degrade on any of more than two hundred different types of paper found worldwide. The chemical composition of the inks is not too water-based, so they don't evaporate while in storage. They're not too acidic, so they don't corrode the metal parts of the cartridge or burn through the plastic container. The formulations are perfect." He stood up and walked over to the white-board. "And they're nontoxic. We made sure that Fido or three-year-old Johnny could even take a few sucks on a Bullock cartridge without undergoing trauma.

"But here's what I'm really proud of: the front end, or what's commonly referred to as the 'printhead,' of the cartridge. That's where it all happens. This is the part of the cartridge where the ink is transformed from lumps to letters."

Roddy drew a dotted line. "Each of these small lines is an electrical resistor," he said. "As ink flows across these resistors, we apply a jolt of electricity, and the resistors instantly boil the ink. Then the ink is vaporized and propelled, or 'jetted,' out tiny holes onto paper."

"The coffee percolator," I said.

"Exactly! In less than a second, that cartridge can spray minuscule dots with breathtaking precision. In that split second, the electrical resistors heat up to over one *million* degrees Celsius. The resistors can get hotter than the surface of the sun. Perfecting that technology took us over a decade.

"Bam, bam, bam," Roddy said, slapping the table in rhythm. "We keep zapping those resistors with jolts of electricity. Eventually, some of those resistors burn out. As a result, certain letters won't form correctly. Overall, the print quality will begin to suffer. Bullock guarantees the resistors will provide the same print quality for the life of the ink supply and no longer."

I studied the cartridge. "Okay. So that's the ink and the front end, which leaves the back end. I assume the back end holds the ink and controls the flow of the ink to the resistors."

"Yep. The ink-containment system, or the back end, has to be calibrated perfectly." He drew an arrow pointing toward the top of the cartridge. "The entire ink supply sits on top of the front end, and we needed a way to deliver the ink to the front end at the right time. We also had to prevent gravity from pulling all the ink out of the cartridge and pouring into the guts of the printer."

"If that happens, I guess the printer is toast," I said.

"Yeah, that's what we call catastrophic failure. The ultimate solution didn't come easily. Again, it took years. We tried everything. We settled on what's known as a constant slight negative pressure, or miniature vacuum. In other words, we've adjusted the pressure inside the disposable unit to be slightly lower than outside the cartridge. This allows a small amount of ink, upon demand, to be pushed out and over the resistors at a steady pace."

"It's truly amazing," I said, hypnotized. "Elegant."

"It really is. We had to make sure that the pressure never got below a certain level. If that happened, it could create a vacuum, and the pen would never deliver ink. That's what we call depriming. There's nothing more frustrating to a consumer than throwing out a full or half-full cartridge just because the doggone ink's stuck.

"The negative vacuum has to be perfect. These cartridges get shipped all over the world. They undergo a wide range of pressures, depending on altitudes and temperatures. We had to do all kinds of tests to ensure, for example, that when an airplane landed in Houston, all the cartridges in the cargo container didn't deprime or undergo catastrophic failure. It took us years to legitimize ink-jet technology. The ink, the front end, and the back end work beautifully together."

"I need to see more on this disposable unit," I told Roddy. "I was told you've been collecting information that I can read about its early development."

"Yes, yes, yes. We've *all* been collecting documents—the whole company. Now I'll bring you to our designated reading room." Roddy escorted me through acres and acres of cubicles. "Everyone has a cube here," he said. "It's all part of our open culture. Engineers, attorneys, secretaries, executives, we all have cubicles. It's intended to help break down the barriers." He paused, realizing that he wasn't talking to anyone. I was crouching on the ground. "Are you all right?"

"Oh, just fine," I said. "Just tying my shoe." At that very moment my

208 ALEX WELLEN

salad-dressing queen from the New York flight walked by. She didn't appear to see me.

It was clear Roddy would play a major role in the litigation. Before I left for the trip, Aaron Reinstein had predicted Roddy would be one of our first depositions. It was proving to be an exciting case. The Rufus matter struck me as about as sexy as it got when it came to high-tech intellectual property and antitrust litigation.

I was lucky to be on the case.

CHAPTER 40

WAS UNLUCKY TO be on the case.

I tried to hide my shock as I thanked Roddy and said good-bye; we would meet again in a couple of hours. The "reading room" was more like a hangar. It resembled something out of the final scene in *Raiders of the Lost Ark,* when the camera pulled back to reveal a gigantic warehouse stockpiled with boxes. The Ark of the Covenant was somewhere in this room. I called Aaron Reinstein.

"Aaron," I said, a bit shaken. "I'm going to need some support out here."

"Okay," he said calmly.

"Apparently, we've asked more than a thousand Bullock employees to submit documents potentially relevant to this case. I'm standing in a warehouse with at least five hundred boxes."

"Yeah, and that's only one location. We have Bullock doing the same thing at its facilities all over the world. We'll strategize about how to deal with these documents when you get home. How did it go with Roddy?"

"Excellent. You were right. He can really tell the Bullock story. It seems the disposable unit *is* the Bullock story."

"That's one of the fundamental questions in this lawsuit—does an ink-jet cartridge have a fixed life?"

"It's a single-use cartridge," I said confidently. "They're easy to use and reliable. Bullock guarantees the print quality for the life of the cartridge, no more and no less. When you're done with the pen, you throw it away."

"That's fine, but should other companies be allowed to modify them? That's the question. Rufus retaliated with an antitrust lawsuit. They say Bullock has committed every antitrust violation under the sun, that we tried to illegally corner the ink-supply market. Rufus doesn't think that a cartridge needs to be an all-in-one deal. Think of it like an automobile. Rufus says, hey, you don't throw away the car when the gas tank is empty, do you?"

I thought about the analogy. "I dunno. I don't think of the cartridge like the gas tank. Isn't the cartridge more like the engine? You'd replace the engine, wouldn't you?"

"Nice," he said. "Now you're thinking. Keep an eye out for early documents that speak to the disposable unit."

I scanned the brightly lit room overflowing with boxes. "Yeah, that's going to be like finding a straw in a haystack."

"Needle," Aaron said.

"I'll get a handle on things here, and I'll see you back in the office on Friday."

I pulled up a chair and a box and began doing what I would likely do for the indefinite future—document review.

The job was exactly what it sounded like: one of the most common yet tearfully boring tasks in litigation. This was the reality of being not only a first-year associate but the *only* first-year associate on the case. My job was to review documents and determine whether Rufus was entitled to see them as part of this lawsuit. It was all part of the specific phase of the lawsuit called "discovery." If Rufus *was* entitled to discover certain documents, it was my responsibility to designate each document with a certain level of confidentiality, then provide, or produce, it to them.

The general rule was, the more confidential the Bullock document, the fewer Rufus people were entitled to see it. The exact rules of engagement were contained in the protective order, or PO. The PO was my friend. The PO would set me free.

The ten-page PO was agreed upon by Bullock and Rufus and signed by the court-appointed judge. It described exactly what both parties were looking for and how to handle the information. The protective order was intended to do just that—to protect Bullock and Rufus from misusing sometimes highly confidential information just because they were suing each other. Disclosing trade secrets and market plans to your competitor was a harsh reality of litigation. In fact, it was so harsh that sometimes parties refrained from suing simply because the risk that the competitor might misuse the information was too high.

The Rufus PO described four standard categories of documents: public, confidential, highly confidential, and attorney-client privileged. I'd become intimate with these categories during my summer internship with Nickel. Besides the occasional interesting project, I'd spent most of that summer reviewing and designating documents.

Public documents were just that. The most proprietary documents, like marketing plans, were designated highly confidential. Data and meeting minutes, for example, were considered simply confidential. The PO made the process sound simple, but unfortunately many of the documents didn't naturally fall into these neat categories. Most of the time it was a judgment call. A judgment call reserved for someone like me—above paralegal status and below a license to practice.

My first box was filled with lab notebooks from the mid-nineties. The engineer writing the entries was apparently experimenting with a new method of delivering ink to the resistors. I designated all the composition notebooks highly confidential. Nothing inside them mentioned the disposable unit. I'd have to go much further back to find that information.

After the notebooks, I moved on to another box filled with e-mail printouts. E-mail was always the most interesting, revealing, and honest of documents. It contained excited utterances. People spoke the truth when they were angry and rushed. Reading this particular engineer's private exchanges, I realized that not in his wildest dreams had he ever figured a lawyer would be reading his e-mail as part of a major lawsuit. Maybe he'd even be unlucky enough to have his e-mail become an exhibit at trial.

It was clear that I was going to review hundreds of thousands of documents. It was also clear that I was going to make some mistakes. Eventually, I'd miss important documents, produce stuff that was irrelevant, and mistakenly designate a confidential document as highly confidential, or a public document as confidential. The good news was that thanks to the PO, my mistakes were forgivable. As long as I discovered the error soon after making it, I could "cure" it: I could kindly ask Rufus to return the document so I could redesignate it properly. This was all very comforting.

There was one mistake, however, that would not be so simple to cure—one mistake that Aaron Reinstein warned me could be catastrophic. I had to make absolutely sure that I did *not* give Rufus "privileged" Bullock information. According to the PO, documents containing privileged information were the only documents both parties were specifically allowed to withhold from one another—thus the "privilege."

There were two types of privileged information: The first was work product. In simple terms, Rufus was not entitled to know our litigation strategies—these documents were considered the product of our legal work and therefore private. Fine. Those documents would be easy to spot.

The more common form of privileged information was attorney-client. Rufus was not entitled to look at a communication in which a Bullock employee requested legal advice or a Bullock attorney rendered it. Here was the perfect bar-exam hypothetical. An e-mail says, "Hi, Bernie-the-attorney. Just wanted to know: Can we design our cartridges so they blow up after the ink supply is finished, or will we get sued?" Now, *that* would be considered an attorney-client-privileged communication. This type of document was *not* something Rufus was entitled to ever see. The law protected attorney-client communications in an effort to encourage attorneys and clients to speak candidly with each other. And boy, did they. Oh, the things that people said to one another, relying heavily on that attorney-client privilege.

Pinpointing, extracting, withholding, or redacting Bullock attorney-client-privileged communications was going to be a challenge. The only way someone could identify attorney-client-privileged communications was to know who Bullock's attorneys were. Whoever reviewed all these documents—me—would need to compile and be familiar with the name of every single attorney who had worked for Bullock over the last twenty years. There would be hundreds. Only then could I start identifying the precious attorney-client-privileged documents.

That handy-dandy PO was also designed to save the day when it came to inadvertently producing privileged information. The PO was based on ethics, trust, and good faith, and if I gave Rufus a privileged document by mistake, I was required to make a formal written request for it back. But even if Rufus abided by the PO and returned all copies of the privileged information, it would probably be too difficult for them to pretend that it didn't happen. By then, the cat was out of the bag. They would know what they had seen and would likely try to get the same information through a legitimate channel.

Here again, I was going to make a mistake. I was bound to produce *something* privileged. It was statistically impossible for a new attorney unfamiliar with a case to review hundreds of thousands of pages without eventually producing something privileged. It was just a question of degree. Would I hand off something innocuous or give Rufus a smoking gun, if there even was a smoking gun? The prospect terrified me.

On the fifteenth box, my cell phone interrupted the deafening silence. It was my mother.

The Oracle never called me on my cell phone. She didn't like the quality of the connection and said people on cell phones always sounded distracted. It was the middle of the day. Perhaps she'd failed to figure in the three-hour time change.

"I'm sorry to bother you at work," she said.

"No, that's okay. What's up?"

"Well, you know that Grandma Mary has been sick lately. We've been visiting her, and so have Aunt Greta and Uncle Stephen. It's been a horror. She's just been getting worse and worse. Now she's in the hospital."

"Oh, Mom, I'm so sorry. Did they say what's wrong?"

"They did some tests. It's not good. They determined that it's lymph cancer."

My eyes began welling up with tears. "Can I help? What can I do?"

"I know, sweetheart. There's nothing you can do right now, but talking to you helps. Sometimes I just have to hear your voice. Call me later when you're off from work, okay?"

We said good-bye, and in my fortress of boxes, I quietly cried.

CHAPTER 41

GRANDMA MARY'S CONDITION worsened. We all visited her at the hospital—me, my parents with Mike, my aunt, uncle, and cousins. Sometimes we met, other times we alternated visits. Sometimes Grandma was undergoing treatment, other times she was in intensive care.

Although she was rarely awake and never alert, I took the subway to Brooklyn and visited her every couple of days. I sat with her, told her about the Bullock story, and what it was like to be an attorney in New York. She died on a Thursday at one-thirty P.M. Doctors resuscitated her five minutes later. In those precious five minutes, her heart stopped, she stopped breathing, and oxygen was unable to get to her brain.

In a coma, with no brain activity, living only on life support, Grandma Mary was truly gone. There was no hope that she would ever recover. The doctors and hospital were resigned to the fact that this was how it was going to be. The family was in shock. It couldn't be that this vital woman would remain totally inert. Every treatment the hospital tried had failed, and to see her attached to life support in a state of isolation was a cruelty we couldn't endure. The question became, what do we do now? Grandma had loved life and loved us. We all knew she would never choose to continue this way. Although we suffered from losing her, we prepared ourselves to let her go.

My father pulled me aside in the hospital. "So there's a problem," he said, shaking his head. "We can't disconnect the life support. Mary didn't designate a health-care proxy. Apparently, in New York, you can appoint an HCP to make medical decisions for you in the event that you're unable to make them yourself. She could have done that at any point while here in the hospital, but she didn't. No one told us."

I panicked. I'd just finished a crash course in wills, trusts, and estates, and the term "HCP" meant nothing to me. What good was taking the bar and being an attorney—a New York attorney—if I couldn't understand the simplest task in the most practical situation?

"Dad, didn't she have a living will?" That was the equivalent of an HCP but was created well in advance of such dire circumstances.

"No. I don't think many people from her generation did. In fact, your mother and I just finished making our living wills."

The comment threw me. This was the very first time my father had verbalized that he and my mother would die.

"In our living wills, we've instructed the hospital not to resuscitate either of us if there's no brain activity. If you don't put that in, the doctors are obligated to do everything in their power to save you. We're stuck. The hospital rules state that the life-support system must continue unless she has an HCP or a living will."

"Dad, I'll look into this."

"It will all be okay," the Optimist said reassuringly. I so much wanted to believe him.

I spent Monday pretending to work on the Bullock case but instead researching New York living wills and health-care proxies. I learned that without either, the only option was to make a written appeal, much like a legal brief, to the hospital board. We would need to outline the reasons why Grandma Mary would have disconnected life support if she could have made the decision herself. I drafted a four-page memo that lovingly described how she lived life to the fullest, how she loved to go dancing, to shop, and to travel. I documented conversations in which she told us of her disdain for doctors and hospitals. Hospitals were for the dying, she'd always said.

I asked my family to write letters to fold in to the appeal. "The letters must be specific," I instructed them. "They must prove as accurately as possible Grandma's words and wishes about life support or being in an irreversible coma." My parents, aunt, uncle, cousins, and Mike wrote letters of appeal, and I determined who on the medical board should receive these pleas. In what was my first legitimate role as pseudo-attorney, I requested the court—in this case, the hospital— to let my grandmother die.

The hospital decision came two days after I filed the paperwork. Our family gathered at the hospital to say personal good-byes, to hold on to each other, to cry together, but mostly to cherish and adore the person we loved so much.

I'd won my first case. It was heartbreaking.

CHAPTER 42

N AN OFFICE the size of a prison cell, there was no privacy. Sitting an arm's length from Hayley, I knew all of her personal business, and she knew mine. If she was arranging a gynecologist visit or a date on the phone, I knew where to be and when to show up. While there were plenty of times we wished for more personal space, I was thankful to have her around during the heartwrenching Grandma Mary saga. Hayley was there from the appeal to the funeral to the mourning. The sadness that overcame me after losing Mary was all-consuming, but Hayley made each day a little easier than the last.

Lately she'd been programming my social life. Hayley's leftovers were my lifelines. Her family was tapped in to New York's best restaurants, exclusive parties, and premier social activities. Sometimes I went with Hayley to a movie premiere or restaurant opening; other times she offered them up for me plus one. One time Gwen even took a train in from Newark and accompanied me to the opera. Over the summer Gwen and I had kept the relationship exclusive. But since the bar exam and Europe, we'd hardly seen one another and spoke once every few weeks. The relationship was finished. We now lived separate lives, in separate cities, and I assumed that she was dating other people. I was.

"I can't decide whether this is too cool for you," Hayley said, getting off the phone.

I put the four volumes of case law down on my desk. "What is it this time? Tickets to the symphony? The opera? Extra orchestra seats to a Broadway show? What? Come on. I've worked my way up. You've even inspired me to buy some new black clothes."

"Okay, fine. Do you want to be a seat filler? I have two tickets."

"Yes," I responded without hesitation. I knew exactly what she was asking. A month ago it was the Emmys, then it was the ESPN Awards, or ESPYs, and last week it was the MTV Awards. She'd been a seat filler for all of them. I was so envious. "Okay, hit me. What is it this time?" I braced for the answer.

"Tonight is the VH1 Fashion Awards," she said, pulling up the website. "Why? 'Because music and fashion have had an immense influence on each other.'"

"Fashion awards? Come on. Give me a break."

"Alex"—she paused—"you're always asking me where all the models go. Well, the models go to *fashion* shows. And supermodels go to fashion shows where they can meet *rock stars*. Let's see." She scrolled through the page. "Prince, the Red Hot Chili Peppers, and the Pretenders are all performing."

"If the people at VH1 need someone to work the fashion awards, I'm sure I can accommodate them."

"Did you catch that?" she asked. "That was a big eye roll. Would you like me to do it again for your benefit? Call up your Jersey girl. You'll get huge points." Hayley didn't know Gwen by name. Besides Gwen, I'd had maybe three or four other dates since arriving in New York, and Hayley was my consigliere. She determined when I should call a woman back, where I should take her for dinner, and whether I should wear my round- or square-toed black shoes. The common New Yorker might be under the impression that I'd integrated into the lifestyle effortlessly, but Hayley knew better.

"But if I take a date to the *fashion* show, how am I supposed to ogle? Can I bring a guy friend?"

"Fine, but you may not get the right models to notice you."

"You're right. This *is* a dilemma."

Two hours later, I was waiting for David Markey outside the Armory, on Twenty-sixth and Lexington, sporting my favorite black clothes and my square-toed black shoes. I chose David because I was realistic about my inability to take a date to the fashion awards without gawking at the supermodels. Plus, together we seemed to be gaining some momentum in the New York social scene.

Just last weekend we'd partied with Mark Wahlberg. Sort of. We didn't exactly *party* with Mark Wahlberg. David's high school friend managed Wahlberg's band. They were in town bar-hopping, so we tagged along.

Actually, the Mark Wahlberg night was pretty depressing. We spent most of the night either squished in the back of his Range Rover as he yelled obscenities out the window, or walking through the streets of New York as he broke beer bottles and peed in alleyways.

When we arrived at a new bar, it was always the same protocol. Someone in his entourage would run inside, identify the gatekeeper, and inform him or her that Mr. Wahlberg and his friends were available to drink, for free, if the bar was willing to give Wahlberg star treatment. Five minutes later, we were escorted into the VIP section, where David and I would watch dozens of drop-dead-gorgeous women line up to meet Wahlberg. At the time he was doing everything in his power to shake his image as a Calvin Klein model and teen idol nicknamed Marky Mark. His band, Marky Mark and the Funky Bunch, was a one-hit wonder, but then came his lead role in *Boogie Nights* and suddenly he was a mega movie star. All night he gave the Funky Bunch the impression that they were cramping his style, and the Funky Bunch gave David and me the impression that we were cramping theirs.

Whatever. Now, on a date or in social circles, either of us could say: "What do *I* do in my spare time? Oh, not much. Let's see. Last weekend I hung with Mark Wahlberg. To meet him he's actually quite immature. Then this week there were the VH1 Fashion Awards . . ."

David Markey and I hoped we'd eventually hook in to the secret New York social society. Then we'd attend all the elite soirees and coveted after-parties. An invitation to the VH1 Fashion Awards was looking like a watershed event.

For a VH1 Fashion Awards seat filler, there were no guarantees. The event was to be televised live, and the massive space in the Armory had to give the appearance that it was full. If a rock star didn't show up or a supermodel decided to leave early to purge, it was a seat filler's responsibility to fill that empty seat. The way Hayley explained it to me was—the seat fillers waited on the sidelines like a ball boy at a tennis match. As needed, we'd sprint to any of the newly open seats in the first fifty or so rows—the ones most commonly caught in the show's sweeping television shots. If and when the important person returned, you were sent to the back of the seat-filler line, or directed to another open seat by the sideline coach.

"Sorry I'm late. I came straight from work." David was wearing a conservative blue suit and a white button-down shirt with the collar loosened. He had a mouthful of Tums. On the outside he was the calm, cool, collected assistant district attorney, but he'd told me that on the inside, his stomach was doing acid flip-flops. He'd been assigned to the Homicide Investigations Bureau, the most coveted assignment. All day long David saw dead people. He could be paged at any time. Then he'd jump into his police-confiscated Range Rover, drive to the crime scene, and determine whether it was murder or suicide. It wasn't a suicide unless David said it was. He often told me about the crime scenes. Each death seemed more gruesome than the next.

"I just came from Hell's Kitchen," he said. "You should have seen this guy. He was *really* dead."

"I don't even want to know," I said. "Are you on pager tonight?"

"I was able to switch," he said. "I stopped at Saks on the way here. These two ties cost me a year's salary. I hate being poor."

"The blue one," I suggested, and he began tying it around his neck.

"RuPaul's boyfriend just invited us to a party," I said as we walked into the side entrance of the Armory. Blue signs directed us to the seat-filler sign-in table.

"There are so many things wrong with that sentence," he said, adjusting the knot in his tie. "Look, that's *your* vibe, man."

"Yeah, well, I was waiting for you, and RuPaul's boyfriend—that's the name *he* used—handed me this card and said come to the after-party."

"That doesn't count. In fact, that invitation is so devastating that it has the effect of canceling any credit we got for hanging out with Mark Wahlberg." David was on to other topics. "See that?" he said, pointing with his chin to a six-foot-tall emaciated brunette. "Bring it."

"You mean Kate Moss–alike? Yeah, bring it," I said, making the corresponding hand motion. We nodded in agreement and frustration. It was destined to be a long night of bring-its. Either you brought it or you kept it. Either you waved it toward you with both hands or pushed it away with one. Either you desired a woman or you didn't. It was black or white. Every woman was a bring-it or a keep-it. Bring her to me or keep her to yourself.

And there were rules. It was simple courtesy to respond to another person's bring-it or keep-it with your own opinion. But the most important rule was, whoever saw the woman first and brought it, got dibs; she was off-limits to everyone else. It didn't matter if the woman didn't know you existed or rebuffed your advances. Take the Kate Moss–alike. Neither of us had a snowball's chance in hell with her, but David brought it, so I had to respect the call. The statute of limitations on a bring-it was two years.

Since law school, David and I talked to each other like this. Sometimes we didn't even need to speak. We'd see a woman that neither of us found attractive, look at each other, and then simultaneously hold out our right hands, low and to the ground, and mouth the words—"keep it." We were snobs. We could afford to be—the woman never knew. New York had the most beautiful women in the world walking its streets, yet David and I were compelled to brand nearly every one of them a keep-it. We'd routinely walk into parties together, scan the prospects, and share a handful of sly keep-its. Yet in that hundred-yard walk from the entrance of the Armory to the seat-filler line, he and I exchanged more than twenty bring-its. The women were breathtaking. Plus, everywhere you looked were celebrities.

"Margo," I shouted to a woman walking by. She suddenly stopped laughing. Her date became silent. "Hey, how's it going? What are you doing here?" I already regretted this conversation.

"Oh, hey," she said as if she'd forgotten my name. "You know, I'm here with Victoria's Secret." She didn't introduce her date. I didn't introduce David. "And you?"

"Oh, a friend passed along some passes," I said, realizing that I'd said "passed passes." Meanwhile, two attractive women walked up to David and confirmed that we were standing in the seat-filler line.

"Good. Well, it's good to bump into you, Alex." She'd remembered my name, but I hated that she'd used it in a sentence. "Have a nice time," she said, as if it were her event. Then she and silent Adonis walked toward their designated seats.

"Bring it," David said.

"Brought it," I said. "And you know what, you can keep it. I told you about her. Was that guy with her wearing earrings in both ears? Anyway, that's the girl I went on a date with, and she stared at me the whole time with this look like 'Entertain me, monkey boy.' "

"You're going to have to narrow the date down a little more."

"You remember Margo," I said. "She's the girl I met in my building the day all my stuff got stolen? I used to call her 'Lucky Girl.' She's a friend of Tony's, the guy who runs the hat store in my building. She was the girl I took to the Dave Matthews concert."

"Of course, Lucky Girl. You guys were going to take her car to the concert at Giants Stadium, but you had to take the bus because you shorted out the electrical system in her car when you tried to jump-start it."

"You'd think after graduating cum laude from engineering school that I'd know whether the positive goes to the positive or the positive goes to the negative. Those were the most expensive concert tickets I'd ever bought. She was *not* happy on the phone when she told me why the car wouldn't start. 'Hi, Alex, it's Margo. Guess we really got our wires crossed the other day,' she tells me."

"She must have been rehearsing that line before she called. It's too good."

"Maybe. But she was pretty quick. That's what I liked about her on the phone beforehand. 'I just received a five-hundred-dollar estimate to replace the damage you caused to my car's electrical system on Saturday,' she tells me. She took my check but never took my calls again.

"At least I bumped into her when I looked good," I said, glancing down at my clothes. "Somehow I always bump into people like her on my way back from the gym."

"She said she's here with Victoria's Secret? She's pretty, but she's no Victoria's Secret model."

"No. She *works* for Victoria's Secret. She always says it that way. I think she likes to leave it ambiguous. She's a copywriter for the catalog. She decides whether the description of the Miracle Bra includes underwire cups, removable push-ups, or adjustable straps."

"You're scaring me."

"Yes, that was the moment I realized that even Victoria's Secret, bras, and boobs can't rehabilitate a bad date."

"Dude, how lame is this? You could end up being *her* seat filler."

I shook my head. The two women eavesdropping behind us found the premonition entertaining. I smiled at the one wearing silver pants. She was very model-esqe—tall and thin, with dark eyes and long caramel hair. The lights dimmed, and the Artist Formerly Known as Prince, formerly known as the Artist, and now again known as Prince, opened the show. He was the perfect musician to open a fashion-awards show. Dressed in tight purple leather from head to toe, he couldn't have weighed over ninety pounds. David and I watched on the sidelines, along with about two hundred other seat fillers. Bill Murray was chatting it up with the attractive blond usher at the front of the line. He looked heavier in person.

A half hour into the program, some of the rock stars and models got antsy, and seat fillers began circulating into their seats. Once David and I got to the head of the line, a woman usher with a radio headset turned to David and said, "I think Sting is going to the bathroom—three C-B."

"What?"

"Row three, center section, seat B. Go, go, go," she said.

"I'll meet you back here at the end," I whispered loudly to David.

David sprinted for the seat. When he reached it, he gave me the thumbs-up. He was in one of the Oscar seats—close to the aisle so he could easily exit and receive his award. Despite his fancy tie, I didn't think David was going to get a fashion award for his Today's Man suit.

We watched Tyson Beckford win the Male Model of the Year award—it was a precious moment. He seemed genuinely grateful to get the statuette, but no tears. A few more models walked up and down the catwalk, followed by Sean Penn delivering ex-wife Madonna the Most Fashionable Artist award. After that, Tina Turner and Elton John took the stage to do a surprise rendition of "The Bitch Is Back."

"You see right there," headset woman said to me as she pointed to a beautiful woman with long dark hair, "right there in front of Carol Alt. That's k.d. lang's band. The drummer is MIA. Go to seven L-G." She flipped through her floor plan.

I quickly took the seat. On the floor was a large paper bag full of CDs, T-shirts, coupons, even a watch. I gave the k.d. lang band member sitting next to me a glance. He gave me an "it's yours" nod. And there I sat for the next two hours. It was a lucky break. Some seat fillers swapped seats a dozen times before they found a home. I got rock-star parking on my first assignment. When the concert was over, I circled my way back to our designated meeting area.

"Tell me you have *something*. Anything," David said to me as he approached.

"Nothing," I said. "Unless, of course, you want to go to RuPaul's boyfriend's—"

"Keep it." He stretched his hand out and paused. We occasionally used the "keep-it-bring-it" convention for matters unrelated to rating women. "We suck. Diner?"

"Diner," I conceded. "Lemme call Arjun. I promised him that if he couldn't come to the awards show, we'd at least fill him in on the details." I dialed his number and placed my palm over the phone. "When he gets here, embellish. Actually, lie."

CHAPTER 43

SOMETHING ABOUT THE lighting and the smell of grilled cheese and tomato makes all New York diners conducive to good conversation. David and I picked a familiar diner close to the Armory. We took our normal seats in our normal booth. Arjun met us inside.

"I don't need to look at the menu," I said to the waitress. "Waffles and ice cream, please."

"Bold move," David said. "I'm having breakfast. Scrambled eggs, and bacon, well done," he ordered. "I'm not kidding. Please make sure the bacon is well done, or I'll send it back."

"French toast," Arjun said, closing his menu. "Please tell me that between the two of you, you met at least *one* girl at this thing?"

"I had no 'in' with those women. I didn't have a scintilla of an 'in.' How about you?" I said to David.

"The same 'in' as I always do—homicide. D.A.'s office."

"Ah, the universal 'in.' Actually, I did have one—the fact that I sat with k.d. lang's band. I used that when I bumped into the seat-filler girl who was standing behind us when we got there. The one with the silver pants. She's good on paper—she's a fit model for Prada." I pulled out the piece of paper from my pocket. "Sophie."

"What's a fit model?" Arjun asked.

"Apparently, Prada designs clothes around Sophie's body. It's Sophie that women are cursing out when they try on clothes. She's from Melbourne, Australia. She says things like 'petrol,' 'bum,' 'lollies,' and 'mate.' "

"Bring it, bring it," David said, recalling what Sophie looked like. "She had nice norgs. That's Aussie for 'boobs.' "

"That's very helpful. Thank you. I'll make a point of mentioning that when we speak. What about you?" I said.

"I don't have norgs," he said.

"No, did you meet anyone?"

"I carded two people," he said. "But I'm not doing that anymore. The business card is pointless. I'm on record that if you card someone, you've guaranteed that she'll *never* call you. It's a lose-lose proposition. Clearly, she's not giving up her number. And even though she's asking for *your* number, she's never going to call. Whatever-whatever."

"Amen, brother. I'll see it when I believe it," I said.

There was a pause. David and Arjun looked at each other and smiled. "You must be biting at the chomp for that to happen," Arjun said.

"Or maybe you'll just burn that bridge when you get there," David added. I gave them a weak smile.

"By the way, David, I'm sure Alex told you how last Friday night ended," Arjun said.

"Yeah, with him throwing up every ten blocks along the West Side Highway," David said.

"That cabdriver was *trying* to make me sick," I said.

"I dunno. I think he was trying to get you home," Arjun said. "We get to the apartment, David, and I go to pay the cabdriver, and Alex is making love to the curb. He's just lying there on the ground in the garbage and pee. Then I have to carry him up those steps. Those god-damn steps."

"I don't know *what* happened," I said. "We were just mixing too much alcohol. What'd we do? Shots of Goldschläger, Jägermeister, Southern Comfort, and Sambuca." I rarely drank. "Oh, man. What were we thinking?"

"Yeah, you may have noticed that I disappeared at one point in the evening," David said. "I think the Goldschläger put me over the edge. I drank about half of it, then I realized I had to get out of there right away. Somehow I found a cab and told the driver where I lived. I could see him checking me out in the rearview mirror. He was definitely worried about whether I'd make the ten-block trip without getting sick. So I pay the man, and I go to leave the cab, and I throw up all over the interior of his door. Did anything happen with that girl you met, Arjun?"

"Nah, she turned," he said. "Then again, I probably would have turned my cheek, too, if she tried to kiss me. Did you notice that her teeth were sort of brown? I don't get it. She didn't smoke. It didn't look like coffee stains."

"Tetracycline," I said. "I saw it, too. I think if you take too much of it at an early age, it can stain your teeth. What a shame. Teeth are so important."

"Teeth and a laugh," David said. "She can't have a brutal laugh. That's why I broke it off with Mona. Besides her name, her laugh was unbearable. Every time she laughed, it sounded like she was coughing. I kept offering her water."

"I spent Saturday afternoon hydrating. That afternoon, I broke down and called Deena, that paralegal you met the day you came by the firm," I said to David.

"Hot," David said flatly. "Young, but hot." Deena was twenty-one. She worked full-time at the firm and went to CUNY's College of Criminal Justice at night.

"You're going to love this," Arjun said. He knew the story.

"This whole thing is your fault," I said to Arjun.

"Dude, I have no idea where they came from," he said.

"As you know, I've been trying to show some restraint when it comes to dating in the workplace. You don't shit where you eat. Right?" Arjun and David nodded in agreement. I'd finally gotten an expression right. "But I should have known. Once I took Deena's number it was only a matter of time before I called. Despite Friday night's lovely alcoholic festivities, she and I go out Saturday night for drinks. Later, she comes back to the loft. Drunk, and out of breath from the walk-up, she decides to stay over.

" 'Do you have something that I can wear?' she asks. 'Grab a pair of boxer shorts from that laundry basket,' I say. She rummages through the basket. 'Uh, Alex,' she says. 'Whose are these?' and she holds up this little purple thong. I'm just as surprised as she is about the mystery underwear. I'm not really dating anyone, not to mention sleeping

with someone, and it's been months since Gwen and I have been together. 'I dunno whose underwear that is,' I say. This doesn't comfort
her.

"So then it starts to get all emotional. 'What am I doing here?' she
says. 'We work together. You probably have a girlfriend.' At this point
I'm somewhere between consoling and annoyed. I say, 'Look, my
roommate and I share those machines. From time to time, friends and
neighbors use our machines. Really, Deena, I don't know where the
underwear came from.'

"She rolls her eyes and says, 'Then why are you acting so guilty? The
more defensive you are, the more it seems like you've done something
wrong.'

"I'm screwed. I can't even pull off innocent when I am," I finished.

"Yeah, I'd like to introduce you to some of the incompetent defense
attorneys I've been up against lately," David said as the food arrived.

THI_RD TRIMESTER

CHAPTER 44

"D O YOU HAVE an appointment?" John Madison's secretary, Sari, asked.

"No, I just started with the firm. My name is Alex Wellen—I'm working on the Rufus matter. I thought I'd introduce myself to Mr. Madison."

She was shocked by my request, a breach of protocol. "He's on the phone right now. When he's off, I'll inform him that you're here."

I peeked into his office. He was facing away from the door, staring out the window of his corner office with the phone cord stretched around his large brown leather chair. All I could see was the crown of his gray head.

Nickel was John Madison's firm (New York University Law, Tier 1). Officially, Madison was the number two guy in the firm, but everyone knew that he ran the place. Aside from the respect his position commanded, John Madison was a physically intimidating man. He was of medium height and had good posture, perfectly combed gray hair, dark, almost black eyes, and a strong chin. He was always impeccably dressed and perfectly manicured. He exuded power. Madison was a true showman. For the past ten years he'd been consistently ranked among the top fifty trial attorneys in the United States. And when it came to the intellectual property world, he was untouchable.

Once he was off the phone, Sari went into his office, said something, waved me in, and ran for her life. She must have been at least intrigued by my intention to shoot the breeze with the boss. I didn't hesitate. I walked right into his office, up to his desk, and extended my right hand. Madison stood up and gave me a strong handshake.

"Hello. I'm Alex Wellen. I'm a first year. I wanted to introduce myself and ask whether you have any assignments that I can help with."

To someone outside the big-law-firm culture, such a request might seem outlandish, but scrounging for work was commonplace during your first few weeks at a firm. It was all part of the integration process—some of us had too much work, while others had too little. When the workload was low, first-year associates were expected to make the rounds and ask if anyone needed help.

Sheer boredom with my Rufus document review responsibilities had prompted me to make the rounds. Three or four of my first-year comrades were also doing the circuit. Occasionally, we'd awkwardly bump into one another in the same office, bearing the same request. This door-to-door solicitation was a generally accepted law-firm practice.

Standing before Madison, I realized I was making a big mistake. There were at least four levels of management that I should've investigated before coming to him for work. Even after I'd exhausted those options, Madison was still probably off-limits. Generally, senior partners and first-year associates didn't associate. If anything, I should have waited until I had something to say to the man. I should have waited until he noticed me. But I walked in with this fantasy that he'd take an instant liking to me, and that would set into motion the perfect mentor-protégé relationship. Wrong.

"What's your discipline?" he asked. This was similar to how dogs greeted one another. He was asking the first question every intellectual property attorney asked a fellow practitioner.

"Industrial engineering," I said sheepishly. At that instant an arm reached into the room and stamped "Tier 2" on my forehead. Madison was a mechanical engineer.

Disappointed with my answer, he moved on to the second most commonly asked question of an intellectual property attorney by an intellectual property attorney: "Litigation or prosecution?"

"Litigation," I said without hesitating—a strange answer for someone who had been practicing law, if you can even do that without a license, for under a month. Madison didn't say anything.

"Yep, litigation," I repeated. "I'd like to be a trial attorney," I said, walking around his office and waving my hands. I meandered over to his golf clubs in the corner of the room, then turned back toward him. "I'd like to stand before a jury and say," I deepened my voice, " 'Ladies and gentlemen of the court . . .' " My heart skipped a beat. My God, what did I just say to the senior-most partner of the firm? The trial attorney of trial attorneys?

I couldn't tell whether Madison was entertained or horrified. He still said nothing.

"Play much?" I asked, pulling out the largest golf club from his bag. I turned toward him, holding it. Now he was mortified.

"Learning," he said in a tone that suggested "put down the club." "You?"

"Oh, no, I don't really play. Would love to learn," I said. Was I suggesting that he teach me? It wasn't likely I'd be joining Madison for an instructional round of golf at his country club anytime soon. It took me a couple of tries, but I managed to jam the club back into his golf bag.

"Well, thanks," I said, making my way for the door. "Sorry to interrupt you. I really appreciate your time."

"Okay," he said, a bit dazed. I bolted past an entertained Sari.

CHAPTER 45

HERE'S NOTHING PATHETIC about dining alone. As long as you have something to read or write, it's perfectly normal. With a book or pen, I'm a sophisticate. I'm a tortured artist. I'm an academic. I'm a high-powered attorney. I'm single. I'm desirable. Sans literature, I'm a fool. I'm the weird guy in the corner staring at everyone. I'm alone. It's the difference between doing something clothed or naked. I think that's why I can't go to the movies alone. Even though the real event happens in the dark with no human interaction, I find those few minutes before and after the movie—the foreplay and the pillow talk—painfully lonely.

These days I was doing a lot of dining alone, so I was doing a lot of reading. Laverne's was only four blocks from my apartment, so if I was really desperate for paper, pen, or prose, it wasn't a big deal to circle back and grab a book, a newspaper, or some legal briefs.

Laverne's striped awning, its white-picket fence, the old family photographs on the wall, the dark-roasted-coffee scent, the wooden tables, the handcrafted cushions on the seats, even the fireplace gave the impression that you'd stumbled across a homey restaurant just off a country road. But tonight the candles on the table and the sound of cabs crushing the snow on Hudson Street made it feel like a New York evening in late fall. Tonight I had reading material. I took my regular seat and began reviewing the to-do list.

"Just you?" Linda said, walking over to my table.

"No, I'm expecting one more," I said. "You're coming tonight, right?"

"Of course. Miss an opportunity to see the Oracle's art and your brother? Never! I get off at eight P.M."

"Perfect. There should still be a few expensive paintings and sculptures left to buy." I smiled and pointed my chin toward the corner, where the only other person in the room was also dining alone. "That's him, right?"

"Of course that's him," she whispered, and walked away. Harvey Keitel could tell that we were talking about him. I smiled. He smiled back. I considered inviting him to the art show but didn't. Laverne's was set in the middle of celebrity row, with the usual suspects. Harvey Keitel lived a block away. Robert De Niro lived across the hall from him. And Chazz Palminteri lived down the street. It was like a scene out of *A Bronx Tale*. All three frequented Laverne's.

Arjun walked in, covered in snow.

"I can't believe it's snowing and it's not even November. This is the wrong night to entertain," I said to him.

"I wouldn't worry," Arjun said, wiping snow off his trademark full-length raggedy brown leather coat. "People will come. We owe them a party. We've been talking about the apartment renovations for months. The bigger challenge will be getting the keg up the steps."

"Oh, I didn't think of that."

"You've truly transformed that store downstairs," Arjun said. "I still can't figure out how you got Tony to move all his crap out. Where did he put all his soaps, jewelry, and doilies?"

"It was a long, agonizing process. Over the past week, day by day, I've removed a few tchotchkes here and a few tchotchkes there. Most of them are in the back storage room. Tony insisted on keeping his hats and figurines on display. He only agreed to move the crap because he's getting ten percent on everything we sell tonight. If the art show starts at seven-thirty, I guess it's safe to assume people will start going upstairs to the after-party around ten?"

"That's a good guess. What did we decide about music?" Arjun asked.

"The DJ is coming at seven," I said. "He's three hundred dollars."

Arjun rolled his eyes.

"What?"

"We don't need a DJ. I have music. The Psychedelic Furs, the Sex Pistols, Fratricide, Ox Baker, Sugar Coated Killers, Fubar." Arjun was going through a punk and hard-core phase. The phase was coming up on its ninth year. I gave him a long look. "Whatever," he said. "You have no taste in music. I've wired your new speakers to the living room. People should stay out of the bedrooms. Between the kitchen, hallway, and living room, we should be able to fit about two hundred people."

"Nice."

"I've starting making the hors d'oeuvres. You owe me a hundred dollars for food. Just like you asked me, it's all going to be traditional Indian finger food—Tandoori chicken, potato and beef samosas, and lamb kebobs." In addition to construction worker, engineer, and MBA candidate, Arjun had recently added chef to his résumé.

"Great. The Oracle is bringing cake," I said.

"What's the story with girls?"

"I've been maintaining the three-to-one ratio," I said.

"Yeah, me, too. I've spread the word at b-school, but the place will still probably be a sausage factory. My friend Laura is bringing her friend Maxine. Don't hit on Maxine."

"Fine. But what number are you?" I asked.

"I'm number one—you were the last person to have sex. Deena the paralegal, right?" I neither confirmed nor denied the allegation. "I haven't had sex in weeks. I'm going through a dry spell. So I get dibs on Maxine."

"Fine. But Deena's off-limits."

"She's coming? She's over the underwear?"

"Yeah, she seems to be having a sense of humor about it, but don't antagonize her."

Arjun pretended to read his menu. "Well, I'm number one, so I get first choice of anyone else there tonight."

The walk back to the apartment was freezing. We were both underdressed, and our blood had thinned over the summer. New York City had skipped fall. What a shame: Autumn was the only season that really mattered. When we arrived at the apartment building, I could see Tony inside, straightening out his hats and figurines. My mother's paintings were hung on the back wall, crooked and unevenly spaced. I'd come back downstairs in a few minutes to orchestrate things.

"It's your turn," Arjun said to me, standing by the door and shivering.

"No way, I'm not taking my gloves off. You have keys. I did it last time," I said.

"It's got to be fifteen degrees out here. I'm not doing it. I've opened the door every time this week."

"I'm not opening it," I said. For the next thirty seconds, we stood there with our hands in our pockets.

"This is ridiculous. Who's going to open the door?" I said. More silence. Finally, Arjun took his hands out of his pockets, took out his keys, and unhooked the house key. Then he walked over to the sewer and dropped it through the grate. He turned around to give me a self-satisfied smile.

I paused in disbelief. "You're an idiot." I opened the door and we went inside. At the top of the steps, I unlocked the door to the apartment and turned on the kitchen light. A rat scrambled by my foot, and I nearly knocked Arjun back down the steps.

"Turn the lights off," Arjun said, as if that would solve the problem. Ever since the weather got cold, we'd been engaged in a full-fledged war with dozens of enormous, brazen rats. They had managed to jimmy their way up the elevator shaft and into our apartment. Last week I'd gotten up in the middle of the night to use the bathroom, only to be confronted in the hallway by a rat waddling toward me with a glue trap stuck to his back. After that, Arjun and I never entered the hallway at night without stomping on the floor to the words "Rat, rat, rat." These days, every time we walked into the apartment, I half expected to find a rat sitting on a stool at the kitchen table, peering over his *New York Times:* "Hey, I'm reading here."

As Arjun suggested, I turned off the kitchen light. The loft looked best at night. The light in each of our rooms spilled out through the transoms and into the hallway and living room. As I walked down the hallway toward the living room, the floorboards creaked. Suddenly, the large industrial heating fan that hung from the ceiling in the living room automatically clanked on. *Bam!* I jumped. I didn't think I'd ever get used to those fans. I definitely wasn't getting used to the four-hundred-dollar monthly electric bills. That's what it cost to heat this glorious commercial space.

Peering through the full-length windows facing Reade Street, I could see our favorite neighbor in the loft across the way. "She's doing it again," I yelled. "Don't turn on the lights."

Arjun darted to my side. "She is *so* hot," he whispered. The waif, who appeared to be in her early twenties, walked over to her dining room table topless, pushed her short blond hair behind one ear, bent over, and snorted a line of cocaine. "It's a shame that women like that don't come to our parties," Arjun said. "I should go over there and invite her."

"What, and shatter our fantasies?" I said. "It's better not knowing her. If she comes to our party, we'll tip her off to our proximity. Plus, what's your in going to be? 'Hi. On behalf of two men familiar with your sex life and drug habits, I'd like to invite you to our soiree this evening.'" She disappeared from view. Arjun went back to preparing hors d'oeuvres, and I went downstairs to put the finishing touches on the gallery.

"Not bad," Tony announced as I walked in the shop. With both hands, he pointed me to the pedestal where five of his troll figurines surrounded my mother's egg-shaped black stone sculpture. The sculpture's name was *Chasm*. "Now, your mother's stone tells a story. *These* are the keepers of the gem."

This mortifying characterization epitomized our ongoing struggle: simplicity versus clutter, American contemporary versus medieval Dungeons and Dragons, elegance versus tackiness. Before I'd left for dinner, there was room to walk in the store, the room was dim, and a dozen spotlights precisely hit six pedestals displaying six of my mother's most dramatic stone sculptures, each a different color. Using simple hand tools and a sense of touch, the Oracle had carved alabaster stone into simple, solid, smooth, geometric shapes that appealed to the imagination. She polished each stone to a beautiful natural luster.

My mother once said, "Every stone sculpture I've created has in it my blood, sweat, and tears." Posted on each pedestal was a small label providing the sculpture's name, size, price, and, at my mother's request, the words "Please touch."

But in the hour I'd spent having dinner at Laverne's, all of my hard work was ruined. Tony had brought up the store lights, repositioned the spotlights, and cluttered the pedestals. He'd placed green soaps all around the green stone titled *Mobius Strip*. He'd positioned jewelry next to the pink stone titled *Inversion*. He'd used the tips on the orange alabaster stone titled *Variegated Column* as hooks for two particularly flamboyant hats.

I picked up one of the custom invitations stacked next to the large fan-shaped white stone titled *Expansion*. "These are the wrong invites," I said, frustrated.

"Yeah, I know that," he said in his snippy British tone. "Those are the only ones I could find."

"But my mother's name is spelled wrong, Tony. It's Carole Wellen, not Carole *Weller*."

"Well, the store's address is right. I paid for half of them, so I can use half of them," he said as he ripped the bottom of the invitation off, discarding the half with the misspelled name and a picture of a sculpture. "I'll do this to the rest of them while you look for the right invitations in the back." Rip, rip, rip. "That is, if you can find them buried among all the stuff you dumped out of my store." I located the reprinted invites, placed them out front, and turned my attention to the wall displaying my mother's paintings.

The acrylics were part of series she'd titled *Patches & Pieces*. The basic designs were both contemporary and traditional, and carried with them an inherent American quality. Inspired by a group of quilters my mother met while living in New England, she'd invented her own patchwork of colors, textures, and bold designs. "I do a series of pieces so I can present the possibilities," she said. She gave them names like *Autumn Tints, Storm Signal, Buckwheat,* and *Grosgrain*. I'd always intended on displaying the twenty medium-sized paintings together, one next to another, like a gigantic quilt, four paintings high and five paintings wide.

"All I ask is that you hang them straight," the Oracle begged me before the show. "Crooked art is never attractive." That task proved to be more difficult than I anticipated. It had taken me all morning, but I managed to get all the paintings in my giant quilt perfectly aligned. By evening, the display was a wreck. I could hear the occupants, *my neighbors,* stomping around in the apartment above the store. Every one of their steps caused a different painting to tip in a different direction. To stabilize each painting, I decided to use two hooks. For the next half hour I added a hook to each painting.

"They're not straight," Tony said as he walked by me with a dozen hats.

"That's impossible, I used this level," I said as I stepped off the ladder. He was right and he was wrong. They *were* straight, but none of them were *aligned.* Because the length of the hanging wire on each painting varied, every painting hung at a slightly different height. Four years of engineering school, and I couldn't line up twenty paintings. The quilt was unbearable to look at. It was getting late.

First I considered nailing all the paintings to the wall. But I didn't want to ruin the wooden frames. I decided to forget about the hanging wire. Using the back edge of the frames, I delicately balanced each painting on the head of two tiny nails. Very little was holding them up, but at least they were straight and aligned. I feared that one big pound from the upstairs neighbors would have a domino effect, causing all twenty glass frames to come crashing down. Then I'd have one big, bloody New York art show on my hands. Who knows, maybe it'd be all the rage.

My parents and Mike walked in as I straightened the last painting. "What do you think?" I said, clenching the ladder with my free hand.

"They look beautiful," my mother said sweetly. "I can't believe you did this." She began strolling through the gallery. This was the first time she'd ever seen her stone sculptures publicly displayed.

"I have a car full of these," my father said, referring to the thirty or so prints Mike was struggling to balance with both hands. We didn't have the time, money, or resources to go the proper route with true lithograph prints. To keep them affordable, my parents made color copies of each of the twenty *Patches & Pieces.* Then Mom signed and numbered them, and Mike helped Dad mat and shrink-wrap them.

Frames were your problem. For us, the costs were minimal. And at twenty dollars apiece, we'd make a 500 percent profit.

"Dad, help him. You can put them over there," I said to Mike, hinting with my eyes that I wanted to camouflage Tony's case displaying glass-blown animals.

"Aren't they great?" my mother said as she watched me page through the color prints.

"These are perfect—some of the color copies are even more interesting then the originals," I said.

"I was thinking the same thing," she said. This was something I admired about my mother. She wasn't insulted by such a comment. The pure artist in her recognized the artistic value of derivative work.

"I think I'm going to buy those trolls over there on the pedestal," Mike whispered in my ear. My face dropped. "I can't think of a more polite way to move them *away* from Mom's sculpture."

"Welcome to my world," I said.

I introduced the family to Tony, who was remarkably reserved for being Tony. Only recently had Tony started to warm up to me. I think he felt bad about setting me up with Margo. By agreeing to sponsor the art show, maybe he thought I'd make enough money to buy that new electrical system for her car. Even though Tony also stood to make some money this evening, you still couldn't help but feel as if you were invading his space.

"Tony, you have such a beautiful gallery," my mother said. "Thank you so much for having us." My mother understood the sacrifices Tony made in order to exhibit her work.

"I think our artwork works nicely together," he said, referring to the figurines guarding her black stone.

"I'm particularly fond of your hats," she said.

Tony smiled. "I have the perfect fur hat for you," he said excitedly, and ran to the back room before I could suggest the big purple silk hat hanging off the orange sculpture.

"It's all so wonderful," my mom said as she admired the wall of paintings.

"Actually, don't stand so close to that wall, Mom."

"I just can't get over it." Her voice cracked slightly. She was moved. I gave her a smile. It had been less than a month since she'd lost her mother, and I wasn't sure she'd ever be the same. Tragedy brings people closer. She and I were spending a lot more time on the phone. I think I helped fill the void—for as long as I could remember, Grandma and Mom had spoken every evening.

"Okay, let's go upstairs," my dad said, interrupting the moment. He was the family navigator. Move along. Places to go. Things to see. We walked out of the shop, made a quick U-turn, and entered the front door to the apartments. My family wore the same expression everyone did the first time they stared at those hundred narrow steps. On the landing between the second and third floor, my mother said, out of breath: "I'll meet you upstairs in a couple of minutes."

"This is awesome," Mike said as he entered the apartment. He was greeted with a big hug from Arjun, who was in the kitchen finishing up the art show hors d'oeuvres. The apartment had never looked better. The dimmers were on low. All along the hallway, Arjun had mounted Gothic-looking candleholders that were lit with scented candles. Lounge music poured in from the living room, where the DJ had already set up. My father, the engineer, began inspecting the new construction, sliding his hand along the freshly erected and painted walls, flipping light switches, and opening and shutting doors. Arjun pulled up beside him and began answering his miscellaneous strapping and Sheetrock questions.

"It's here!" a voice cried from my room. When I walked in, Mike was fully reclined in The Chair, his eyes closed, as two rolling balls vibrated up and down his spine. He let out a long, inappropriate sigh of ecstasy. "Mom, you have to try this," he said as our mother found her way to my room. Mike released the leg rest and reset The Chair. Then, with an uneasy look, my mother settled in.

Flashes of anguish overcame her face as she arched her back in time with the massage balls creeping slowly down her back. In between jabs of pain, she begged me to turn it off. "This thing is obscene," she said to me as she frantically looked for a way to lower her legs and prop herself out.

"But haven't you always said there's something irresistible about a good chair?" I said.

"Well, not *that* chair," she said. She and Mike went to the kitchen to help Arjun bring the food downstairs. I found my dad in the living room. He was completing his inspection of the walls.

"We put soundproofing in that one," I told him.

"You guys did a nice job."

"You mean we did a nice job paying twelve thousand dollars to the building contractor, electrician, taper, transom guy, and door hanger," I said. "Here, these are for you." I handed him a box containing two expensive ties. Between Father's Day, birthdays, and my father's predisposition not to spend a penny on himself, I didn't think he'd bought himself a tie in ten years. He needed them. I was subtly trying to help him revise his résumé and wardrobe. He'd been out of work for two months.

"Oh, thank you. These are great," he said, holding them up.

"So, anything interesting lately?" I said. No "How's the job search?" or "Any good leads or offers?" I wanted to be helpful and interested yet respectful. It was all in the posturing. I didn't offer career advice. I was a cheerleader and support service. The ties were gifts for good luck, not reprimands from the dressing police. My résumé advice was directed at the format, not the substance.

"I've sent out about a hundred letters and résumés." I'd never considered that image of my father. "I haven't heard much. The right thing will turn up," the Optimist said.

"Did you use that Mail Merge function that I showed you? I found it helpful with my law-firm search."

"Yes, I did. Thank you. I'm meeting with someone tomorrow. They need a director of engineering and manufacturing. It's an aerospace company in Trenton, about an hour from the house." I was excited. Not so much about the job interview, but that we were talking. We'd always talked, but not like this. We'd spent the majority of the last twenty-five years talking about me. Sure, I'd listened to him discuss day-to-day events with my mother, and I'd occasionally asked him about his job, his interests, and his life, but given the crossroad in both of our careers, the relationship was changing. We were having a breakthrough. He was talking, albeit briefly, and I was listening. We'd always been friends, but now we felt more like peers.

Dad went downstairs to start welcoming guests. I showered, shaved, and put on the most chic outfit I could think of—a three-button black suit, black shirt, square-toed black shoes, and a solid azure tie. No hair gel. Never hair gel. I was a power lawyer by day and an art manager by night.

When I got downstairs, the small shop was packed. Twenty or so people were inside drinking wine and eating Arjun's hors d'oeuvres. I could see Nickel friends and Linda the pie maker. David Markey was there with a new girl. Tony was outside smoking with a few friends. It had stopped snowing and turned out to be a perfect, brisk early-winter New York evening.

As I walked in, I could see my mother in the corner of the room. She was in her element, surrounded by family, friends, and artwork. She looked more beautiful than ever. She was glowing, her eyes smiling in a way I'd never seen before.

All my life, I'd told people how alike she and I were. From the way we looked to the way we laughed to the way we occasionally argued. But the major difference between Mom and me was that she was an introvert and I was an extrovert. The Oracle didn't like crowds. She didn't like social gatherings. Even the hour trip to New York from Toms River was an angst-filled, exhausting pilgrimage for my reclusive mother. The Oracle wanted to be either with her immediate family or by herself. Tonight was the exception. She was the center of attention. She owned the room. I walked up to her.

"I think there are three requirements of art," she told Aaron Reinstein. "That it speaks to you. That it evokes a response. And that it sticks."

"Well, I think your work is wonderful," he said.

"Thank you, Aaron, I'm glad you enjoy it."

I put my hand on her back. She smiled and disengaged herself from the group.

"Cheers," she said to me. We clinked wineglasses.

"So we *haven't* sold anything yet," I whispered.

"That's not the point. It's always been about the artwork—just having people appreciate it. I'm thrilled that you did this for me. Seeing my work displayed is enough for me."

Arjun walked up with a friend of his family. "This is Yasmine," he said excitedly. She was a stunning petite Indian woman with big brown eyes and a slim figure. "Our parents have been lifelong friends. They grew up together in Dubai. Yasmine's a lawyer. She went to Yale Law [Tier 1]," Arjun gushed. "Which firm are you with again, Yasmine?"

"Willis, Conrad," she said softly. I refrained from mentioning my miserable experience interviewing with that firm. "I want to manage your artwork, Mrs. Wellen," she said. "Whatever your son is charging, I'll take half. I've already persuaded that man over there that he *must* own the white stone." She was motioning to *Expansion* and Aaron Reinstein, arguably the wealthiest person in the room.

"I'm afraid we're going to have to let you go," my mother said to me gently. Arjun was beaming. In one sweeping exchange, Yasmine had endeared herself to all three of us.

"She's no Tuesday girl," Arjun whispered to me as he steered Yasmine toward some new people. He'd used "Tuesday girl" as our long-standing description of a woman you found attractive, on average, once a week. Yasmine was no Tuesday girl.

The Oracle gave me a knowing glance as we watched Arjun introduce Yasmine to some more people. There was something special about her. I'd never seen Arjun like this before.

Linda the pie maker stood a few feet away from us. She looked lost. I tapped her on the shoulder and introduced her to my mother. Linda showered her with compliments.

"Thank you. Oh, look, and this is my other son, Mike," my mother said. Mike gave Linda a big smile. Thanks to a plateful of pies, they were old friends.

"These are my favorites," Linda said, pointing to the *Patches & Pieces* collection.

"Have you seen the prints?" Mike asked. "I can help you pick one out, if you'd like." He put out his arm to escort her to the print rack.

"Just give it to her. Don't charge her," I heard my mother whisper to Mike.

I pulled my mother aside and said with a smile, "Hey, Mom, do you realize that your artwork's for sale here, or are you giving it all away?"

"I'm not really giving *that* much away. Although I did give Tony a few prints he liked. He's been so kind and helpful." My expression said otherwise. She laughed. "You have to understand that it was a sacrifice for him to push aside his own artwork to show mine. I want him to know how much I appreciate that."

"Okay. But why did you give *her* a free print?" I motioned with my chin in Linda's general direction.

"There's something strange about that woman," she confided. "I can't pinpoint it, but I feel like she wants something from me. So I gave her a print." Others began to crowd around us.

Overall we sold twenty prints, not including the one Mom gave Linda. Aaron did in fact buy *Expansion*. After subtracting costs for food, wine, invites, prints, and 10 percent commission to Tony, we made about a thousand dollars. By ten P.M., most everyone had migrated to the apartment. My family said good-bye, and I began the other half of the evening.

By the time I reached the top of the steps, my head was spinning. I'd already had a few too many glasses of wines, and the night was still young. I struggled to open the door to the apartment, as it was wall-to-wall people bobbing their heads to house music. Arjun was waiting for me.

"WE GOTTA DO SOMETHING ABOUT BUZZING PEOPLE IN!" he screamed.

"WHAT?" I screamed back.

"THE INTERCOM, I CAN'T HEAR IT. COME INTO THE HALLWAY." He pointed to the door. We moved the conversation outside the apartment. "That's better," he said. "I'm not going to prop the door open downstairs. Who knows who will walk in? We should take turns either manning the intercom or standing downstairs."

"I'll take the intercom in the living room," I said. "First lemme get a drink." I began to walk back in.

"Dude," Arjun said, grabbing my arm. "You're going to have to keep your head planted up against that intercom speaker. It's hard to hear it buzz. The DJ is deafening, and the police have already come to the apartment. They got a complaint about the noise. They cut us a break. I promised we'd keep it down. I told you this DJ thing was a bad idea. I'll go talk to the DJ again now."

I found the makeshift bar in the kitchen. David was making himself a Ketel One vodka and tonic.

"BOMBAY SAPPHIRE AND TONIC FOR YOU?" he offered. I nodded and began scanning the room. "Keep it," he whispered in my ear. I'd breached etiquette. I was studying a brunette in the corner whom David knew I was too embarrassed to bring, so he was calling me out.

"Hey, I was still deliberating on that girl," I whispered back defensively.

Suddenly the music died down. Presumably Arjun's handiwork. "Well, when you're done, you can keep it. By the way, your silver-pants girl from the VH1 Music Awards is here. She looks good. What kind of party is this? You invite your friends over so they can all meet the girls you're dating? I swear that I just saw that Deena-girl from your firm."

"Yeah, that was an error."

"I thought you guys weren't seeing each other anymore, at least not since the underwear incident. Whatever. I wouldn't worry too much. Neither girl is going to be an option for much longer. Arjun's friends are all over silver-pants girl and Deena's already wrecked. Guys are flocking to that girl, and she loves it. You can tell she's trouble."

"What's the deal with your girl?" I said, changing the topic. "She's smoking."

"Wendy? Beautiful face, but I can't tell whether she's a little 'big.' "
"Big" was an adjective we reserved for below the waist. "It's those god-damn black pants. I just can't tell. More to follow."

I took my drink and began weaving down the hallway toward the in-tercom. A few people away, Deena and I spotted each other. She tucked a piece of short blond hair behind one ear to reveal her beautiful light green eyes. Tonight Deena had this sexy Ann Taylor thing going. The top two buttons of her white button-down shirt were undone. Deena had natural beauty and wore very little makeup. Without saying a word, I reached through the crowd and grabbed her hand. Tripping over people, we reached the intercom and kissed softly. I could taste the rum on her lips.

"Here's what we need to do. We need to have sex in your room right now," she said, louder than I would have preferred.

"Are you serious? My bedroom is the center of this party. I can't," I said. "It's too crazy. Plus, there are people here from the firm." I began scanning the room for Aaron Reinstein. Suddenly, silver-pants girl began approaching with a friend. "Deena, I can't go anywhere. I have to stand by this intercom for a while."

"Come on." She clamped her knees around my right leg. "We have to go right now. I'm going crazy. Let's go, let's go."

I rolled my eyes, smiled, and took a sip of my drink. "Deena, you're too drunk."

"And you're not drunk enough. You're such a prude," she said.

"Look, I can't go right now." Her expression changed from playful to annoyed. "We can do it later. Maybe in the bathroom?" I counteroffered.

"Listen. I'm going to your room, and I'm having sex in five minutes. You're welcome to join me." She about-faced and inadvertently brushed by silver-pants girl, who was wearing skintight red leather pants tonight, accentuating her long, thin legs.

"You remember Deirdre from the VH1 Awards," Sophie said. We nodded hello. Deirdre was very plain. Or at least she looked very plain next to Sophie, who was striking in her form-fitting outfit. Unlike the first night we met, tonight she wore her caramel hair up, accentuating her long sexy neck and tiny facial features. All of a sudden the music kicked back in. "THIS IS A GREAT SPACE," she yelled. Despite all the noise, I could still hear hints of her Aussie accent.

"YOU LOOK GREAT," I said to Sophie. Deirdre rolled her eyes and walked away.

"I'm the type of girl who looks better without clothes," she whispered seductively. I got a chill. My face revealed that she'd caught me off guard. "I'M JOKING," she said quickly. "JOKING." She wasn't.

"OF COURSE YOU ARE. IT'S TOO LOUD IN HERE, LET'S GET SOME AIR. I'M SUPPOSED TO WATCH THE DOOR DOWNSTAIRS. PLUS, I WANT YOU TO SEE SOMETHING."

We went downstairs. At the bottom of the steps, I removed the block of wood that someone had used to keep the front door propped open. Tony was outside smoking again.

"I love your mother," he said. "I love her. She gave me *three* prints. They're beautiful."

"My mom really likes you, too, Tony. The show was great, thanks for your help. Is it okay if we go in?" He obliged.

Sophie immediately gravitated to the sculpture in the far corner. "*Stone Kebob,*" she said, reading the small label on the pedestal. "It's so smart."

"Yeah, that's my brother's favorite. Mom knows Mike loves it, so she wrote 'NFS'—not for sale. Between my mother's disincentives and her print giveaways, it's a wonder we made money at all. She made *Stone Kebob* with pieces of stone left over from previous projects. The translucent white stones turned out to be perfect onions, the green ones peppers, and the orange one a tomato."

"I love those brown stones she used for steak. They're perfect. Now I'm in the mood for steak and chips."

"Yeah, she's amazing," I said as I poured us two glasses of wine from the leftover merlot. "My mother looked at that brown stone and thought: Now, that looks like a piece of steak. She chiseled away at it, put it in this sculpture, and it's hard to imagine it as anything but a piece of steak. My father gets kudos for successfully drilling a perfect hole through each and every piece without shattering any of them. Once they stuck this golden skewer through the center of the stone and mounted it on this stand, there was no mistaking. It was *Stone Kebob.*"

The personal art tour lasted another ten minutes. I learned that Sophie wasn't in Manhattan for work. She was taking six months off to travel as part of what she called the World Tour. Given Australia's proximity to everything else in the world, long holidays were common.

On the way out of the store, I had Sophie pick her favorite print from the *Patches & Pieces* collection. She chose the one titled *Hot-Crossed Buns*.

We began our ascent up the narrow stairs. Between all the drinks and steps, I was starting to feel dizzy. Halfway up, I could see two women making their way down. It didn't take long before I realized it was Deena and her friend Janet. Janet was ahead of Deena, leading her down the steps. Deena was smashed. It was then that I realized how bad things looked. I'd rebuffed Deena and disappeared with another woman. There was nowhere to hide.

Deena looked right at me, then turned to Janet. "This is classic," she said.

Now we were ten steps apart. I gave her an upbeat "Hey there."

Deena ignored me, and Janet gave me a look as if to say "Let it go." Deena stopped next to Sophie. Deena was about five-four. With heels, Sophie had about six inches on her. "What's that?" Deena said, pointing to the print Sophie carried.

"Oh, Alex gave me one of his mum's paintings," Sophie said, repositioning the print so Deena could see. "It's beautiful," Sophie added. Deena paused. The volume of the party temporarily spiked, and Arjun appeared at the top of the steps. He looked worried for me. Deena continued down the stairs. Sophie and I were frozen in our tracks. After about ten more steps, Deena turned around.

"Was that your underwear?" she said to Sophie.

"Deena," I begged.

"Pardon me?" Sophie asked.

"They looked about your size," Deena said, sizing up Sophie. "To avoid this problem in the future, I'd recommend that you refrain from wearing underwear. I generally don't. Just ask Alex. Or better yet, see for yourself." Then, leaning all of her weight on Janet, she mooned Arjun, Sophie, and me. "Good night," she said, as if to say, "I'll be here all week. Please tip your servers and try the veal."

"Deena. Wait!" I said, lunging forward. "Don't go." Aiming to take two steps at a time, I slipped and skidded down four steps on my ass. Hugging the banister, I steadied myself. By then, Deena was gone.

Arjun came running down the steps. "Are you okay?" he asked, laughing.

"Yeah, I'm good," I said, checking myself over. Then the adrenaline kicked in. I'd fallen down four steps, but I could have easily tumbled down forty. The back of my head, my back, and my butt already ached.

"Okay, then, I'm going to go back upstairs and leave you two alone," he said. He gave Sophie a smile.

"And how are you?" I asked Sophie.

She was also laughing. "Fine. Thank you. Are you sure you're okay?"

"Oh yeah. I'm fine. Listen, I know this sounds clichéd, but I can explain."

"What?" she said, helping me up. "You can explain that your girlfriend found someone else's undies in your bedroom and she thinks they're mine?"

"And if I told you that wasn't my girlfriend, and that the underwear was all part of one big misunderstanding, would that rehabilitate things at all?"

"Yeah. Now I think you're a saint. Come on, let's go upstairs and get you some ice."

CHAPTER 46

THE FIRST CASUALTY was my CD collection. Lying in bed, I could tell the stack of CDs on the bookshelf next to my useless law textbooks was considerably shorter. The second casualty was my light gray carpet. There was a path from the door of my bedroom to my bed where guests had tracked in mud and sleet. I was the third and most substantial casualty. Besides being severely hungover, I was bruised from head to toe, thanks to my trip down the steps. The phone rang, and at the other end of the line was the fourth casualty.

"Hey, what are you doing?" came Deena's voice. "Is now a bad time?"

I looked over at the clock. It was eleven-forty-five A.M. "Now's fine. I was just getting up. How am I doing? I'm in traction. That fall down the steps put me over the edge."

"You fell?" she asked.

"Please don't tell me that you missed that part?"

"I don't remember much from last night. But Janet tells me there was a full moon," she said with regret in her voice.

"You'll be pleased to learn that from my point of view, the lighting was very flattering. I'm sorry about last night."

"Me, too. We both had too much to drink," she said. "Janet also tells me that up until that point, I was having a great time." Deena and I promised to make some plans to get together soon and said good-bye.

I stumbled into the hallway. Footprints were stamped all along the bottom of our newly painted walls, where last night's socialites had taken to flamingo stances as they sipped their drinks and made conversation. Beer bottles, cups, and cigarettes littered the hallway. "God, people just stubbed their cigarettes out in the hallway," I mumbled. "That is so rough."

Arjun was in the kitchen making eggs for Yasmine. "Are you alone?" he asked.

"I'm alone," I said. "No cheese, Arjun. Egg whites only. Good morning," I said to Yasmine as I gave myself a quick once-over to be sure I was decent. Everything seemed to be in place.

"Good morning," she said cheerfully. "Do you know that you have rats?"

"Yeah, we know. We've got big, huge sewer rats." I poured myself a cup of coffee. "Why, did you see one?"

"No, but Arjun and I heard one last night, scuffling underneath his futon. We didn't sleep at all."

"Oh, so the two of you *didn't sleep at all*," I said slyly. Yasmine didn't dignify the remark. Arjun, with his back to us, continued to beat my egg whites. "I keep having this recurring nightmare where I wake up and there's a rat sitting on my chest, staring me down. What do you think it means?" I asked her.

"Let's see. The rat represents the ugly weight of the world. He's staring at you because it's you versus him, and he's sitting on your chest because that's his way of applying pressure and stress," she said.

"Good answer," I said.

"Can we change the topic to something more interesting?" Arjun asked. "Take, for example, that soap opera in the stairwell last night." He flipped Yasmine's omelette. "I can't believe you were able to recover with Sophie after that scene with Deena."

"Arjun, I think you've beaten those eggs enough," she said.

"I want them to be fluffy," he responded.

"I go to New York Sports Clubs, too," Yasmine said, reading my tank top. "The gym is fine, but the locker rooms are gross."

"I agree. I can't go anywhere people comb their hair naked," I said. "I don't get it. It's all just one big penis parade in the men's locker room."

"Thank you for that," she said. "Alex, what are all these containers on the shelf? Amino acids, weight gain, creatine. Are you a workout fanatic?"

"I'm trying something," I said.

"Yeah, he's trying to get rock-hard abs," Arjun said. "He wants a six-pack. What are you up to now? A two-pack?" I feigned a smile his way and took a sip of coffee.

"You're quite the perfectionist," Yasmine said. "Your room is perfect, your job is perfect, your clothes are perfect, and now it's time to go for the perfect body. Am I wrong?"

"No," Arjun answered for me.

"Actually, I hadn't thought about it that way," I said.

"I'm not saying, I'm just saying," she said.

"I wouldn't say my life is exactly 'perfect.' Anyway, once I fail the bar, everything will be different."

"Here we go again. *Once! Once!* You're so annoying. Yasmine, tell him he's not going to fail the bar."

"You're not going to fail the bar," she mimicked.

"Yeah, this coming from a Yale Law, Willis, Conrad attorney," I said.

"You're not going to fail the bar," she said in the same dismissive tone. "So, this guy fails the bar. Minutes after finding out, he's called into one of the senior partners' offices of the big law firm. 'Sit down and shut the door,' the partner says. There are three other senior partners sitting in the room with him. 'I understand you failed the bar,' he says. There's a pause. The associate begins to panic. 'Well, join our private club. Everyone in this room failed the first time. Now, get a grip, buckle down, and pass next time.' "

"Is that true?" I asked desperately.

"It's an urban myth. But it always gave me comfort while I waited for the results."

"Speaking of urban myths," I said, "did you hear about the guy who was taking the bar and keeled over midexam with a heart attack? I heard that most people kept on writing, and the two people who took the time to see if he was okay failed because they weren't given back any of the time they lost helping him."

"Yeah, yeah, yeah. In the version I heard, the two people actually passed," Yasmine said. "I guess the urban myths surrounding the bar have gotten more dire since I took the exam."

"And when was that?"

"Two years ago."

"I heard that one year, people were taking the California bar, and there was a minor earthquake," I said. "They all had to evacuate the building and ultimately retake the exam."

"Yep. Acts of God are not an impossibility defense," Yasmine said. Statutes and case law rolled off her tongue as if she'd just taken the bar. This woman was a ninja. This was what I was up against. Oh, yeah, I'd failed.

CHAPTER 47

"JOHN MADISON HERE!"

"Who?" I asked. He was talking over a speakerphone and had said his name so quickly I couldn't be sure who it was.

"John Madison!" he barked. He was angry. Livid.

"Oh yes, of course, Mr. Madison, excuse me," I said.

"I'm looking at one bill for forty-eight hundred dollars and another for fifty-three hundred dollars. Both have your initials next to them. Both are charges from Westlaw electronic legal services. Both are for the month of October. And those are just the two numbers jumping off the page. There are at least five other substantial Westlaw charges here. What's wrong with you?"

"I—"

"Do you have any clue how expensive Westlaw is? Didn't you receive Westlaw training in law school? In addition, didn't *we* train you on how to conduct efficient and reasonable electronic legal research?" I opened my mouth to respond, but he was picking up speed.

"A.W.! A.W.! A.W.! In all the Bullock bills I've reviewed in the last five years, I've never seen the initials 'A.W.' Now I see them everywhere. Alex Wellen, Alex Wellen, Alex Wellen. Do you realize that, in addition to your unconscionable Westlaw bills—which my firm must now subsidize—for the month of October, you've billed Bullock more hours than any other attorney in this firm?"

"Actually—"

"No, you can't possibly understand." His voice got louder. "Nickel has fifteen matters open for Bullock. That means we are handling *fifteen different lawsuits* for Bullock. Rufus is just one of them. More than forty of my attorneys are working on different Bullock matters. But somehow, in the two months that you've been here, you've billed the most hours. And you're a first-year associate; you don't even know anything.

"Last month, besides the Westlaw charges—which I can't pass on to the client—you managed to charge Bullock for *seventy-four hours* of legal research. At one hundred fifty dollars an hour. Do you actually think I'm going to charge Bullock over eleven thousand dollars in legal research?

"On October third you worked nine hours on the Rufus matter. I don't see any authorization for more than seven hours of work. And your billing descriptions are abominable." He began reading directly from the bill: "October thirteenth: 'Researched distinction between collateral estoppel and res judicata in Fifth and Sixth Circuits. Discussed answer with Aaron Reinstein.'

"That particular description goes on for another two sentences." Now Madison was yelling. "You've got to be out of your fucking mind if you think I'm going to send that description to the client. I've been an attorney for thirty-five years, and *I* don't even understand what it is that you did that day. Your billing increments make my mind want to explode," he screamed. "I'm looking at October twentieth. How can you work two-point-one-six hours? How? Explain that to me, if you would."

"Oh, what I was doing there was breaking it into ten-minute intervals, then converting that length of time into decimals. So two hours and ten minutes is about two-point-one-six hours."

"I'm a fair man. I make this phone call *once*. Consider it a courtesy call. Frankly, I don't know whether I can afford to have someone like you working at my firm. I've arranged for you to be retrained on how to conduct electronic legal research with our head librarian, Cindy Rogers."

He took a breath. I took the opportunity to try and defend myself. "If I could please just have an opportunity to respond."

"By all means," he said quickly. "By all means."

In that precious moment I wanted to deliver the most eloquent rebuttal imaginable. I wanted to tell Madison that I *had* in fact received considerable training in how to conduct electronic research, and that I was good. In fact, so good that even though I'd billed seventy-four hours, Bullock was getting a bargain. It would have taken a number of my fellow first-years twice as long to conduct the same research.

I wanted to tell him that I'd conducted all my research at Aaron Reinstein's request. I wanted to tell him that *my* research was crucial in the Rufus matter. I wanted to apologize for my billing descriptions and billing increments but inform him that I hadn't been trained to do it any other way. That I didn't know I needed written authorization from a partner to work on a Bullock matter for more than seven hours in one day. That I didn't know my billing increments needed to be rounded down to fifteen-minute increments because they converted to decimals better.

Overwhelmed by a number of possible defenses, I failed to utter a single coherent sentence. "I didn't realize that . . . as far as legal research is concerned . . . Wait, let me back up, the collateral-estoppel issue was critical to the Rufus case because—"

"Please see Cindy Rogers this afternoon," he interrupted.

"All right. Thank you," I said. With nothing more than a grunt, the line went dead. I held the phone by my ear for another ten seconds. Then, hands shaking, I put the handset down quietly. Did I just thank him?

"What's wrong?" Hayley said to me. The office was so small, I was sure she'd overheard everything. "Are you okay?"

"Just give me a sec," I said, staring out the window.

"Come on, it can't be *that* bad."

"I think I was almost fired."

"How can you almost be fired?"

"I dunno. Just give me a sec, okay, Hayley?"

"Who was that?"

"Madison. He says I can't bill for shit, I don't know how to do legal research, and that I might be too big a liability to the firm."

"You're exaggerating. Don't be dumb."

"No, really. I wish I were." Aaron Reinstein's office was next to ours. The door was open. I knocked on it to get his attention. I closed the door and told him what had happened.

"Look, Bullock is Nickel's largest client," Aaron said. "They're Madison's baby, and they account for a disproportionate amount of

Nickel's work, and that's not particularly a good thing. We can't afford to lose them as a client."

"He said my initials were all over the bills."

"Yeah, it's that time of the month. This is how it works. At the beginning of every month, Sari prints out the bill. She always prints it out on blue paper. Then we all hold our breath while Madison sits at his desk with a cup of black coffee and pages through it. Everything we bill gets put into that report. It summarizes who worked on what, when. Madison may not be involved in the day-to-day research, motion practice, and low-level strategizing, but he's always watching. Nothing gets past him. He scrutinizes every charge right down to the last penny."

"The last Nickel?"

"Yeah, well put. He has to keep Bullock happy, so he gives them some preferential treat. Special bulk rates, if you will. It's all contained in the memo."

"What memo?"

"You didn't get the memo?"

"No. Is this a joke?"

"My bad, my mistake. The memo outlines the proper way to bill Bullock. I think Madison hopes that this billing protocol will become the model for all Nickel clients. Every one of his billing rules is embodied in one authoritative memo. Here, I'll print it for you right now." Aaron hit a couple of keys on his keyboard. "There are rules about how to write your billing descriptions, when to obtain authorization for overtime, what's considered acceptable billing subject matter, and even proper billing increments. I can't believe you billed Bullock two-point-one-six hours." He started laughing.

"Am I the only new attorney on this matter?"

"It's just you and me on this case right now. And nothing's been happening for some time. In September you did a little work, but I'm sure this month the bill was three or four times thicker than usual."

"What a nightmare."

"Electronic legal research is a sore subject for Madison. It's not as if he prohibits it altogether. He knows Westlaw is a necessary evil, but that's a place he says we can minimize costs. It's the Achilles' heel in his grand plan to streamline Bullock's costs. It's all in the memo."

Aaron grabbed the ten-page memo off the printer. He began reading the bullet points aloud. " 'Use the books in Nickel's library before logging on to Westlaw. Photocopy pertinent cases from the books; don't print them from Westlaw. It costs two cents a line to print the cases.' Madison says Nickel's margin on photocopying always trumps the breakeven of passing Westlaw printing costs directly off on the client."

I hadn't done any of the things mentioned in the memo. I hadn't started with the books, economized on the printing, searched the smaller databases, or minimized my time online. "I knew that electronic research was expensive, but I didn't think I'd spent tens of thousands of dollars."

"Yeah, that's bad. I blame myself for not monitoring your electronic research more closely. Generally, I'm accustomed to large bills, but yours are through the . . . Rufus."

"Very nice."

In law school, electronic legal research was free. I spent reckless hours online researching cases and statutes, reading articles and lawyer bios, and printing anything that struck my fancy. Ah, the good old days.

Then there were my three limited real-world experiences with electronic research. In Judge Hudson's and Judge Lexington's offices, like the rest of the federal government, they had an agreed-upon flat rate with the services, so cost wasn't a factor. And then there was my internship with Nickel. That summer I'd done minimal legal research; plus Nickel was courting me. They weren't about to reveal their dark side, even had I run up some minimal Westlaw charges.

So I was tricked, and that was the point. Like any addictive drug, electronic services like Westlaw and LexisNexis gave away a few samples (or, in this case, years) for free. But before you knew it, you were hooked. Hooked with Nickel, Madison, and Bullock supporting your bad habits. And because Westlaw and LexisNexis had cornered the market, they were able to charge exorbitant fees. The day that I graduated from "educational purposes" to "commercial use," Westlaw billed Nickel for every minute I spent, every database I searched, and every line I printed.

"I don't think you realize that five minutes searching and printing cases from the largest electronic databases can easily run up hundreds of dollars," Aaron said.

"I have a problem, don't I?"

"That's the first step," Aaron said, smiling.

"Perhaps I need an intervention."

"Isn't that what just happened with Madison? Congratulations," he said. "Getting yelled at by Madison is a rite of passage. I know it's the most clichéd expression in the book, but one day you'll laugh about this. Come on, I'm laughing already. Plus, in a firm with two hundred attorneys, at least Madison knows who you are."

"Yeah."

CHAPTER 48

DESPITE MY DRESSING-down, I still wanted to be an attorney. I wanted Nickel business cards. I wanted Nickel notepads with my name at the top. I wanted to sign legal documents. I wanted to be on the letterhead.

But these were the possessions and rights of someone licensed to practice under New York law. Nickel hadn't hesitated to move me to New York, give me an office and secretary, and pay me a six-figure salary, but what seemed like trivial items—business cards and pads— were off-limits without a passing score. I was forbidden from even ordering them. Yeah, that was all I needed—to be rebuffed by the guys in the office-supplies department.

It was mid-November, and the results were imminent, according to BAR/BRI's most recent letter.

TO: All July BAR/BRI New York Candidates

Our phones have been ringing with inquiries as to when the New York results will be coming out. According to the State Board, you should expect your results between November 18 and 28.

The question that I am always asked is "What should I do in the event that I do not pass the exam?"

First, the odds are great that you will pass. In fact, the New York State average pass rate during the last five years for first-time takers has been about 80 percent. Second, because most passing and failing papers are right on the border, the odds are overwhelming that should you not pass, you will pass the next time. In the event that you do not pass, we suggest you set up a phone appointment with a BAR/BRI attorney. The attorney will review your scores and recommend a study program and plan of action. There is no cost or obligation for this service.

If it turns out that you need to take the exam again, relax for a while before you begin your intensive review. The BAR/BRI New York bar-review course begins at all locations on December 29.

At the end of the course, we sent you a good-luck postcard on taking the exam. Well, this is a good luck letter on passing the exam. Few of you would regard the studying, taking, and waiting to have been a fun process. Fortunately, the waiting is almost over, and soon you will be a member of the New York Bar.

Best of luck with the results.

Sincerely,

Steven R. Rubin

As much as I wanted some resolution, purgatory wasn't such a bad place to hang out. I'd grown accustomed to not knowing, to not being able to do anything about it. Every once in a while I even managed to forget.

"Were you just singing into your Dictaphone?" Hayley asked as she walked into the office.

"It must be boring for my secretary to transcribe information for this attorney-client-privilege log. I figured I'd give her a little something special. My last ten entries were to 'New York, New York.' " Hayley laughed. "Did you know that last year the New York State bar lost six hundred exams?" I asked.

"What do you mean?"

"Six hundred answers to essay number five mysteriously disappeared from headquarters in Albany. It says in this article that somehow the blue books got mixed in with some old test booklets sent to be recycled."

"When do you do any work?" Hayley asked.

"I always work. This article was just forwarded to me by e-mail. Anyway, somehow the bar examiners graded the exams without six hundred answers to essay five. As a result, there are these thirty-one borderline cases. 'Borderline' meaning those thirty-one scores were ten points above or below the pass rate. New York requires that all borderline cases be regraded. Then they take the two scores and average them. Here's where it gets good. One of the borderline cases is this girl Suzanne Finkelstein. They go to regrade her exam, and they want to include her answer to essay five, but of course, they've lost her original answer. So the board takes all of the other borderline cases where they *didn't* lose the answer, and they give Finkelstein the highest score from that lot. She still fails."

"Are we almost done?"

"Almost. Like any good nonlicensed attorney, Finkelstein sues New York and wins." I began reading from the *New York Law Journal* article. " 'The trial court judge ruled that the alternative method was "arbitrary, capricious, and a denial of her equal protection." The score measured her performance "based on the performance of others, rather than the petitioner herself." '

"Finkelstein was the first applicant in New York bar-exam history to force the State Board of Law Examiners to pass her," I said. "But it was a hollow victory."

"Why?" Hayley asked out of courtesy.

"Because New York State decided to appeal the case, and the retake rolled around in February, so the pissed-off board forced Finkelstein to retake the bar anyway. She won on appeal and passed the second time."

"Can we call?" Hayley asked.

"I guess." Maybe I'd done it the first time, but I had no idea it would become ritual. Every day we called the bar examiner's office and listened to the prerecorded message on the speakerphone. It was the same as yesterday, the day before that, and the day before that: "You've reached the Office of the State Bar Examiners of New York in Albany, New York. The results for applicants who have taken the exam administered on July thirtieth and thirty-first of this year will be available between November twenty-second and December fifteenth. Applicants will receive notification by first-class mail. This message will be updated when more information becomes available."

CHAPTER 49

THE CEILING FAN blew hot recirculated air on my face. I pulled the sheets up over my head and wished things were different. I was already exhausted. How could I face people at work? Ever since Madison chewed me out for improperly billing Bullock, I'd spent every day either hiding in my office or sneaking around, hoping to avoid him.

"Rat, rat, rat," I said, then stepped into the hallway. The hardwood floors creaked as I tiptoed down the hallway to the bathroom. The shower felt good, but it didn't revive me. I was in a daze, not tired.

The A train arrived as I stepped through the turnstile. I sat in the corner of the subway car, replaying the incident with Madison. Almost fired. Told, over a speakerphone, between expletives, that I was probably too much of a liability for the firm. It had taken what felt like a lifetime to get this job—and in just two months I was about to lose it.

Across the street from the firm, I stopped at Café Europa, or "Café Rip-You-Off-A," as I'd come to know it, for my overpriced morning cup of Colombian Hazelnut Supreme. The woman standing in front of me looked oddly familiar—I presumed she worked at Nickel. We paid at adjacent registers, and then it hit me. I closed my eyes tightly. She was Madison's secretary, Sari.

I'm sure Sari knew everything. She probably knew everything before Madison did—she was the one who printed out the Bullock bills. Come to think of it, I was sure the whole right wing of the law firm was privy to my lashing because Madison had put me on speakerphone. Sari and I gave each other a polite smile at the condiment table. I procrastinated with the cream and sugar in order to stagger our exits.

We walked toward the firm, me a few steps behind her. Then she stopped in her tracks and turned as if we were in midconversation. "You know, his bark is worse than his bite," she said. "You should know that about him."

A rush of adrenaline hit me. "Really?" I said desperately. "I can't tell you how much it means to hear you say that. Thank you." We began walking together toward the firm.

"I know you must be upset. But you shouldn't be. This always happens. Once a month the bills get printed, and there are new victims. When I saw the size of the Rufus bill this month, I *knew* we were in for a doozy. Don't get yourself crazy. Four other associates and even a partner got phone calls like yours. Maybe not as bad, but that's just because you were first on his hit list. I'm sure he's over it by now. If you can, try not to let it get you down."

I held open the door to our building for her. "Thank you again," I said. "I appreciate what you're saying, Sari. I guess you can say I'm a bit disillusioned over my choice of professions."

"Oh, don't be. Don't make it out to be more than it was."

We stepped onto the elevator with two men I didn't recognize. Maybe they were Nickel employees, maybe not. We both knew better than to continue our conversation.

I got off a floor before her, tipped my head, and mouthed, "Thank you." Sari smiled and then shifted her eyes toward the floor of the elevator. I felt better than I had in weeks.

I walked past five offices. All of them had their lights off. New York law-firm hours generally didn't begin until after nine A.M. I relished those fifteen to twenty minutes when I could sit down, decompress from the commute, sip my coffee, and read the paper.

My office was dark, too. Hayley hadn't arrived yet, and thankfully, that annoying little red message light on the telephone wasn't illuminated. It just meant more work.

I took a sip of coffee and began logging on to the network. I could feel the caffeine and sugar rush to my fingertips. Scanning my e-mail inbox, there were no new assignments, and according to my electronic calendar, I had one meeting. It was Tuesday, time for my fourth and final one-hour mandatory Westlaw training session. I'd taken this particular course six times—once a year in law school, once before my Nickel internship, once during new-associate orientation, and now. The truth was, everything you needed to know about Westlaw could be taught in about forty-five minutes.

But I didn't mind the sessions. Matt, the Westlaw instructor, was very laid-back. Cindy Rogers, the head librarian, had filled him in on my "circumstances," and luckily, Matt wasn't on some power trip to teach me a lesson. He briefed me on Nickel's billing rates, reviewed a few Westlaw hot-keys, and gave me some basic tips on how to conduct electronic legal research economically and efficiently. Then he promised to tell Cindy that I was progressing beautifully. She would in turn fold that information into Madison's weekly Wellen status report.

Matt and I made a plan. Using his free password, we spent the sessions conducting actual Bullock-Rufus legal research, so I could do my job without showing up on Madison's reports. Our goal was to eliminate or at least minimize the appearance of my initials for two months. We figured that would give Madison some time to cool off and me some time to rehabilitate my credibility. Nickel was making Westlaw a fortune. A little free research wasn't going to hurt anyone.

Today could have just as easily been yesterday or tomorrow. It was looking like another ten- to twelve-hour day of reviewing, designating, and producing documents, and conducting legal research. Joy. Aaron

Reinstein was writing a motion to compel Rufus to produce certain ink-testing documents, so I planned to use my last free Westlaw session conducting research to support his legal papers.

The phone rang. "Alex Wellen," I said in a raspy voice.

"Morning. It's David. Did I wake you?"

"What?"

"I'm just kidding—you sound half asleep."

"Yeah, I'm not much of a morning person."

"Well, this will wake you up. The bar results are out." I panicked. "The *Pennsylvania* bar results are out. And they're pitiful."

"Really? How do you know?"

"My dad faxed me the pages from the *Pennsylvania Law Journal*. Brace yourself. The pass rate was fifty-eight percent."

"You're kidding."

"Check this out. Dougen failed. Richey and Fitzsimmons failed, and geez, they're getting married next month. Silverstein failed. Allen failed. Hey, how do you like that. Allen failed." I could hear him paging through the fax. "Schnaider failed."

"Schnaider failed?" I said in disbelief. Timothy Schnaider was law review, trial team, and had graduated with highest honors.

"And those were just the names I was looking for. Is there anyone you're wondering about?"

The Pennsylvania bar results were a terrible, horrible car accident. Yet I couldn't resist rubbernecking. I didn't want any of my law school colleagues to fail, not even the most annoying, arrogant, and cutthroat ones. If for no other reason than I wanted to feel like my graduating class as a whole was properly prepared for the bar exam.

Until recently, the Pennsylvania bar exam was known as the "cake bar." Similar to New Jersey's exam, the essay section was limited to the six MBE topics. But former Pennsylvania was even *easier* than New Jersey. The New Jersey essay section required a minimum score. The former Pennsylvania essays were graded pass/fail. That meant as long as a former Pennsylvania applicant made a good-faith effort to answer the essay section with a few coherent paragraphs containing some legalese, he or she was welcome to become a member of the illustrious Pennsylvania Bar.

But right before I graduated, everything changed. Pennsylvania's State Bar of Law Examiners decided to borrow from New York and make the essay section a legitimate challenge. They changed it from pass/fail to graded and began testing applicants on nineteen topics specific to Pennsylvania law, not simply six MBE courses. Most of my colleagues from law school, like me, had spent the summer memorizing thousands and thousands of state-specific laws.

This was the second time Pennsylvania had administered its new format. The February results had been even worse. But February's pass rates were typically lower than July's—by as much as 25 percent—mostly because many of the people taking the exam then were taking it for the second time. And, sadly, plenty of second-timers were third-timers and fourth-timers. The new format and the abysmal results were a rude awakening for Pennsylvania candidates, and a rude awakening for many of my friends. It was different when we were talking about bar-exam statistics. Now there were names that went along with the numbers. A 58 percent pass rate meant nearly half of them failed. David was right. I was wide awake.

"I don't think I'm curious about anyone," I said, restraining myself.

"Yeah, it's bad," he said, half listening. "Oh look, Sanders, Sutton, and Travis failed."

"David, tell me who passed." Even though the substance, format, and grading of the New York and Pennsylvania bar exams varied considerably, I hoped the results could give me some insight into how some of the top Temple Law students performed.

"Okay. Let's see . . . London, Loren, and LeMann passed. Ronald Morris passed—no surprise there. Mehra passed. Powell, Trenton, Wells, and Welsh passed. Whoa! Royal failed. Stash failed. I can't believe Stash failed. Come to think of it, I can't believe I dated Stash."

"Stash failed? Dude, this is lame. I'm done," I said.

"Me, too."

"I've heard that the New York pass rate was too high last year, and that they plan to raise the bar," I said. "We may be headed for dismal results, too."

"People say that every year. I can't worry about it. If you pass, don't call me. Don't call me if you fail, either. I mean, call me if you fail if you want to call me. But if I fail, I'm not gonna call you. Then again, I guess you'll know from the newspaper. All right, let's just both check the newspaper and only call each other if we both pass."

"Otherwise what? We never talk again?"

"You know what I'm saying," he said.

"I do. I gotta go. That's my other line. The single ring means it's an internal call. In other words, more work. I'll talk to you later." The caller ID said "John Madison." I braced myself and switched lines.

"Hey, it's me," Sari whispered.

"Whew. You got me all nervous. What's happening?"

"I just wanted to give you an update. I spoke with Mr. Madison this morning."

"You did? About what?" I was worried.

"About everything. I've been working for Mr. Madison for fifteen years." I didn't like that Sari still called him "Mr. Madison." "I have the greatest respect for the man, and in turn, he trusts me. Actually, he started the conversation. I guess for whatever reason, you were on his mind. Plus, he knew I'd overheard everything. He said, 'Do you think I was too hard on that Wellen kid?'"

"He said that?"

"Yeah. So I said yes. I said, 'Alex didn't deserve that phone call. So he made a few mistakes. It wasn't completely his fault. Aaron Reinstein should take some responsibility.'"

My heart dropped. Getting Aaron in trouble was the last thing I wanted to do. "You mentioned Aaron Reinstein?"

"I can't remember. But then I said, 'You know, you should apologize.'"

I cringed as the nausea set in. "You told Madison that he should apologize?" I didn't want Sari to think I didn't appreciate her help, even though I didn't appreciate her help. "That *really* wasn't necessary, Sari. I don't know what to say."

"It was no problem. I said, 'You should apologize.' And he said, 'Should I?' And I said, 'Yeah, you should do it today.' And then he went back to reading his newspaper. So I don't know what he's going to do, but he'll probably say *something* to you soon."

"O-kay. Again, I don't know what to say. I didn't want you to go to any trouble. This is all too much."

"Look, I speak my mind with Mr. Madison. He listens to me. And when I want him to— Wait . . . wait . . . I have to go. I think he's coming." We said good-bye.

In preparation for my meeting with Matt-the-Westlaw-guy, I decided to do some preliminary research on the motion to compel the Rufus ink-testing documents. I took my usual route to the library—the long, circuitous one that avoided walking past Madison or Sari. I found a few cases on point and decided to read them in my office. I piled up six thick case-law books and began slowly maneuvering my way back to my desk. Turning a blind corner, I nearly knocked Madison over.

"Mr. Madison," I said without stopping.

"Alex, hold on." The books were heavy. A shot of adrenaline hit me. I hoped he couldn't hear my heart beating. "First of all, you can call me John. Listen, I might have come down on you a little hard the other day, but what I wanted you to realize is that I have to give my clients the best work product for the best value. You understand what I'm saying, don't you?"

"I do."

"I've put a short memo together on how to bill Bullock. Have you read it?"

"I just got a copy, and yes, I've definitely read it." I adjusted the books and considered putting them down on the floor if this was going to take a while.

"Just stick to those rules, and you'll be fine."

"I understand." I considered justifying my former actions. "I understand," I said again.

"Good. And I see you're going to the books first. Excellent idea." He smiled.

"Thanks."

Madison walked away. I steadied the books with one knee and regained my composure. "Hey there," I said awkwardly to an unfamiliar associate who walked by.

It wasn't beautiful, perhaps even a bit backhanded, but it still qualified: It was an apology. Madison and I now had some sort of relationship.

"In addition to your Westlaw use, Madison wants me to review your time sheets on a weekly basis," Aaron Reinstein confided in me. "Here's your chance to change his perception of you. He's watching."

I know. But now that I've got his attention, my God, I hope I pass the bar.

CHAPTER 50

ON THURSDAY, NOVEMBER 29, at ten-thirty A.M., Hayley and I called the bar examiner's office, and the prerecorded message was different. We both became flushed: "Applicants will receive results to the exam administered on July thirtieth and thirty-first of this year beginning Saturday, December first."

I spent the better half of Saturday, December 1, sitting on my front stoop, waiting for the mailman. Nothing. On Monday morning I prepared for the inevitable. I put on my favorite suit and tie for good luck and walked into work fully aware that for better or worse, my status was about to change. It was time to come out of my burrow, and if I, Punxsutawney Alex, saw my shadow, it meant nine more months of the bar. The first phone call came early that morning.

"*Thank God* there was so much criminal procedure on that exam."

"Hey, David. You passed?" I said, stealing his thunder.

"I passed. It's a beautiful thing."

"I can't believe it. That came out wrong. Congrats. This is huge.

How did you find out so early? Who gets the mail at eight-forty-five in the morning?"

"The District Attorney's Office. My bureau chief made a phone call to Albany this morning. Nineteen of us passed. Two failed."

"Let's see, that's about ninety percent. Not bad."

"Maybe if you're comparing that percentage to the national average, but we're *all* supposed to pass. At one point I heard it's two strikes and you're out. Now the rumor is the two people who failed are gone."

"Done?"

"That's what I'm told. What's the rule at Nickel?"

"If you ask our recruiter, no one at Nickel has failed the bar in six years. I think that's bullshit. I'm not supposed to fail, and that's that. They've already moved me out here, paid me twenty-five thousand dollars for three months' work, and given me an office and a secretary. I'm told they recently preordered business cards."

"You should go home and get the mail."

"I thought you weren't going to call unless we both passed."

"I've changed the rules. Go home and end the misery."

"Or start the sequel: The Bar Strikes Back. My people will be in touch."

For those of us who didn't have a bureau chief in the District Attorney's Office, there were basically three methods of delivery. The slowest was the *New York Law Journal*. The results would be published by midweek.

The fastest method was the Internet, but the State Board of Law Examiners hadn't worked out the kinks on its website yet. In particular, they had underestimated how neurotic and desperate future lawyers could be. Sam Weaver, for example, logged on to the home page on Friday, a full twenty-four hours before the results were rumored to be published. All weekend, Sam and thousands of other desperate wanna-bes simultaneously made attempts to reload that page. The denial-of-service attacks repeatedly brought the servers crashing down. As of Monday morning the results hadn't been posted.

I went to the firm library to avoid discussing the impending results with Hayley. When the coast was clear, I went over to one of the library computers and tried the website. The browser timed out, saying that it was unable to connect to the server. I never considered having a friend check for me. Finding out, at least initially, was going to be a private matter. And the only way that was going to happen was the third method of delivery—snail mail.

When Arjun and I realized the results weren't coming over the weekend, we made a plan for Monday. He had Mondays off from b-school, so he promised to call me at work if a suspicious letter arrived. At that point I'd come home and open the letter. He was not allowed to read the results to me over the phone. I had to know first.

I made a point of not disclosing to Arjun any of the telling physical details or dimensions about the letter. In particular, I withheld any information concerning its thickness, lest he know the results the moment he pulled it out of the mailbox.

All my life, the envelope-thickness rule was the same. Thick was good, thin was bad. College applications, law school applications, job interviews—all the good results came in a thick envelope welcoming me aboard and asking me to fill out some follow-up paperwork. A thin envelope always meant "Thanks but no thanks."

For the bar-exam results, however, I'd heard the rule was reversed: A thin envelope contained a simple congratulations welcoming the person into the New York Bar, and a thick letter contained a long rejection and a new bar application. Geez, a new bar application! "Sorry you failed. Are you okay? Good, here's a new application. See you in February."

I guess the bar examiners sent the rejection letter and application together in the interest of saving postage. I shuddered at the thought. After spending tens of thousands of dollars on my legal education, I would have gladly shelled out the postage in advance in exchange for a little decency. Getting a failing grade would be hard enough. Getting a new application would be devastating.

I hit the reload button on the Internet browser and watched it time out again.

"Alex Wellen, please call 6473. Alex Wellen, 6473." That was my extension. Someone was paging me to my own phone. It had to be Hayley. It was time. I called her on the library phone.

"Your secretary is looking for you. She says that Arjun called," Hayley said.

"I figured."

"Apparently, he was asking all kinds of questions about the thickness of the envelope," she said. This was a bad sign. For some reason, I didn't think he'd be asking that question if the envelope was thin. "What are you going to do?"

"What are you doing?" I asked.

"Me, I'm out of here. I live five blocks away. I have to know. I'm sure you passed. I'll talk to you soon."

"Thanks. I'm sure you passed. Good luck."

I hit the refresh button again on the Internet browser, but still no luck. I spent a few more minutes pretending to do work, then made my way back to my office. On the way, I passed Sam's office. He was slouched in his chair, staring out the window, clearly in a state of shock.

"Sam, are you okay?"

"I failed."

"You're kidding."

He gave me a look.

"*You* failed?"

He gave me another look. "Diane, my girlfriend, just dropped the letter off. Here, take a look for yourself," he said, tossing me the letter. "This is unbearable."

Dear Candidate:

You are hereby notified that you did not pass the examination for admission to the Bar held on July 30–31.

The dates and deadlines for the next examination can be found in the enclosed application packet. If you plan to take that examination, the enclosed form, together with a certified check or money order in the amount of $250, payable to "State Board of Law Examiners," must be received in this office at least 60 days prior to the date of the examination OR 21 days from the date of this letter, whichever is later.

Within 30 days from the date of this letter, you may direct a written request for any or all of the following items below to the Board's office at the above address. Items (2) and (3) will eventually be published in the *New York Law Journal*. The required fees, which must be in a *separate* certified check or money order from the application fee, are noted below.

1. Copies of your essay answers ($40)
2. Copies of the essay questions ($15)
3. Samples of above-average answers by successful applicants ($15)

Sincerely,

Nancy O. Carpenter

Executive Secretary

Enclosure

The thick-or-thin rule was true. All that studying, whining, complaining, stressing, quizzing, driving, drinking, and this was how it ended for Sam.

"Sam, I'm so sorry."

"Me, too," he whispered. "Everyone in the firm is going to know." He continued to look out the window. "How am I supposed to walk out of here today? How am I supposed to walk back in?"

It was a peculiar situation—within the hour I might find myself in the very same circumstances. What could I possibly say? What would I want to hear? Nothing. There was nothing to say. I wanted to be comforting, but all I could think of was myself. God, if Sam (Georgetown Law, Tier 1) failed, then so did I. This was proof that anyone could fail.

"Again, I'm sorry," I said. I put my hand on his shoulder and left the room. As I walked by his office, Aaron Reinstein mumbled something in my direction.

"Excuse me?" I made a U-turn into his office.

"Hayley passed," he repeated, pretending to write something. Aaron knew exactly how much bar-related angst I'd been experiencing over the past two months. Working so closely together on the Bullock case, we'd become good friends.

"She instructed me *not* to tell you, because she said it might freak you out," he said smugly. He snapped his fingers. "Earth to Alex."

"Yeah, yeah. I hear you loud and clear. Excellent."

"You're an idiot. I'm sure you passed. Go home and get this over with so I can send you back to Helix."

I'd always assumed that when the results came, I'd book home. But now, faced with the imminent and inevitable, I was in no rush. I took the leisurely route to the subway, replaying the legal career alternatives that would have enabled me to beg off embarrassing bar results. Had I clerked for a judge, for example, I would have avoided the potential humiliation of failing the exam in front of two hundred colleagues. A clerkship would have enabled me to get the results in private and then partake in a stealthy retake.

I stepped onto the A train, sat in the corner of the car, leaned my head against the wall, and closed my eyes. I was so strung out, exhausted, disgusted, frustrated, angry, anxious, and emotionally drained. After the train made two stops, I noticed the only other passenger in the subway car—a filthy homeless man lying across four seats. He opened his eyes and gave me a warm smile. I smiled back and exited the train at my stop.

"Hey, Arjun," I said, out of breath. "What's up?"

"What does the thickness of the envelope mean?" Arjun was at his computer with his back to me. For the last three weeks, he'd been engrossed in some computer role-playing game.

"Where's the letter?"

"Over there," he said, pointing to the hallway. "Up higher." Arjun, who was six foot three, had thumbtacked the letter about eight feet up the wall.

"Idiot." I took a running jump for the letter and missed it. Finally, I grabbed it in between my fingertips.

It was thin.

My heart started beating quickly. I ran into my room and closed the door. Lying on my bed, with both hands outstretched, I held the envelope above me. Ten seconds passed. I tore at it, unfolded the letter, and read the first sentence: "You are hereby notified that you passed the examination for admission to the Bar held on July 30–31."

BIRTH

CHAPTER 51

OUTGOING MESSAGE: "HI, IT'S ALEX. I PASSED. DO WHAT-EVER."

"Password? Beep, beep, beep, beep. You have nine new messages." You're popular, people love you, you're important.

"First message. Received yesterday at six-thirty-four P.M. Yo, it's David. I just got your message. Bring it, bring it, bring it. Nice job. Congratulations. Let's meet later for a BAR/BRI book-burning brewski. Did I just say 'brewski'? I apologize. That was uncalled for. Call me on the cell. Beep. End of message. Message erased.

"Next message. Received yesterday at seven-oh-one P.M. Aaron calling. What did I tell you? Wasn't I on record that you were going to pass? This is great news. As a reward, you get no increase in pay. You're now liable for legal malpractice. And you're officially up for partnership . . . in *nine* years. Nah, I'm just kidding. Not really. No, I'm serious. I'm kidding. I'm not. Feel free to show up tomorrow whenever you've sobered up. Beep. End of message. Message erased.

"Next message. Received yesterday at seven-twenty-two P.M. You did it, man. We knew you'd do it. I'm so proud of you. This is your kid brother. We're all so happy for you. Actually, that's not true. No one else is even home, but *I'm* psyched. You won't be surprised to learn that the Oracle prophesied this result, but I didn't want to say anything. I didn't want to jinx you. Alex-phone-home! I love you. Bye. Beep. End of message. Message erased.

"Next message. Received yesterday at eight-oh-five P.M. Congratulations. It's me, Linda, from Laverne's, but I guess you knew that. So, today at work I overheard a customer say that the bar results were out, and I just had to call you. I just knew you'd pass. I'm making you dinner. It's going to be incredible, and I'm not taking no for an answer. See you soon. Beep. End of message. Message erased.

"Next message. Received yesterday at nine-thirty-one P.M. It's Mom. I know Mike just left you a message. I cried when I heard the news. I'm so proud of you. Our hopes and prayers were with you. All that work and struggle paid off—you're on your way now . . . unstoppable . . . We love you. Call us. Beep. End of message. Message erased.

"Next message. Received yesterday at nine-forty-nine P.M. Hey, wanker. So now what? You think you're a big shot? You think this means that chicks are going to go with you? Even if it does mean visiting your stair-climbing, old-girlfriend-underwear-throwing, rat-infested apartment. It's Sophie. Call at your leisure. Beep. End of message. Message erased.

"Next message. Received yesterday at ten-ten P.M. Good evening. It's Owen Thompkins. I know you came to my office seven years ago with your invention for a double-sided table-tennis paddle. It always bothered me how I just took your eight hundred dollars and then discouraged you from pursuing your dreams. Well, now look who's got egg on his face. In short, I misjudged you, and I'm sorry. You rule. Beep. End of message. You've pressed an invalid number. I'm sorry, there is no message to replay.

"Next message. Received yesterday at eleven-eleven P.M. As a long-standing member of the New York bar for all of two years, it is an honor to welcome you aboard. I always knew you'd pass. Here's Arjun. Yasmine and I are at the Opium Den in the East Village. It's time to pay the piper. We're doing one shot of Jägermeister for every country in Europe that you convinced me that you failed the bar. And no, I am not dragging your sorry ass up our stairs at the end of the evening. Congratulations. Can't wait to see you. Beep. End of message. Message erased.

"Next message. Received today at twelve-oh-one P.M. Hi, my dear, it's Gwen. I just got your message, and I am overjoyed for you. I was waiting to get a copy of the *New York Law Journal* before calling you. I'm assuming you saw the paper, and that's how you heard my good news as well. I also passed New Jersey, so I'm doubly happy, I guess. Although I think in all my angst and anxiety, I caught the flu, so I'm under the weather. I hope you're out celebrating. I'm incredibly proud of you. There was never a doubt in my mind as far as you were concerned. I miss you. Talk to you soon. Bye. Beep. End of message. Message erased.

"Next message. Received today at twelve-forty-five P.M. John Madison here! I'm looking at the most recent Bullock bill. It says here that you conducted 8.12417 hours of electronic legal research on November twenty-ninth. What have I told you about billing this client? Do you want me to cry? Because I'll cry. And when *you* open the John Madison floodgates . . . Okay, fine, I do a terrible John Madison, but I'm drunk. It's Hayley, if you didn't already figure that out. Listen. Do me a favor. When you get into the office tomorrow, turn on my desk light and computer. In my top right drawer is a pair of glasses. Take them out and put them on my desk. That should buy me some time in the morning. Be good and don't vomit. Bye. Beep. End of message. Message erased."

CHAPTER 52

THAT SUMMER CLOSE to ten thousand people took the New York bar exam, and 68.4 percent, or sixty-five hundred, of them passed. The good news: The pass rate for first-timers like me was better—76.5

percent passed. The bad news: Even that pass rate was down from last year by nearly 3 percent. Was this year's exam more difficult? Were the candidates less qualified? BAR/BRI said no and no, but we'd never really know.

The final phase of bar admission was upon me. Before being sworn in and allowed to practice, I'd have to complete a lengthy questionnaire that included affidavits of good moral character, an affirmation of legal employment, and proof that I'd graduated from law school. Then there was a short, informal interview conducted by a member of the Committee on Character and Fitness. The rumor was that your application could get bounced if you had an outstanding parking ticket or you defaulted on a student loan. After that, we had to attend a two-hour orientation about legal ethics, the importance of pro bono work, and bar associations. If I wanted to be admitted to the New York bar before next summer, I'd have to get my application in right away. Swearing-in ceremonies were done on a rolling basis.

Drudgery. That was the life of a first-year associate at a major law firm. So what if I passed the bar. I spent the day after the results doing exactly the same thing I'd done the day before—reviewing, flagging, designating, and producing documents for the Rufus matter. Two days after the results, Nickel took all the new first-year associates, except for Sam, to a congratulatory lunch at an expensive restaurant. It was a very nice gesture.

If you're going to be immersed in drudgery, I've always said, go for extreme drudgery. And there was no better way to capitalize on that opportunity than to fly across the country and sit in a windowless warehouse poring over decade-old engineering notebooks, marketing plans, and business records. My next trip to Helix, Oregon, I made alone. But in mid-December it came time to review the business records of some of the Bullock bigwigs, and Aaron Reinstein decided to join me.

Even though Aaron and I were now good friends, this still was my first business trip with a senior-level attorney, and I was consumed with paranoia. It hadn't taken long to learn that being panic-stricken was fundamental to being an attorney. Everyone on the case was scared of something. Looking at John Madison's billing memo, you could tell he was terrified of losing Bullock as a client. Aaron went to work every day wondering whether I would make some sort of amateur mistake that could cost him his job. And I spent my days convinced I'd disclose something confidential to the wrong person.

Paranoia seeped into every element of my life as an attorney. Every conversation during every meal in every restaurant was fraught with danger.

"Helix is a company town," Aaron warned me on the flight over. "You never know who's sitting next to you—maybe he works for Bullock, or maybe she's a Rufus attorney working on the case. The waiter's wife could be a Bullock employee. As a general rule, keep your mouth shut."

As the seniormost attorney on the matter, Aaron was obligated to put the fear of God in me. I didn't resent him for it. He was the closest I'd ever had to a big brother. It was a pleasure traveling with him. Instead of sitting coach, booking cheap motels, and eating fast food, we lived large. Thanks to his frequent-flyer miles, he traveled everywhere in business class and was kind enough to upgrade me in both directions. We dined at great steakhouses, smoked cigars, and drank martinis. We worked hard. We played hard.

"The problem with this city is that we can get in anywhere," I said to him as the bouncer waved us into the Engine Room, one of Seattle's hottest clubs, on Friday night. It had been Aaron's idea to fly from Helix to Seattle for the weekend. On Sunday night we'd make our way back to Helix to review more executive files.

"Yeah, this club is pitiful," Aaron said. "We're nobodies, and they still just let us in."

"Do they even *have* a VIP list?" I asked.

"I don't think so. It's mind-boggling. This would *never* happen in New York. I can't respect a city that doesn't use some discretion."

Inside, we did the same thing that men always do in bars. We stood in the corner, sipped our overpriced drinks, and assessed a multitude of women that we'd never talk to. Keep it, keep it, keep it, bring it, bring it, bring it. Aaron quickly picked up on the system. I pounded drinks in an embarrassing and juvenile effort to keep up with Aaron.

After about an hour, my low tolerance to alcohol caught up with me. At one point I lost Aaron and met this sexy Native-American woman named Natalie. We laughed. We danced. We drank. I mentioned that my hotel had a twenty-four-hour hot tub, and before I knew it, we were in a cab back to the Best Western.

"I'm going in," she said, pulling off her clothes in the reception area of the hotel. The Jacuzzi was in her sights.

"Wait, wait, wait," I begged her as hotel guests looked on. Once I convinced her not to skinny-dip in the hot tub, we went back to my hotel room, kissed, groped, and passed out. There was some morning sex, then some more sleep.

Aaron's hotel room was four down from mine. I gave him a visit around ten A.M. Natalie was still asleep. "How ya doing?"

"No, the question is, how are *you* doing?" he said, wide-eyed.

"I'm good. I'm good."

"I go downstairs to get breakfast this morning, I'm waiting for the elevator, and this guy comes up next to me. We're both just standing there, waiting. Suddenly, we hear all these sounds. There's moaning, a little yelling. And it all seems to be emanating from *your* room." He started laughing. "I'm in my room reading briefs this morning, and you're in yours doing, well—"

"Aaron, these were exceptional circumstances. I never meet women in bars."

"Aren't *you* supposed to be the one working? *I'm* the senior associate, and you're the first year. Where is she now?"

"In the room. She seems very nice. Last night she mentioned that there's this big fair in town. We have no social plans. Maybe she can call a friend and we can all go." Aaron hesitantly agreed. Ultimately, there was no friend, and the three of us spent a nice romantic day walking around the local craft fair.

"I was going to a community college up until about a year ago," Natalie told us over an expensive dinner. "I quit because I found out the real money is in fishing boats."

"Excuse me?" Aaron asked. He hadn't spoken in about an hour.

"Yeah, I spend a few months of the year in Alaska, living and work-ing on a commercial fishing vessel. I'm a slimer."

"Didn't I mention that?" I asked Aaron.

"I work on the production line, gutting fish. The fishing vessel pays my room and board. They even bus me up to Alaska. If you're on a good boat and it's a good harvest, you can make a killing."

"How much?" Aaron asked.

"Let's see. We had a good season. I made a little over forty thousand dollars in five months, and that's nothing. The guys harvesting the fish can make that in one month."

"Are there many other women on these ships?" I asked.

"Most of the harvesters are men. Maybe half the processors are women."

"And what do you do the remaining seven months of the year?" I asked her.

Natalie laughed. "Collect unemployment." Then she took a sip of wine.

Aaron didn't plan on making too many treks to Helix after that. It had nothing to do with the Natalie incident; it just didn't make sense to send a senior associate cross-country to review documents. Now that we were done with all the executive files, Aaron planned to stay put for a while. There would be plenty of traveling in the deposition phase.

The day I got back from Helix, Aaron informed me that drudgery loved company. Sam had been assigned to the Rufus case. "The two of you leave for Helix in the morning," Aaron said.

Sam had one more chance to pass the bar before picking another career, or at least another firm. Nickel figured that document review was about as low-maintenance an assignment as it got. These days I was a finely tuned document-reviewing machine, averaging about ten thousand pages per day. In a split second I could tell whether a docu-ment should be designated attorney-client privileged, public, confi-dential, highly confidential, or the new category, highly confidential future-product information. Often the code names of the Bullock projects instantly tipped me off. Bullock had a long tradition of naming all of its projects after candy bars. Projects like "Kit Kat" and "PayDay" were flagged confidential. "Milky Way," however, was considered highly confidential future-product information.

Because I was the idiot savant of Bullock document review, Aaron asked me to mentor Sam—an awkward assignment, given our already strained friendship and the bar review results. Sam and I began spending endless hours together, reviewing and designating documents. We flagged each document with the agreed-upon color code: purple flags signified highly confidential future-product information; red was highly confidential; yellow was confidential; green was public; and blue was privileged. Eventually, paralegals would come in and stamp each page of every document flagged red, for example, with the words "Highly Confidential." After that the pages would be numbered, copied, and shipped, or "produced," to Rufus. Rufus was about to receive millions and millions of Bullock pages.

Sam and I couldn't talk about the Bullock case in public, and we couldn't talk about the bar, so we spent most of our Helix meals in silence. Aaron had whipped me into such a paranoid frenzy that I couldn't even keep it together in the safest place in the world—Bullock's headquarters.

"Hey, Alex, I'm hungry. I'm gonna make a run to the vending machines. Can I grab you a . . . *Snickers,*" Sam said, smiling.

"Shhhhhh! What's wrong with you! Dude, you're *freaking* me out," I whispered loudly. "Snickers" was the code name for Bullock's most highly confidential future product.

I was spending so much time in Helix that I stopped checking out of the Ramada Hotel. At thirty-nine dollars a night for deluxe accommodations, it was just easier to keep the room and leave a change of clothes. The airline tickets, however, weren't cheap. All of our trips to Oregon were impromptu, and that meant never buying a ticket with a seven-day advance. Each full-priced round-trip ticket cost Nickel, or rather Bullock, a fortune. That is, until John Madison started looking at the December bills and realized that it was cheaper to send all the

boxes east. That month *Aaron* got the earful. Because document review consumed my time and legal research didn't, I'd been managing
to stay under Madison's radar.

As the litigation picked up steam, so did the number of boxes being
shipped from Helix to New York. In late December, Bullock began for-
warding documentation from its manufacturing plants all over the
world. The Nickel partners realized that hundreds of boxes would
eventually turn into thousands, and the firm was going to need some
help. They decided to hire six full-time attorneys to review, designate,
and produce Bullock documents. They came through a legal temp
service—I'd never heard of such a thing. I'd become somewhat of
a snob about document review and I was skeptical about using temp
attorneys. "We're going to build our whole case around these documents, and so will Rufus," Aaron had counseled me. "I can't empha-
size how important this work is."

As document review boy extraordinaire, I was assigned by Aaron to
train the temp attorneys. The first thing I did was have each sign a
confidentiality agreement. These six temps were about to become
privy to Bullock's most precious secrets, and I couldn't risk having
Loose-Lips Temp Number Four inadvertently utter the code name
"Butterfinger." I spent the next week baby-sitting them in a Nickel
conference room, answering their every question. After reviewing hundreds of thousands of highly confidential documents, I could name
and describe every Bullock engineering and marketing project by its
internal code-name, dating back twenty years to the inception of ink-
jet technology in 1978.

"What do you designate engineering lab reports?" one asked.

"Is Benny Sawtelle a lawyer?" asked another. "I think this document
might be attorney-client privileged."

"What is the Reese's Pieces Project?" said a third, handing me a
document.

"Flag this one purple. Reese's Pieces contains highly confidential
future-product information. Wait a minute," I said, paging through the
document. "This printout is in color. And it's signed in ink." That's when

I realized that even Bullock was feeling overwhelmed by the ferocious pace of the Rufus litigation. Apparently, because it had become too expensive and too time-consuming, Bullock had unilaterally decided to stop copying its documents and was shipping us *originals*. Aaron charged me with pricing out every document service in New York City capable of copying, scanning, and cataloging millions of pages.

The temp process started out slow. Each attorney averaged about five hundred pages per day. But once my gaggle of lawyers was satisfyingly self-sufficient, and the reproduction and electronic scanning services were in place, I moved on to other equally riveting first-year-associate litigation work. Like privilege logs. Privilege logs were charts outlining all of the attorney-client-privileged information that Bullock was withholding, without telling them what we were withholding. Creating a privilege log was painstaking, mind-numbing work. For every document we withheld or redacted, we had to log who wrote it, who received it, when, and generally what it was about; then we'd hand the privilege log over to Rufus. That way they could attempt to challenge our decisions in court. My Bullock privilege log was already a hundred pages long and described more than a thousand documents that I had no intention of ever handing over to Rufus.

Soon it became necessary for Nickel to rent out commercial space on one of the other floors in the building. It was designated our war room. On one side of the room, temp attorneys would review and produce Bullock documents. On the other side, Sam and I would start reviewing documents that Rufus sent us. They were trickling in at about four boxes a day. By contrast, we were sending Rufus about seventy-five boxes a day. I couldn't wait to see Rufus's docs. Finally, a rare opportunity to peer into the inner sanctum and peruse their pitiful research and development work, marketing plans, and business records. My blood boiled as the Rufus story came together—they planned to piggyback on Bullock's precious technology. Pirates!

With the Rufus matter exploding in size, John Madison decided to add a dozen Nickel attorneys to the lawsuit, in addition to the temp attorneys, paralegals, and administrative assistants. Soon he divided the twenty of us into teams—ten of us on defense, and ten of us on offense.

"Wellen," he said, like a professional coach. I was looking right at him yet was still startled by the call to action. "You're on defense. You've met the Bullock engineers, inventors, and managers. You're intimate with the inner workings. You know the Bullock story." The fact that I knew that Bullock's first cartridge, code-named "Baby Ruth," shot ink out of twelve nozzles, held four milliliters of ink, and printed ninety-six dots per inch made me critical.

I hoped that defending the Bullock story might eventually mean defending Bullock inventors. And that meant depositions, the next logical step in the discovery phase. Rufus would soon discover whether Bullock's executives, managers, and engineers supported the Bullock story. It was unheard of for a first-year associate at a major Manhattan law firm to do deposition work in a multimillion-dollar lawsuit. Depositions ordinarily came in your third or fourth year of practice. But my prospects were good.

I'd been seeing a lot more of Madison lately. The Rufus matter was heating up, and that meant more and more team meetings and strategy sessions. Until I met Madison, I'd always assumed senior partners lived the good life, working bankers' hours, doing ministerial jobs like reviewing bills and entertaining clients, and stepping into a litigation at the last possible moment to try the case before a jury. Not Madison. He worked around the clock. He was always on call. In fact, it was the late evenings where I observed Madison exhibit his greatest flashes of brilliance. Without hesitation, he could pinpoint the relevant legal issue and dispense the most savvy litigation strategy. Madison was smart, creative, and fearless. Law school professor William McGovern was my first scholar, and John Madison was my second.

At about the same time, Madison seemed to be rethinking his impression of me. Lately, he'd been assigning me to some special legal-research projects. He trusted me. And from what I could tell, he liked me.

"Alex, can you please stay," Madison said one night as he adjourned our weekly Rufus meeting. "Listen, you forgot to include partner approval on your December nineteenth entry. I put it in for you."

"Thanks. I'm surprised I missed that." Over the past few months Madison had gone from scrutinizing my bills to reading them out of sheer curiosity. I knew every one of his billing rules cold. I'd become the billing king, and we both knew it.

"I have two extra tickets to the Giants game this Sunday. It's the last game of the season. I try to circulate them around the firm. They're yours if you'd like them," he said. "Unless, of course, you're a Jets fan."

"Are you kidding? I love the Giants," I said, praying he wouldn't follow up with a tough question like "Name one player on the team." Look, I was all man, but my inability to name six living professional football players had proven emasculating in the past. I blamed my father.

"Thanks, I'll take them," I went on. "Are you going?"

"I haven't missed a game in six years. I'm bringing my son, Ron. Sari has the tickets at her desk. Just drop by and pick them up." I had less than a week to familiarize myself with relevant football-statistics fodder.

CHAPTER 53

I T WAS IMPOSSIBLE to go to Laverne's these days without Linda reminding me that she owed me a gourmet dinner to celebrate my results on the bar. Over and over I tried to politely decline, but she wouldn't have it. I sensed that she didn't have many friends, and when she started running through the potential menu, I buckled. We made Thursday-night plans.

That Thursday the weather was awful. It was sleeting, and by the time I found a cab and made my way to Linda's apartment on the Upper East Side, I was nearly half an hour late.

As soon as she opened the door, it was clear I'd made a terrible mistake. There she stood, busting out of a black evening gown, with full makeup and her hair up. All she was missing was the diamond tiara.

Linda gave me a kiss on the cheek. "You didn't have to bring wine," she said. It was a good thing I'd passed on the flowers. "I'll take your coat. Have a seat in the living room."

Two or three dozen candles were lit and positioned all over the room. Between the scented honey candles and whatever was roasting in the oven, the apartment smelled exquisite. I took a deep breath and then began sneezing uncontrollably.

"Are you allergic to cats?" Linda asked as she handed me a glass of wine.

"Only a little." My eyes began to itch.

"I'll put Sheila in the bedroom. Dinner should be ready in a half hour. You're going to love it."

"What are we having?" I asked her as my sneezing attack subsided.

"It's going to be a surprise," she said as she took a seat close to me on the couch. Over the next twenty minutes, we covered all the major topics we had in common—pie making, the bar exam, and the Oracle's artwork. After our second glass of wine, we sat down to dinner. Linda had prepared an elaborate seven-course meal. We started off with a seared tuna appetizer, followed by roasted butternut-squash soup. With very little left to say, I peppered her with questions about the ingredients, preparation, and presentation of the meal.

"This is an arugula salad with goat cheese, walnuts, apples, and a raspberry vinaigrette dressing," she said. She dreamed of one day publishing a cookbook.

"This is too much," I told her as she placed a small dish of lemon sorbet before me.

"We're halfway through," she said, delighted. I furtively checked my watch as Linda reached into the oven for our entrées. It was nine-thirty-five P.M. I'd made plans to meet Sophie in upper midtown at ten-thirty P.M. I was going to be late.

"Honey-glazed pork tenderloin with mint carrots," she said proudly. My mouth began to water.

"You went to too much trouble," I told her. She watched me eat. "This is remarkable. Aren't you going to eat?" I said.

She took a big sip of wine. "There's no other way to say this," she said. "But I may be falling in love with you, Alex. It's fine if you don't feel the same way, you probably don't, but I needed to tell you this."

I cradled my head in my hand. We both just sat there.

"Don't feel bad for me," she said.

"I'm just taking this in, that's all. I mean, we don't really know each other. I had no idea that you felt this way."

"I'm not sorry I told you," she said.

"No, no, I'm glad you told me." Take it back. Take it back. "I'm glad." At that point she didn't need to hear me say that I thought we had nothing in common, that there were at least ten years between us, and that I didn't feel any chemistry. I skipped directly to the conclusion. "I don't think we can have a romantic relationship, Linda. Have I ruined everything?"

"How can you ruin everything when there's chocolate-almond torte?" she said, getting up out of her seat. She hadn't had a bite of her pork tenderloin.

"Please don't be upset," I said.

"I'm not upset. I'm relieved. I'm relieved that I told you." Neither of us was relieved. The room was silent, awkward. I sneezed three times to change the mood. "When you're finished, we can have dessert and lattes in the living room," she said.

"You're going to kill me, but I have to go. I made some plans for later this evening. I underestimated how sophisticated the meal would be. I can cancel the other plans. It's not a big deal. I feel so badly. You went to all this trouble. And me leaving has nothing to do with what we were just talking about. I swear."

"I know. That's fine. I'll wrap dessert up for you. Alex, don't worry. Let's not make this a big deal." Five minutes later, Linda's cat was roaming the apartment, and I was in the hallway with a tinfoiled block of chocolate-almond torte.

The cab dropped me off at the Au Bar a few minutes before ten-thirty. The abrupt ending to my evening with Linda had put me back on schedule. Tonight I planned to pop the question to Sophie: Will you accompany me to a Giants football game hosted by senior law partner John Madison? After waiting twenty minutes and leaving her two cell-phone messages, I convinced the bouncer to let me get out of the sleeting snow and cruise the bar to make sure Sophie wasn't already inside. She wasn't. I hadn't seen her in a couple of weeks. She was a tough person to get ahold of. Plus, the nature of our relationship was to call whenever, for whatever. If we got together, causal sex was assumed.

After close to an hour, I called it quits. I was soaked, freezing, and disgusted. Just then Sophie pulled up in a cab.

"Sorry, my cell phone was dead," she said unapologetically.

"What about a pay phone?"

"Alex, your number's programmed into my phone, and the phone was dead. Plus, there were heaps of traffic. I don't know what you want me to do," she said, annoyed. I handed the woman behind the counter fifty bucks for our admission and another ten to hold our coats. The dynamic of my relationship with Sophie had changed ever since I used her Prada discount to buy clothes at Barney's. She'd insisted that I use it, and I'd regretted the whole thing. Now she acted as if I owed her; as if I dated her *for* the discount.

The Au Bar was for models and ridiculously rich people. I was neither. Sophie fit in, with her slim figure and midriff showing. She looked fantastic. I decided to forgive her. We really didn't know each other, and it was too early in the relationship to be having an argument.

"We'll fix everything with shots," she said, relieved to see the bar. Each of us did two shots of tequila. Then we ordered drinks and began dancing. Sophie started to loosen up. In fact, so much so that halfway through our second song, she threw up on my black square-toed shoes. Apparently, she hadn't eaten all day. We agreed to take a cab downtown to my apartment, where she could freshen up.

"At your last party, I never got a chance to try this thing," she said, jumping into The Chair. Geez, lady, you may only weigh one hundred and ten pounds, but be careful. "Turn me on."

I flipped the switch and propped up her feet. The mechanical rolling balls crept down her spine. She let out a sigh of ecstasy. It was interesting, the extreme reactions The Chair evoked. "We should do it *in* this chair. Have you already?"

"No," I said, evaluating whether it could hold both our weights. I straddled her, placing each knee on an arm of the chair. We began kissing. I moved down her neck. She let out another sigh—maybe it was me, and then again, maybe it was The Chair.

"Wait, wait, wait," she said, panicked.

"What?"

"Get off, quick." I did. She threw up on The Chair. "I'm sorry."

"Don't worry about it. It's pleather." We went to bed and tried to sleep.

At four-twelve A.M. Sophie said, "Ugh, I can't take it." Both of us had spent the last twenty minutes quietly scratching. "I keep getting bitten by something." She threw off the covers.

"Me, too," I said. "I must have bedbugs." She was in no mood to joke. "I'm sorry about this, Sophie. There must be a couple of mosquitoes in here."

"What's that sound?" she whispered. Lying completely still, we slowed our breathing and listened. A tiny scratching sound could be heard at my bedroom door.

"I think it's a rat eating the carpet under my door. This happens all the time," I said, realizing that I hadn't comforted her at all. "Don't worry." I pulled up the covers. "Even if he eats *all* the carpet, he's still too big to burrow underneath the door. He never gets in."

I DID NOT invite Sophie to the football game with Madison. She probably wouldn't have accepted anyway.

As there was no significant other significant enough to bring, I went with a safe bet. Mike had never been to a professional football game, and I figured I'd earn some cool-brother points for serving up box seats courtesy of the guy running one of the biggest intellectual property law firms in the world. Mike was thrilled.

"Okay, so you remember everything that we went over on the phone," I said to him as he got off the bus from Toms River.

"Yeah, yeah, yeah. John Madison, senior partner, second in command of the law firm, hated you, now he might like you, New York University Law, Tier One."

"And what do you know about the Rufus case?"

"I don't know anything about the major ink-jet lawsuit between Bullock and Rufus that, might I mention, was written up in the *New York Times.*"

"You read the *New York Times?*"

"Mom's idea. I'm just here to watch the football game," Mike continued. "Alex never talks about his work. I've never been to a football game." He sounded like he was reading the text off cue cards.

"Excellent. You'll do fine. Did you eat?"

"Nope. Can we go to Laverne's? I love their French toast with strawberries. Plus, I could see Linda. Does she work today?"

"I don't know. But we can't go to Laverne's." I paused. "I don't really go there anymore. Mom didn't tell you?"

"No."

"Linda confessed to me about a week ago that she's interested in starting a romantic relationship."

"With you? Really?"

"I told her I was flattered, I asked if we could be friends, and everything seemed copacetic. Then yesterday I got this angry letter saying that I wasn't holding up my end of the bargain and that our friendship was feeling very one-sided. The Oracle is helping me craft a polite but firm response.

"We're already in midtown," I continued. "Why don't we just get something to eat here, then we'll take the bus to Giants Stadium."

I couldn't care less about missing kickoff, but when we got to the stadium, I frantically dragged Mike to the seats for fear of disappointing Madison. "How could you miss the kickoff?" I could hear Madison saying. We arrived just in time. Madison had season tickets. His seats were on the fifty-yard line. In the box below us were network televi-

sion cameras. We all quickly made our introductions, as it was freezing. With the windchill factor, it felt like single digits. I sat between
Madison and Mike.

"Oh, and one more thing," I whispered to Mike. "Don't bring up the
whole speakerphone incident."

Mike reached into his pocket and handed me a note. I took my
gloves off to read it. "Do you think I'm an idiot?" it said. I laughed.

"I have two more identical notes in my pocket," he said. "Just in
case we need them later."

I spent the first quarter of the game waiting for the perfect oppor-
tunity to share with Madison my newly acquired football knowledge.
He finally gave me something to go on, mid–second quarter. "Thank
God for Fassel. That's all I have to say," he said.

"Yeah, it's been like night and day ever since Head Coach Jim Fassel
rejoined the New York Giants in 1997. Fassel was an assistant Giants
coach years ago, wasn't he?"

"Yeah, I think so," Madison said. "Barber and Toomer, the two of
them are absolutely on fire today. Did you see that last catch?"

"Totally." I nodded. For all I knew, Barber and Toomer was a mid-
size Manhattan law firm.

"Ron's making a beer run. Do you want?"

I hated beer. "Sure," I said, reaching for my wallet.

"Not necessary," Madison said, waving me off.

"Mike, do you want anything?" I whispered.

"Hot chocolate, maybe?" Mike said innocently.

I really didn't want Madison's son to become our errand boy. "I can
help, Ron," I offered. Ron was a junior at Cornell. I knew that
Madison was pushing him to apply to law school.

"I got it," Ron said politely.

By halftime Madison was starting to warm up. "I want you to be
heavily involved in the defensive deposition process. You'll sit second
chair on the first few, but I'm going to need you to do some of them
on your own. There are going to be dozens."

"That would be great," I said.

"Let me explain to you a little about the dynamic. You're going to be *defending* depositions. That means Rufus will ask the questions, put their case together, and you'll sit there and make objections for the record. Do not underestimate how difficult this is. Defending a deposition is arguably more difficult than taking one."

"Okay."

"Rufus will ask questions, and you will object to the *form* of the question. That's generally the only type of objection you can make. So when the question is asked and answered already, argumentative, compound—meaning it contains more than one question—or ambiguous, you make an objection."

"Have you stopped beating your wife?" I said. Madison gave me a look. "I object to loaded questions like that, right?"

"Yes, yes. That question assumes facts not already in evidence—that the witness admitted to beating his wife at some point prior. You'd make the objection that the question lacked foundation, then politely request that opposing counsel rephrase the question."

"Do I have to make the objection before the deponent answers?"

"Usually, yes. The record reads better that way, and frankly, it will tip off the person you're defending that there might be something wrong with the question. But if you can't get your objection in right away, it's not always a big deal. The person deposed will still probably answer the question. It's not like being in court."

"I'm just making a record of objections for the future," I said.

"Damn! What's wrong with you?" Madison said as the Green Bay Packers intercepted the Giants' ball. "Right. The theory goes: We're all here, the deponent should answer the question, and we can figure out later whether he or she understood and answered the question correctly. There *is* one exception," he said seriously. "Privileged information. Never let the Bullock witness disclose attorney-client-privileged or work-product information. This is where it's crucial that you make the objection *before* the witness speaks. When the question calls for privileged information, you *must* prevent the witness from answering. You *never* want to disclose attorney-client-privileged information. Nice kick."

"Yeah," I said.

"That's the key," he continued. "Block Bullock attorney-client-privileged information from getting out, and make sure all of your objections are on the record. If you don't get them on the record at some point, you could end up waiving our chance to make the objection in the future, and the record won't properly reflect the witness's testimony. Then, when I'm at trial, I'll be stuck with that crappy answer."

"Got it."

"It truly is an art to be able to analyze a question and make timely objections. Most young attorneys object too much. It's always good to drive opposing counsel crazy with objections, but if you object *too* much, you'll rattle the witness. You need to strike a delicate balance."

"So, hearsay objections, relevance objections: I can't make any of those during the depositions?"

"Nope. Besides calls for privileged information, you can't make any substantive objections. The purpose of the Bullock deposition is for Rufus to gather facts and build their case. Opposing counsel can ask the witness anything likely to lead to the discovery of admissible evidence. In other words, anything. But make them work for it. You don't have to be confrontational or defensive; be as cooperative and forthright as possible, but it isn't an open and unfettered question-and-answer session. Opposing counsel is not your friend. Do not make small talk with them on breaks, in the hallway, or on the way to the bathroom. Remember, litigation is war."

"Okay."

"Think of it like a football game." I hoped the forthcoming sports analogy would be obvious. "You're playing defense. Occasionally, you can make an interception, but your primary goal is to prevent the other team from advancing down the field and scoring. You can't win the case for us when you're playing defense, or when you're defending a deposition. Just make sure you prevent Rufus from scoring. Shit! Are you an idiot?" He was talking to the field. The Giants nearly fumbled. "The key to these Bullock depositions will be sitting down with the witnesses ahead of time."

"We're like their coach," I said, extending the analogy.

"No, no, no!" he said, annoyed. This time he wasn't referring to the game. Geez, this guy was a time bomb waiting to go off. "We *do not* coach our witnesses, Alex. Coaching is unethical. We *prep* our witnesses." He took a sip of beer. Yeah, but who was going to prep me?

"Tell the witness to listen to the questions," he continued. "Tell him not to look at you before answering every question, otherwise it will look like you coached him. Tell him not to volunteer information, to answer only the question being asked, and that means making sure he narrows the answer down to specific time periods and events. Tell the witness not to kill himself trying to recollect something. If he doesn't remember, he doesn't remember. Make sure he doesn't speculate." I wished I had a pen.

"There are only five answers to a deposition question," he said. "Yes, no, I don't know, I don't remember, or a short explanation."

"That's very helpful." My head was spinning. The audience erupted in cheers. The Giants had scored a forty-yard field goal.

"And if you remember anything I said today, remember this—make sure the witness *always* tells the truth. Start the preparation off with that one rule—always tell the truth." Madison went back to watching the game. Mike was falling asleep. The Giants lost, 25–34.

Had I accepted an engineering job at a place like Bullock fresh out of college, who knows if I ever would have met the legends of ink-jet technology, the Roddy Helms of Bullock. But three years of law school had changed all that. Now these engineering pioneers needed me. I was their legal protector.

Finally, I was someone's attorney.

CHAPTER 54

"I DO SOLEMNLY SWEAR that I will support the Constitution of the United States and the Constitution of the State of New York. That I will faithfully discharge the duties of the office of the Appellate Division of the First Department of New York, according to the best of my ability."

I repeated the oath, lowered my right hand, put it together with my left, and began clapping along with about three hundred other future lawyers in the courtroom. Mine was a good, solid, authentic clap. I smiled over at the Oracle, the Optimist, and the Child Prodigy, who were also clapping enthusiastically. I couldn't help but think of the Oracle's advice: "Happiness shouldn't be your goal, but you should find it along the way." It felt like a lifetime ago that the four of us were all at law school graduation. A lot can happen in nine months. Now I was officially a counselor, an esquire, an attorney, a lawyer, whatever. I was licensed to practice. Born slightly premature and jaundiced, but otherwise healthy.

The Rufus case now consumed my life. And I liked it. I was billing over two hundred Madison-approved hours a month. Billing that much meant working tons more. The hours were long, but I was enamored by my lifestyle. I was the bicoastal, high-powered New York attorney that I'd always dreamt of becoming. I lived in a beautifully renovated loft in Tribeca, and I was a player in a high-tech multimillion-dollar intellectual property and antitrust litigation.

I wondered how long I could do this. Would drafting legal briefs, arguing motions in court, and preparing my colleagues for trial be enough? Even if I was on the firm's rocket docket, trying a case before a jury was at least seven or eight years away. Could I really wait that long? Whatever I decided, passing the bar meant I had a license to make that choice. Whenever I wanted, I could get on with my life. With a clear conscience, I could quit if I wanted. I wasn't stuck in a New York State bar-exam holding pattern.

"Don't be such a lawyer." I heard that a lot lately. "It's 'attorney,' " I corrected my critics. "But aside from that, thanks. You're right, I *am* being such an attorney." And even though it bothered me to admit it, I was a better attorney thanks to the bar. I had a better grasp of the law in general. There were certain topics that I'd never quite understood in school. Now I did. There were certain subjects that I'd never even studied in school. Now I had. I realized that law school, the bar, and the practice were the perfect trifecta. Each phase complemented the next, and the process of becoming an attorney proved empowering.

Life was starting to look like one big hypothetical, or at least a series of strung-together fact patterns and but-for legal analyses.
Whether I was considering an invention, renting an apartment, or
preparing for my own mortality, nothing looked the same anymore.
Now, when my cell phone overheated, I wondered whether Motorola
was exposing me to an unhealthy level of microwave electromagnetic
radiation. Perhaps I was on the verge of a major class-action product
liability lawsuit.

For the last ten years I'd been engaged in an epic battle. Call it me
versus standardized test scores, me versus Tier 2, or simply, me versus
mediocrity. And despite all my bellyaching, I relished the fight.
Usually, ingenuity and persistence enabled me to prevail. Sometimes
it was a double-sided table-tennis paddle.

Then came the bar exam, a different animal altogether. For the bar,
you *had* to pass. There was no way to beat or trick the system. *There
were no table-tennis paddles.* I found myself on unfamiliar ground, and
insecurity kicked in. Somehow, passing the bar became the only way
to validate everything that I'd done before and everything that I'd do in
the future. "Just let me pass," I bargained. "If I pass, everything will be
okay."

What I didn't anticipate was the wait, and how profoundly that time
period would change my life. In those four months I was subjected to
far greater challenges than the bar itself. I was stripped down and
forced to reexamine who I was and who I wanted to be. I discovered
that my performance on the bar did not dictate my place in the universe. Perhaps I'd be singing a different tune had I failed the exam. I
hoped not.

"They can never take away your education," the Oracle always told
me. "They" rattled, challenged, starved, and confused me. They tested
me. They made me want it, and they made me wait. Maybe they
couldn't take away my education, but whoever "they" were—for that
period of nine months—they came close to taking away my self-
esteem, to making me think a law degree was worthless without a license. And that simply wasn't true. I liked the law. And it didn't matter
where I learned it or whether or not I practiced it.

AFTERBIRTH

AFTERBIRTH
(EPILOGUE)

Following the swearing-in ceremony, I spent the next seven months reviewing documents. Day in and day out, I tagged Bullock documents with green, orange, red, and purple flags. I must have designated close to a million pages. On my one-year anniversary at the firm, the discovery phase of the Bullock lawsuit at last shifted to deposition mode. For months I second-chaired depositions alongside attorneys like John Madison and Aaron Reinstein. It was the first chair's job to defend a Bullock witness by objecting to inappropriate questions asked by opposing counsel. It was my job, as second chair, to pass the first-chair notes. My brain was packed with Bullock factoids, so I was supposed to see problem areas three questions away and tip off the first chair with a terse note.

It was nerve-racking stuff. Note passing was an art. Some attorneys wanted more information. Others wanted less. Madison became impatient with too many notes. For Aaron, there were never enough. Right around Thanksgiving, Madison invited me to his private club, we drank Scotch, and he informed me that I was ready to defend my first deposition. Aaron volunteered to second-chair. It was a thrill. For the first time in my life, my objection would be noted for the record. I was finally an attorney.

But in the months following my one-year anniversary with Nickel, I found myself wondering whether I wanted to be an attorney at all. It wasn't as if I hated being an attorney. It wasn't that the hours were too long or that I felt stuck in the profession. My legal career was still on the rocket docket. I was taking depositions in a multibillion-dollar law-suit and hobnobbing with the seniormost partner in the firm. The law practice could be very exciting. Advocating on behalf of your client could be pretty heady stuff. And it wasn't as if there was this one defin-ing moment that triggered my choice to leave the practice. Eventually, I just decided that the "deal" no longer interested me. I was unwilling to endure daily drudgery in exchange for a highly lucrative job and an extravagant lifestyle. I was not going to live my life in billable hours, and I was not going to spend the next nine years working to become a partner in a business that really didn't suit me. Already I'd spent too many days pushing paper in the profession. Perhaps that was par for the course for a young associate at a large firm in a major litigation, but it wasn't for me. I can't entirely explain it. Maybe it's a character flaw. Or maybe it's simply a feeling of being propelled outward by a great natural force, catapulted into a new life-form. Whatever it was at the time, once I was all set in the profession that I'd so struggled for, I needed my freedom. I wanted something else. I needed something more creative.

That's when my close friend and law school colleague Lukas Reiter came to me with a proposition: "I know about this new cable televi-sion network that's about to be launched. We should pitch them a show."

"I'm in," I responded, without knowing a thing about pitching a net-work or producing a television program. I didn't know the name of the network, and I didn't have the faintest idea what we'd pitch. The yet-to-be-launched network was Ziff Davis television, or ZDTV—now TechTV—a channel devoted to technology. At the time, Ziff Davis was one of the leading technology publishers in the world, with magazines like *PC Magazine* and *Yahoo! Internet Life.*

Lukas and I went to work on creating a television program. Midway through our second year in practice, we formed Eleven Eleven Productions and developed a show called *CyberCrime*—a weekly newsmagazine program that explored high-tech crime in the Digital Age. Even though neither of us had any journalism training or experience, and even though neither of us knew anything about the topic, it was an opportunity for both of us to apply what we knew. I was an engineer practicing intellectual property law, and Lukas was a star prosecutor. We were a natural fit. In the early days, we joked that I was the "cyber" and he was the "crime." We both sensed that high-tech crime was about to play a big role in everyone's lives. The Oracle had always taught me that a good idea at the right time can take you pretty far. It did. The *CyberCrime* concept quickly sold and Lukas and I remain deeply indebted to family and friends who supported us, and to the ZDTV executives who had the foresight and willingness to take a chance on two attorneys who didn't know the first thing about producing television.

Interestingly, all of the Nickel attorneys I've mentioned eventually left the firm. Aaron, Hayley, and even Madison all lateraled to other big New York firms. As for Sam, he decided to leave the firm after failing the bar a second time. I heard that he passed on his third try.

Over the next five years, TechTV grew to become an international cable television network reaching seventy countries and more than eighty million homes worldwide, and *CyberCrime* became an award-winning program that recently celebrated its hundredth episode.

People are usually surprised when I tell them that I left the law and moved to San Francisco to work in television. It's true, Lukas and I took a substantial risk. We were both willing to leave the secure, prestigious jobs that we'd worked so hard for to pursue something we knew nothing about. But it wasn't a blind leap. In many ways, we'd been training for that fateful ZDTV pitch meeting our whole lives. Whether it was as students on the trial team or the student bar association, whether it was overcoming the bar exam or pursuing the practice, we didn't know it, but the law was preparing us for our next career, and even the one after that.

For me, inventing a television program came along a natural progression that started with a table-tennis paddle. Nine months after conception, I was an attorney. And in the afterbirth, there are always some things you must leave behind. I left the law practice, but not the law. I'll always be an attorney. I'm proud to have gone to law school and grateful for my experiences in the practice. My law professors succeeded—whatever the circumstances nowadays, very little can prevent me from "thinking" like an attorney. Even though I no longer practice, I happily pay my bar dues, as the prospect of retaking the bar still sends me into cold sweats. I offer my experiences as consolation to those undergoing the pressures of the big test.

ACKNOWLEDGMENTS

I am so grateful to friends and family who provided undying help and support as I wrote this book.

To my mother, who read dozens of drafts, sent me detailed notes, strategized with me on the phone for countless hours, told it to me like it was, and always remained my biggest fan. To my father, whose optimism has infused my life. To my brother, Mike, whom I love, respect, and admire like no other. To my entire family, who didn't bargain for this revealing book yet supported me every step of the way.

To Kris Kosach, for her uncompromising patience, support, and love.

To all of my wonderful friends, who read various drafts of the manuscript and gave me such insightful and honest feedback. Matt Richtel, Lukas Reiter, Brad Stone, Alan Tenenbaum, Jennifer London, Henry Sawtelle, and Jennifer Granick—I can't thank you enough.

To Temple Law School, I can think of no better place to study the law. I'm eternally grateful to the gifted faculty and administration for providing me with the best education an attorney could ask for.

And finally to my publisher, Shaye Areheart, and to my editors, Jake Morrissey and Teryn Johnson, for inspiring me to write a better book. Thank you for investing so much of yourself in this labor of love.

ABOUT THE AUTHOR

ALEX WELLEN co-created, executive-produced, and co-hosted the award-winning high-tech crime newsmagazine program *CyberCrime* on the TechTV cable television network. His columns, breaking news stories, and contributions appear in print, radio, and television, including NBC News, ABC News, CNN, and MSNBC. He's currently an independent producer and freelance writer living in San Francisco.